Whillans Tax Tables

Budget Edition

Edited by
Claire Hayes CTA
Shilpa Veerappa ATT

LexisNexis® UK & Worldwide

United Kingdom	RELX (UK) Limited trading as LexisNexis®, 1-3 Strand, London WC2N 5JR and 9-10 St Andrew Square, Edinburgh EH2 2AF
LNUK Global Partners	LexisNexis® encompasses authoritative legal publishing brands dating back to the 19th century including: Butterworths® in the United Kingdom, Canada and the Asia-Pacific region; Les Editions du Juris Classeur in France; and Matthew Bender® worldwide. Details of LexisNexis® locations worldwide can be found at www.lexis-nexis.com

First published in 1948

© 2020 RELX (UK) Limited

Published by LexisNexis
This is a Tolley title

ISBN for this volume: 9781474313957

Printed and bound by CPI Group (UK) Ltd, Croydon, CR0 4YY

Visit LexisNexis at www.lexisnexis.co.uk

Foreword

Since 1948, when George Whillans produced the first edition of his tax tables this publication, which still bears his name, has provided tax practitioners with concise, quick and easily accessible information about rates, allowances and other useful information across all the main taxes.

This edition is updated to reflect the announcements in the 2020 Budget, which was held on 11 March, together with any subsequent changes relating to the package of temporary, targeted measures introduced by the Government to support businesses and individuals through the period of disruption of the coronavirus (COVID-19) pandemic. A number of announcements in the Budget related to this Government support but two of the notable tax announcements included in this edition are the reduction in the lifetime limit for entrepreneurs' relief, which has been renamed as business asset disposal relief, and the continuation of the main rate of corporation tax at 19%, superseding the planned reduction to 17%.

See https://covid19.tolley.co.uk/ for the Tolley COVID-19 Toolkit

Andrew Hubbard

Editor-in-chief *Taxation Magazine*

Disclaimer

While every care has been taken to ensure the accuracy of this work, no responsibility for loss or damage occasioned to any person acting or refraining from action as a result of any statement in it can be accepted by the authors, editor or publisher.

Administration

Bank base rates

Period	Rate
from 19 March 2020	**0.10%**
11 March 2020–18 March 2020	0.25%
2 August 2018–10 March 2020	0.75%
2 November 2017–1 August 2018	0.50%
4 August 2016–1 November 2017	0.25%

Due dates for tax

Capital gains tax

Generally

Normally 31 January following end of year of assessment. (TMA 1970 s 59B).

Disposals of UK residential property by UK residents and by UK branch/agency of non-residents

For disposals after 5 April 2020, 30 days after date of completion of sale.

Disposals of UK land by non-residents and by UK residents in the overseas part of a split tax year

For disposals after 5 April 2019, 30 days after date of completion of sale.

Non-resident CGT disposals

For disposals before 6 April 2019, 30 days after the date of completion of sale if not registered for self-assessment. (TMA 1970 s 59AA).

(See also *Extended due dates* under **Income tax**, see p 2.)

Corporation tax

SEE TOLLEY'S TAX COMPUTATIONS 115.1.

Must be paid electronically.

Generally (TMA 1970 s 59D)

9 months and 1 day after end of accounting period.

Instalments for large and very large companies (TMA 1970 s 59E; SI 1998/3175)

A '**large company**' is any company whose augmented profits (see p 64) for the accounting period exceed £1.5m (but from 1 April 2019, do not exceed £20m, see below), both thresholds being proportionately reduced for accounting periods of less than 12 months and divided by 1 plus the number of any active 51% group companies. Any company which pays the bank levy is also a large company unless, from 1 April 2019, it exceeds the £20m threshold resulting in it being a very large company (see below). A company is not a large company in respect of an accounting period if its total liability for that period is not more than £10,000, or if its profits for an accounting period are £10m or less (both limits proportionately reduced for accounting periods of less than 12 months) and it was not a large company (or from 1 April 2019, a very large company, see below) in the 12 months preceding that accounting period. For most large companies (those with no ring fence profits) the amount of each instalment for a 12 month accounting period will be one quarter of its total liability. The amount of each instalment for any accounting period longer than 3 months but shorter than 12 months is calculated using the formula 3 x CTI/n where CTI is the amount of a company's total liability for that accounting period, and n is the number of months in the accounting period. The due dates of instalments are as follows:

    1st instalment: 6 months and 13 days from start of accounting period (or date of final instalment if earlier);
    2nd instalment: 3 months after 1st instalment, if length of accounting period allows;
    3rd instalment: 3 months after 2nd instalment, if length of accounting period allows;
    Final instalment: 3 months and 14 days from end of accounting period.

For accounting periods beginning on or after 1 April 2019 revised payment dates apply to a '**very large company**' which is one whose augmented profits exceed £20m (proportionately reduced for accounting periods of less than 12 months and divided by 1 plus the number of any active 51% group companies). A company is not a very large company in respect of an accounting period if its total liability for that period is not more than £10,000 (proportionately reduced for accounting periods of less than 12 months). The due dates of instalments are as follows:

    1st instalment: 2 months and 13 days from start of accounting period (or date of final instalment if earlier);
    2nd instalment: 3 months after 1st instalment, if length of accounting period allows;
    3rd instalment: 3 months after 2nd instalment, if length of accounting period allows;
    Final instalment: 3 months after 3rd instalment, if length of accounting period allows.

Close companies: tax on loans or benefits to participators

9 months and 1 day after the end of the accounting period. To be included in instalment payments for large and very large companies (see above) (TMA 1970 s 59E(11)).

Income tax

SEE TOLLEY'S TAX COMPUTATIONS 26.1.

Payments on account (TMA 1970 s 59A; SSCBA 1992 ss 11A, 16; SI 1996/1654)

A payment on account is required where a taxpayer was assessed to income tax in the immediately preceding year to an amount exceeding the amount of tax deducted at source in respect of that year (subject to a de minimis limit, see below).

The payment on account (which includes Class 4 NIC) is made in 2 equal instalments due on:
- (a)   31 January during the year of assessment, and
- (b)   31 July in the following year of assessment.

This is subject to a relaxation for 2019/20 as part of the Government's assistance to taxpayers during the COVID-19 pandemic. The second self-assessment payment on account for the 2019/20 tax year is deferred from 31 July 2020 to 31 January 2021. No interest will be applied for the period between 31 July 2020 and 31 January 2021.

No payments on account are required where either:
- (a)   the aggregate of the liability (including Class 4 NIC) for the preceding year (net of tax deducted at source) is less than £1,000; or
- (b)   more than 80% of the taxpayer's income tax and Class 4 NIC liability for the preceding year was met by tax deducted at source (including PAYE).

Note that payments on account are not required for Class 2 NIC.

Final payment (TMA 1970 s 59B, Sch 3ZA)

Balance of income tax due for a year of assessment (after deducting payments on account, tax deducted at source if any and (before 2016–17) credits in respect of dividends, etc) is due on:

31 January following end of year of assessment (TMA 1970 s 59B(4)).

Class 2 NIC is also due through the self-assessment system no later than 31 January following end of year of assessment.

Extended due dates:
- (a)   If a taxpayer has given notice of liability within 6 months of the end of the year of assessment, but a notice to make a return is not given until after 31 October following the end of the year of assessment, the due date is 3 months after the notice is given (TMA 1970 s 59B(3)).
- (b)   If tax is payable as a result of a taxpayer's notice of amendment, an HMRC notice of correction or an HMRC notice of closure following enquiry, in each case given less than 30 days before the due date (or the extended due date at (a) above), the due date is on or before the day following the end of a 30-day period beginning on the day on which the notice is given (TMA 1970 s 59B(5), Sch 3ZA).
- (c)   If an assessment other than a self-assessment or simple assessment is made, tax payable under the assessment is due on the day following the end of a 30-day period beginning on the day on which notice of the assessment is given (TMA 1970 s 59B(6)).

The extensions under (b) and (c) do *not* alter the due date for *interest purposes* (see p 4).

Final tax payable under simple assessment:
- (a)   If a taxpayer is given notice of the simple assessment after 31 October following the end of the year of assessment, the due date is 3 months after the notice is given (TMA 1970 s 59BA(4)).
- (b)   In any other case, due date is no later than 31 January following end of year of assessment (TMA 1970 s 59BA(5)).

Harmonised interest regime see p 4.
Interest on overdue tax see p 5.
Interest on overpaid tax see p 6.
Penalties see p 13.
Remission of tax see p 6.

Inheritance tax

(IHTA 1984 s 226)

Chargeable transfers other than on death, made between:

6 April and 30 September	–	30 April in next year.
1 October and 5 April	–	6 months after end of month in which chargeable transfer is made.

Relevant property settlements periodic and exit charges

	–	6 months after end of month in which chargeable event occurs.

Chargeable events following conditional exemption for heritage etc property and charge on disposal of trees or underwood before the second death:

– 6 months after end of month in which chargeable event occurs.

Transfers on death:

Earlier of   (a)   6 months after end of month in which death occurs, and
               (b)   delivery of account by personal representatives.

Tax or extra tax becoming payable on death:
Chargeable transfers and potentially exempt transfers within 7 years of death.

– 6 months after end of month in which death occurs.

PAYE and NIC

(SSCBA 1992 ss 11A, 15; SI 2001/1004; SI 2003/2682)

Employer's tax and Class 1 NIC payable under PAYE	In-year payments – 14 days after end of tax month or quarter to which it relates (extended to 17 days where payments are made by electronic means). Final payment for tax year – 19 April following deduction year (extended to 22 April where payments are made by electronic means).
Class 1A NIC	19 July following year in which contributions due (extended to 22 July where payments are made by electronic means).
PAYE settlement agreement and Class 1B NIC	19 October following year to which agreement relates (extended to 22 October where payments are made by electronic means).
Class 2 NIC	Contributions based on an annual liability are due through the self-assessment system no later than 31 January following the tax year[1].
Class 4 NIC	See under income tax on p 2.

[1]   Those who do not pay through self-assessment will be sent a bill by HMRC. Voluntary payments may still be made.

Paying HMRC

HMRC have a number of bank accounts. The respective accounts to which payments should be made from UK bank accounts for the main taxes are as follows:

Tax	Account name	Sort code	Account number
Self-assessment/ capital gains tax	HMRC Shipley	08 32 10	12001020
Self-assessment/ capital gains tax	HMRC Cumbernauld	08 32 10	12001039
Corporation tax	HMRC Shipley	08 32 10	12001020
Corporation tax	HMRC Cumbernauld	08 32 10	12001039
PAYE/ Class 1/ Class 1A NIC	HMRC Cumbernauld	08 32 10	12001039
Class 2 NIC[1]	HMRC NICO	08 32 20	12001004

[1]   If taxpayer does not pay through self-assessment.
[2]   Where both Shipley and Cumbernauld can apply and a taxpayer does not know which accounts office he normally pays, generally he should send payment to Cumbernauld. For details of other taxes see the list of taxes at www.gov.uk/topic/dealing-with-hmrc/paying-hmrc.

Harmonised interest regime

SEE TOLLEY'S TAX COMPUTATIONS 13.1, 222.1.

(FA 2009 ss 101–104, Schs 53–54A; SI 2011/701; SI 2011/2391; SI 2013/280; SI 2013/2472; SI 2014/992; SI 2014/3269; SI 2015/974, SI 2019/918, SI 2019/921)

A harmonised interest regime is being phased in for all taxes and duties and currently applies to:
— income and capital gains tax self-assessment amounts including penalties from 31 October 2011,
— CIS late return penalties from 6 October 2011,
— tax agent dishonest conduct penalties from 1 April 2013,
— annual tax on enveloped dwellings and penalties from 1 October 2013,
— PAYE and CIS in-year amounts for 2014–15 onwards from 6 May 2014 (including penalties),
— stamp duty reserve tax and penalties from 1 January 2015,
— diverted profits tax and penalties from 1 April 2015,
— Class 2 NIC from 6 April 2015,
— capital gains tax on disposals of UK land (where not included in a self-assessment) from 6 April 2019,
— various DOTAS penalties from 1 June 2019,
— penalties for offshore evasion from 6 September 2019,
— loan charge from 1 October 2020.

For annual PAYE payments such as Classes 1A and 1B NIC HMRC will continue to charge interest on any amount which remains unpaid after the due date.

Appointed Day Orders will be made in due course to align the treatment of interest and penalties for inheritance tax purposes with other taxes (F(No 2)A 2015 s 15).

The measure provides for differential interest charged and paid by HMRC to be based around the Bank of England base rate. The current late payment rate is:

Late payment interest	Rate
from 7 April 2020	**2.60%**
30 March 2020–6 April 2020	2.75%
21 August 2018–29 March 2020	3.25%
21 November 2017–20 August 2018	3.00%
23 August 2016–20 November 2017	2.75%
29 September 2009–22 August 2016	3.00%

The current repayment rate is:

Repayment interest	Rate
from 29 September 2009	**0.50%**

Late payment interest runs from the start date to the date of payment. The start date is generally the date on which the amount becomes due and payable, but special rules apply as follows:

Where an amount is due as a result of—
(a)   an amendment or correction to an assessment or self-assessment; or
(b)   an HMRC assessment in place of, or in addition to, an assessment made by the taxpayer; or
(c)   an HMRC assessment in place of an assessment which ought to have been made by the taxpayer,

the start date is the date it would have been if the original assessment or self-assessment had been complete and accurate and made on the date (if any) by which it was required to be made, and the tax had been due and payable as a result of the original assessment or self-assessment.

Repayment interest runs from the start date until the date the payment or repayment is made. The start date in the case of an amount paid to HMRC is the later of—
(i)   the date the amount was paid to HMRC; and
(ii)   the date on which the amount became due and payable to HMRC (in a case where the amount has been paid in connection with a liability to make a payment to HMRC, and it is to be repaid by them).

The start date, in the case of an amount which has not been paid to HMRC and which is payable by virtue of a return or a claim having been submitted, is the later of—
(1)   the date (if any) on which the return or claim was required to be submitted; and
(2)   the date on which the return or claim was submitted.

The start date in the case of the carry back of losses or averaging claims is 31 January following the *later* tax year in relation to the claim.

Interest on overdue tax

See p 4 regarding the **harmonised interest regime** and the taxes to which this currently applies. The provisions on interest on overdue tax continue to apply to taxes where the harmonised interest regime does not yet apply, and applied to other taxes before the transition to the harmonised regime.

NICs Class 1A, 1B, 4, stamp duty and stamp duty land tax

Interest runs from the due date (see p 2 for income tax and p 1 for capital gains tax) to the date of payment, on the amount outstanding. Interest is payable gross and is not tax deductible.

Period	Rate
from 7 April 2020	**2.60%**
30 March 2020–6 April 2020	2.75%
21 August 2018–29 March 2020	3.25%
21 November 2017–20 August 2018	3.00%
23 August 2016–20 November 2017	2.75%
29 September 2009–22 August 2016	3.00%

Corporation tax

SEE TOLLEY'S TAX COMPUTATIONS 110.1.

Interest runs from the due date (see p 1) to the date of payment. For instalment payments by large and, for accounting periods beginning on or after 1 April 2019, very large companies, a special rate of interest runs from the due date to the earlier of the date of payment and nine months after the end of the accounting period (after which the normal rate applies).

Corporation tax self-assessment

Period	Normal rate
from 7 April 2020	**2.60%**
30 March 2020–6 April 2020	2.75%
21 August 2018–29 March 2020	3.25%
21 November 2017–20 August 2018	3.00%
23 August 2016–20 November 2017	2.75%
29 September 2009–22 August 2016	3.00%

Period	Special rate for instalment payments (except where still unpaid nine months after end of accounting period)
from 30 March 2020	**1.10%**
23 March 2020–29 March 2020	1.25%
13 August 2018–22 March 2020	1.75%
13 November 2017–12 August 2018	1.50%
15 August 2016–12 November 2017	1.25%
16 March 2009–14 August 2016	1.50%

Income tax on company payments

Period	Rate
from 7 April 2020	**2.60%**
30 March 2020–6 April 2020	2.75%
21 August 2018–29 March 2020	3.25%
21 November 2017–20 August 2018	3.00%
23 August 2016–20 November 2017	2.75%
29 September 2009–22 August 2016	3.00%

Inheritance tax[1]

Interest runs from the due date[2] (see p 2) to the date of payment.

Period	Rate
from 7 April 2020	**2.60%**
30 March 2020–6 April 2020	2.75%
21 August 2018–29 March 2020	3.25%
21 November 2017–20 August 2018	3.00%
23 August 2016–20 November 2017	2.75%
29 September 2009–22 August 2016	3.00%

[1] Appointed Day Orders will be made in due course to align the treatment of interest and penalties for inheritance tax purposes with other taxes.

[2] Where higher IHT is payable as a result of IHTA 1984 Sch A1 or the F(No 2)A 2017 domicile changes, interest runs from the last day of December 2017 if later than normal payment date.

Interest on overpaid tax

See p 4 regarding the **harmonised interest regime** and the taxes to which this currently applies. The provisions on interest on overpaid tax continue to apply to taxes where the harmonised interest regime does not yet apply, and applied to other taxes before the transition to the harmonised regime.

NICs Class 1A, 1B, 4, stamp duty and stamp duty land tax

Calculated as simple interest on the amount of tax repaid. The supplement is tax-free.

Period	Rate
from 29 September 2009	**0.50%**

Inheritance tax

(IHTA 1984 s 235)

Repayments of inheritance tax or interest paid carries interest *from* the date of payment *to* the date on which the order for repayment is issued.

Period	Rate
from 29 September 2009	**0.50%**

Appointed Day Orders will be made in due course to align the treatment of interest and penalties for inheritance tax purposes with other taxes.

Companies

Corporation tax self-assessment

SEE TOLLEY'S TAX COMPUTATIONS 109.1.

Normal rates

Rates on overpaid corporation tax in respect of periods after normal due date (SI 1989/1297 reg 3BB).

Period	Rate
from 29 September 2009	**0.50%**

Special rates

For instalment payments by large and, for accounting periods beginning on or after 1 April 2019, very large companies and early payments by other companies, a special rate of interest runs from the date the excess arises (but not earlier than the due date of the first instalment) to the earlier of the date the repayment order is issued and nine months and one day after the end of the accounting period, after which the normal rate of interest (as above) applies.

Rates on overpaid instalment payments and on corporation tax paid early (but not due by instalments).

Period	Rate
from 21 September 2009	**0.50%**

Direct recovery of debt

(F(No 2)A 2015 Sch 8)

From 18 November 2015 HMRC are able to secure payment of tax and tax credit debts directly from debtors' bank and building society accounts (including funds held in cash in Individual Savings Accounts) that have a minimum aggregate credit of £5,000. HMRC will only take action against debtors who owe over £1,000 of debt, and will only put a hold on the funds in the affected account up to the value of the debt. Safeguards in place include a face-to-face visit with an HMRC officer, a specialist unit to deal with cases involving the vulnerable, and availability of appeal to the County Court.

Remission of tax

(Concession A19)

By concession, arrears of tax may be waived if they result from HMRC's failure to make proper and timely use of information supplied by the taxpayer or, where it affects the taxpayer's coding, by his or her employer. The concession also applies to information supplied by the Department for Work and Pensions affecting the taxpayer's entitlement to a retirement, disability or widow's pension. The concession only applies where the taxpayer could reasonably have believed that his or her affairs were in order and (unless the circumstances are exceptional) where the taxpayer is notified of the arrears more than 12 months after the end of the tax year in which HMRC received the information indicating that more tax was due.

Special relief

(TMA 1970 Sch 1AB para 3A; FA 1998 Sch 18 para 51BA)

A statutory 'special relief' is available which allows HMRC to give effect to a claim for repayment or discharge of an amount of tax that a person is liable to pay, but which the person believes is not due or, if it has been paid, was not due, where the usual time limits for such relief have expired. Relief is only available to taxpayers in receipt of an income tax or corporation tax self-assessment determination made by HMRC in the absence of a self-assessment return being submitted, and where the following specific conditions are met: (a) it would be unconscionable for HMRC to seek to recover the amount or to refuse to repay it if it has already been paid; (b) that the person's tax affairs are otherwise up to date, or arrangements have been put in place to HMRC's satisfaction, to bring them up to date as far as possible; and (c) the person has not previously claimed special relief, or its concessionary predecessor equitable liability, whether or not such a claim was successful. This latter condition may be waived in exceptional circumstances. There is no time limit for claiming the relief.

Certificates of tax deposit

From 23 November 2017 the scheme is closed for new purchases, but existing certificates will be honoured until 23 November 2023. Any certificates remaining after this date should be submitted to HMRC for refund. HMRC will seek to repay the balance of any certificate remaining unpaid and unclaimed. If they are unable to contact the current certificate holder after reasonable effort the balance will be forfeited.

Certificates were available to purchase by individuals, partnerships, individual partners, trustees, personal representatives and companies for the payment of income tax, Class 4 NIC, capital gains tax, inheritance tax, or petroleum revenue tax, but not payment of corporation tax, PAYE liabilities, or tax payable by companies etc on disposals of high value UK residential property, see p 64. Interest is paid gross and is chargeable to tax. It will only be paid for the first six years of a deposit. A deposit bears interest for the first year at the rate in force at the time of the deposit and for each subsequent year at the rate in force on the anniversary of the deposit. HMRC provide an interest calculator tool on their website.

Date of deposit	Amount	Held for (mths in yr)	Pay't of tax %	Cashed %
6.3.09–	Under £100,000	No limit	0.00	0.00
	£100,000 or over	under 1	0.00	0.00
		1–under 3	0.75	0.25
		3–under 6	0.75	0.25
		6–under 9	0.75	0.25
		9–12	0.75	0.25

Student loan deductions

Plan 1

	Percentage of income above the threshold	Threshold
2020–21	**9%**	**£19,390 per year** **£1,615 per month** **£372 per week**
2019–20	9%	£18,935 per year £1,577 per month £364 per week
2018–19	9%	£18,330 per year £1,527 per month £352 per week
2017–18	9%	£17,775 per year £1,481 per month £341 per week
2016–17	9%	£17,495 per year £1,457 per month £336 per week
2015–16	9%	£17,335 per year £1,444 per month £333 per week

Plan 2

	Percentage of income above the threshold	Threshold
2020–21	9%	**£26,575 per year** **£2,214 per month** **£511 per week**
2019–20	9%	£25,725 per year £2,143 per month £494 per week
2018–19	9%	£25,000 per year £2,083 per month £480 per week
2017–18	9%	£21,000 per year £1,750 per month £403 per week
2016–17	9%	£21,000 per year £1,750 per month £403 per week

Postgraduate loans

	Percentage of income above the threshold	Threshold
2019–20 and 2020–21	6%	**£21,000 per year** **£1,750 per month** **£403 per week**

Filing dates

Corporation tax

SEE TOLLEY'S TAX COMPUTATIONS 118.2.

(FA 1998 Sch 18 paras 14, 15; SI 2003/282 reg 3(2A))

The return must be filed on the latest of the following dates—
- (a) 12 months from the end of the period for which the return is made;
- (b) where the company makes up its accounts for a period not exceeding 18 months, 12 months from the end of that period;
- (c) where the company makes up its accounts for a period exceeding 18 months, 30 months from the start of that period;
- (d) 3 months from the date of issue of the notice requiring the return.

All company returns must be filed online. Computations and, in most cases, accounts must be submitted in iXBRL format. Micro-entities have the option to file simplified accounts.

Income tax and capital gains tax

(TMA 1970 ss 8, 8A, 12AA; SI 2003/2682 reg 186)

Self-assessment returns

Basic position for paper returns.	On or before 31 October following end of tax year.
Basic position for electronic returns.	On or before 31 January following end of tax year.
Paper return and notice to file return issued after 31 July but on or before 31 October following end of tax year.	Within 3 months of date of notice.
Electronic return and notice to file return issued after 31 July but on or before 31 October following end of tax year.	On or before 31 January following end of tax year.
Paper or electronic return and notice to file return issued after 31 October following end of tax year.	Within 3 months of date of notice.
Paper return and taxpayer wishes tax underpayment of less than £3,000 to be coded out.	On or before 31 October following end of tax year.
Electronic return and taxpayer wishes tax underpayment of less than £3,000 to be coded out.	Before 31 December following end of tax year.

Returns relating to disposals of UK land

Returns relating to disposals of UK residential property by UK residents / UK branch or agency of non-residents	For disposals after 5 April 2020, 30 days after date of completion of sale.

Returns relating to disposals of UK land by non-residents and by UK residents in the overseas part of a split tax year	For disposals after 5 April 2019, 30 days after date of completion of sale.

Non-resident capital gains tax

(TMA 1970 s 12ZB)

For disposals before 6 April 2019, 30 days after the date of completion of sale via online NRCGT return. For disposals after 5 April 2019 the rules for disposals of UK land by non-residents and by UK residents in the overseas part of a split tax year apply.

Withdrawal of self-assessment notice

(TMA 1970 s 8B)

HMRC may withdraw a notice to file a self-assessment tax return in certain circumstances. The statutory power has effect for returns for 2012–13 onwards. Penalties for failure to make a return may be cancelled.

Simple assessment

(TMA 1970 ss 28H–28J, 31AA)

From 2016–17 HMRC may make an assessment of an individual's or trustee's income tax or capital gains tax liability without that person first being required to complete a self-assessment return. HMRC will instead assess their tax liability on the basis of information already held. The assessment notice must include details of the information used and the amount of tax due. The assessment may be appealed or queried without formal appeal. HMRC may withdraw a simple assessment notice.

Penalties

Penalties — modernised penalty regime

A modernised penalty regime is being rolled out to all taxes and duties with the exception of tax credits. The penalty regime in force in respect of various defaults is set out below.

Inaccuracy in return or other document

(FA 2007 Sch 24 para 1)

Applies to	Commencement date	Penalty details
IT, CGT, CT, VAT, CIS, NIC Classes 1 and 4[1]	Return periods starting 1 April 2008 where the return is due to be filed on or after 1 April 2009	Penalty based on potential lost revenue Careless inaccuracy — 30% Deliberate but not concealed — 70% Deliberate and concealed — 100%
IHT, SDLT, SDRT, other taxes, levies and duties (except tax credits)	Return periods starting 1 April 2009 where the return is due to be filed on or after 1 April 2010, or where the liability arises on or after 1 April 2010; for IHT in respect of deaths from 1 April 2009	*Reductions for disclosure*[3] Unprompted disclosure minimum penalties nil, 20% and 30% Prompted disclosure minimum penalties 15%, 35% and 50%
Class 1A NIC	2010–11 returns	
Corporation tax credit, return by registered pension scheme	Return periods starting 1 April 2009 where the return is due to be filed on or after 1 April 2010	
Annual tax on enveloped dwellings	2013–14 returns	
Non-resident CGT[4]	6 April 2015	
Class 2 NIC	6 April 2015	
Apprenticeship levy	6 April 2017	
Disposals of UK land	6 April 2019	
Digital Services Tax	1 April 2020	
IT, CGT but offshore matter Extended to IHT and offshore transfers (see note)[2]	6 April 2011 (see note)[2]	Penalties above are increased by either 0%, 50% or 100% depending on the territory concerned (see table on p 14 for a list of territories in each category) Statutory limits for reductions for disclosure apply

[1] From 2013–14 for RTI purposes an inaccuracy in any full payment submission can attract a penalty. HMRC may issue one penalty notice for multiple inaccuracy penalties in a year.

[2] From 1 April 2016 the offshore penalty regime is amended to include IHT. From 1 April 2017 for IHT transfers and from 6 April 2016 otherwise, the regime also applies to domestic offences where the proceeds are hidden offshore. From a date to be appointed the territory classification system will be updated to reflect the jurisdictions that adopt the new global standard of automatic tax information exchange and there will be four levels of penalty instead of three.

[3] In December 2017 HMRC announced a restriction on quality of disclosure penalty reductions where taxpayers take 'a significant period (normally 3 years) to correct or disclose the inaccuracy'. They will restrict the penalty range by 10% above the minimum before working out the reductions. It is not clear when the 3-year period starts.

[4] Applies up to 5 April 2019. Replaced by returns for disposals of UK land.

Inaccuracy in return or other document as a result of third party providing incorrect (or withholding) information

(FA 2007 Sch 24 para 1A)

Applies to	Commencement date	Penalty details
IT, CGT, CT, VAT, IHT, CIS, NIC Classes 1 and 4, SDLT, SDRT, other taxes, levies and duties (except tax credits)	1 April 2009 where the return is due to be filed on or after 1 April 2010	100% of potential lost revenue Subject to reduction for disclosure as for inaccuracies above
Class 1A NIC	2010–11 returns	
Annual tax on enveloped dwellings	2013–14 returns	

Failure to notify HMRC of an error in an assessment (within 30 days)

(FA 2007 Sch 24 para 2)

Applies to	Commencement date	Penalty details
IT, CGT, CT, VAT, CIS, NIC Classes 1 and 4	1 April 2008 where the return is due to be filed on or after 1 April 2009	30% of potential lost revenue *Reductions for disclosure*[1] Unprompted disclosure minimum penalty nil Prompted disclosure minimum penalty 15%
IHT, SDLT, SDRT, other taxes, levies and duties (except tax credits)	1 April 2009 where the return is due to be filed on or after 1 April 2010	
Class 1A NIC	2010–11 returns	
Annual tax on enveloped dwellings	2013–14 returns	

[1]   In December 2017 HMRC announced a restriction on quality of disclosure penalty reductions where taxpayers take 'a significant period (normally 3 years) to correct or disclose the inaccuracy'. They will restrict the penalty range by 10% above the minimum before working out the reductions. It is not clear when the 3-year period starts.

Failure to notify chargeability

(FA 2008 Sch 41)

Applies to	Commencement date	Penalty details
IT, CGT, VAT, NIC Class 4	1 April 2010	Penalty based on potential lost revenue Failure to notify — 30% Deliberate but not concealed — 70% Deliberate and concealed — 100%
CT	Accounting periods ending on or after 31 March 2010	*Reductions for disclosure*[2] Unprompted disclosure minimum penalties nil (within 12 months late), 10% (more than 12 months late), 20% and 30% Prompted disclosure minimum penalties 15%, 35%, 50%
Other taxes, levies and duties (not IHT, SDLT, SDRT)	Obligations arising on or after 1 April 2010	
Diverted profits tax	Accounting periods beginning on or after 1 April 2015	
Digital Services Tax	Obligations arising on or after 1 April 2020	
IT, CGT but offshore matter Extended to offshore transfers (see note)[1]	6 April 2011 (see note)[1]	Penalties above are increased by either 0%, 50% or 100% depending on the territory concerned (see table on p 14 for a list of territories in each category) Statutory limits for reductions for disclosure apply

[1]   From 6 April 2016 the offshore penalty regime is amended to apply to domestic offences where the proceeds are hidden offshore. From a date to be appointed the territory classification system will be updated to reflect the jurisdictions that adopt the new global standard of automatic tax information exchange and there will be four levels of penalty instead of three.

[2]   In December 2017 HMRC announced a restriction on quality of disclosure penalty reductions where taxpayers take 'a significant period (normally 3 years) to correct or disclose the inaccuracy'. They will restrict the penalty range by 10% above the minimum before working out the reductions. It is not clear when the 3-year period starts.

Failure to make returns on time

(FA 2009 Sch 55; FA 2010 Sch 1; SI 2003/2682)

Applies to	Commencement date	Penalty details
IT, CGT, NIC Class 4[5]	6 April 2011	Initial penalty £100 Failure continues for more than three months — with notice — £10 per day for up to 90 days Six months late — greater of 5% of the tax due and £300 12 months late — same penalty as for 6 months late unless deliberately withholding the return Deliberate withholding of the return more than 12 months — 70% of tax due (minimum £300) Deliberate and concealed withholding of the return more than 12 months — 100% of tax due (minimum £300)
Return by Registered Pension scheme	1 April 2011	*Reductions for disclosure*[1] Unprompted disclosure minimum penalty 20% and 30% Prompted disclosure minimum penalties 35% and 50%
Annual tax on enveloped dwellings	2013–14 returns due 1 October 2013	
Stamp duty reserve tax	1 January 2015	
Class 2 NIC	6 April 2015	
Non-resident CGT[6]	26 March 2015	Penalties as above (*except* the £10 daily penalty)[6]
Disposals of UK land	6 April 2019	Penalties as above
CIS returns	6 October 2011	Initial penalty £100 After two months — £200 Six months late — greater of 5% of the tax due and £300 12 months late — same penalty as for 6 months late unless deliberately withholding the return Deliberate withholding of the return more than 12 months — 70% of tax due (minimum £1,500) Deliberate and concealed withholding of the return more than 12 months — 100% of tax due (minimum £3,000) *Reductions for disclosure*[1] Unprompted disclosure minimum penalty 20% and 30% Prompted disclosure minimum penalties 35% and 50% Special rules apply to the first returns made on registration for CIS so that the maximum total penalty that can apply for the initial and second fixed penalties for all such returns is £3,000. Subsequent tax-geared penalties may still be incurred. Where a CIS return only relates to persons registered for 'gross payment' a tax-geared penalty after 6 months or 12 months cannot apply. In these cases the person is liable to the fixed amount penalty.
PAYE Real Time Information and Apprenticeship levy. Failure during a tax month to make a return on or before the filing date (normally the date employee is paid)	6 October 2014 in relation to 2014–15 onwards for employers with 50 or more employees 6 March 2015 for employers with fewer than 50 employees	First failure in a tax year — nil Second and subsequent failure in tax year 1–9 employees — £100 10–49 employees — £200 50–249 employees — £300 250 or more employees — £400[2] Failure continues for more than three months — with notice — 5% of tax due New employers only: A failure in the 'initial period'[3] — nil

Applies to	Commencement date	Penalty details
IT, CGT but offshore matter Extended to offshore transfers (see note)[4]	6 April 2011(see note)[4]	Penalties above for a return later than 12 months which has been withheld are increased by either 0%, 50% or 100% depending on the territory concerned (see table on p 14 for a list of territories in each category) Statutory limits for reductions for disclosure apply

[1] In December 2017 HMRC announced a restriction on quality of disclosure penalty reductions where taxpayers take 'a significant period (normally 3 years) to correct or disclose the inaccuracy'. They will restrict the penalty range by 10% above the minimum before working out the reductions. It is not clear when the 3-year period starts.

[2] Before 6 April 2020 employers will not incur penalties for delays of up to 3 days in filing PAYE information. HMRC take a more proportionate approach and concentrate on the more serious defaults on a risk-assessed basis.

[3] A penalty will not be issued to a new employer if their first FPS is received within 30 days of making the first payment to their employee(s) (known as the 'initial period'). After that, normal penalties rules will apply if there is a failure to file on time.

[4] From 6 April 2016 the offshore penalty regime is amended to apply to domestic offences where the proceeds are hidden offshore. From a date to be appointed the territory classification system will be updated to reflect the jurisdictions that adopt the new global standard of automatic tax information exchange and there will be four levels of penalty instead of three. Proposed to be extended to IHT failures.

[5] HMRC will accept reasonable excuses from taxpayers who are generally compliant without further investigation.

[6] Applies up to 5 April 2019. Replaced by returns for disposals of UK land. Does not apply to an elective return made under TMA 1970 s 12ZBA. HMRC confirmed in June 2017 that they no longer issue the £10 daily penalty and such past penalties will be withdrawn.

Failure to pay tax on time

(FA 2009 Sch 56; FA 2010 Sch 1)

Applies to	Commencement date	Penalty details
PAYE[1], NIC Class 1, CIS[2], student loan deductions	2010–11 liabilities (on a risk assessed basis at present)	Penalty based on number of late payments in a year applied to the amounts paid late 1 late payment — nil 2, 3, 4 late payments — 1% 5, 6, 7 late payments — 2% 8, 9, 10 late payments — 3% 11, 12 late payments — 4% Any amount paid 6 months late — 5% Any amount paid 12 months late — 5%
NIC Class 1A and 1B (SI 2001/1004 reg 67B)	2010–11	31 days late — 5% 6 months late — 5% 12 months late — 5%
Tax due by Registered Pension schemes	Payments due 30 September 2010	31 days late — 5% 6 months late — 5% 12 months late — 5%
IT, CGT payable under self-assessment	6 April 2011 for self-assessment for 2010–11 onwards	31 days late — 5% 6 months late — 5% 12 months late — 5%
Annual tax on enveloped dwellings	2013–14 payments due 31 October 2013	31 days late — 5% 6 months late — 5% 12 months late — 5%
Stamp duty reserve tax	1 January 2015	31 days late — 5% 6 months late — 5% 12 months late — 5%
Class 2 NIC	6 April 2015	31 days late — 5% 6 months late — 5% 12 months late — 5%
Apprenticeship levy	15 September 2016	1 day late — 5% 5 months late — 5% 11 months late — 5%
Pension scheme overseas transfer charge	9 March 2017	31 days late — 5% 6 months late — 5% 12 months late — 5%
Disposals of UK land where not included in self-assessment	6 April 2019	31 days late — 5% 6 months late — 5% 12 months late — 5%

Applies to	Commencement date	Penalty details
CGT exit charge payment plan[3]	6 April 2019	31 days late — 5%[3] 6 months late — 5% 12 months late — 5%

[1] It had been intended to charge automatic in-year late payment penalties for RTI from 6 April 2015 but HMRC confirmed that late payment penalties will continue to be reviewed on a risk-assessed basis rather than be issued automatically. From 2014–15 a 'tolerance' of £100 has been introduced for PAYE in-year late payment penalties. Where the difference between the total of all the amounts that the employer is due to pay to HMRC for a tax period and the amount paid over for that period is no more than £100 the employer will not be liable to a late payment penalty.

[2] From 2014–15 a 'tolerance' of £100 has been introduced for CIS in-year late payment penalties. Where the difference between the amount that the contractor is due to pay to HMRC for a tax period and the amount paid over for that period is no more than £100 the contractor will not be liable to a late payment penalty.

[3] Penalty applies from day after date on which the amount is payable under the plan, if that is later than the date specified in TMA 1970 s 59B.

Offshore penalties — territory categories[8]

Category 1

Anguilla	Estonia	Japan	Poland
Aruba	Finland	Korea, South	Portugal[4]
Australia	France[2]	Latvia	Romania
Belgium	Germany	Liechtenstein (from 24 July 2013)[7]	Slovakia
Bulgaria	Greece	Lithuania	Slovenia
Canada	Guernsey[3]	Malta	Spain[5]
Cayman Islands	Hungary	Montserrat	Sweden
Cyprus	Ireland	Netherlands (not including Bonaire, Sint Eustatius and Saba)	Switzerland (from 24 July 2013)[7]
Czech Republic	Isle of Man	New Zealand (not including Tokelau)	USA (not including overseas territories and possessions)[6]
Denmark (not including Faroe Islands or Greenland)[1]	Italy	Norway	

[1] Faroe Islands and Greenland are in Category 2.
[2] Includes overseas Departments of France; the overseas collectivities of France are in Category 2.
[3] Includes Alderney and Sark.
[4] Includes Madeira and the Azores.
[5] Includes the Canary Islands and other overseas territories of Spain.
[6] The overseas territories and possessions of the USA are in Category 2.
[7] SI 2013/1618 changed the level of penalties which may be charged for 14 specified countries from 24 July 2013. This is to reflect the entry into force of tax information exchange and enhanced tax cooperation agreements with those countries. Liechtenstein and Switzerland were previously in Category 2.
[8] From a date to be set by Treasury Order the territory classification system will be updated to reflect the jurisdictions that adopt the new global standard of automatic tax information exchange.

Category 2

Territories not listed in Categories 1 or 3 (other than the UK) will be in Category 2. Crown Dependencies and Overseas Territories of the UK are, unless listed, in Category 2.

Category 3

Albania	Costa Rica	Kyrgyzstan	(Before 24 July 2013) *Saint Lucia*[2]
Algeria	Curaçao	Lebanon	(Before 24 July 2013) *Saint Vincent and the Grenadines*[2]
Andorra	Cuba	Macau[1]	(Before 24 July 2013) *San Marino*[2]
(Before 24 July 2013) *Antigua and Barbuda*[2]	Democratic People's Republic of Korea	Marshall Islands	Seychelles
(Before 24 July 2013) *Armenia*[2]	(Before 24 July 2013) *Dominica*[2]	(Before 24 July 2013) *Mauritius*[2]	Sint Maarten
(Before 24 July 2013) *Bahrain*[2]	Dominican Republic	Micronesia, Federated States of	Suriname
continued on next page			

(Before 24 July 2013) *Barbados*[2]	Ecuador	Monaco	Syria
(Before 24 July 2013) *Belize*[2]	El Salvador	Nauru	Tokelau
Bonaire, Sint Eustatius and Saba	Gabon	Nicaragua	Tonga
Brazil	(Before 24 July 2013) *Grenada*[2]	Niue	Trinidad and Tobago
Cameroon	Guatemala	Palau	United Arab Emirates
Cape Verde	Honduras	Panama	Uruguay
Colombia	Iran	Paraguay	
Congo, Republic of	Iraq	Peru	
Cook Islands	Jamaica	(Before 24 July 2013) *Saint Kitts and Nevis*[2]	

[1]   China and Hong Kong are in Category 2.

[2]   SI 2013/1618 changed the level of penalties which may be charged for 14 specified countries from 24.7.13. This is to reflect the entry into force of tax information exchange and enhanced tax cooperation agreements with those countries. 12 of the countries highlighted in this table are in Category 2 from 24.7.13.

Offshore assets moves

(FA 2015 Sch 21; SI 2015/866)

Applies to	Commencement date	Penalty details
Offshore assets move from a specified territory to a non-specified territory where IT, CGT or IHT penalty under FA 2007 Sch 24 para 1, FA 2008 Sch 41, or FA 2009 Sch 55 above already applies for a deliberate failure (see table below for a list of specified territories)	27 March 2015	50% of amount of original penalty

Offshore assets move penalties — specified territories

Andorra	Curaçao	Japan	Qatar
Anguilla	Cyprus	Jersey	Romania
Antigua and Barbuda	Czech Republic	Korea, South	Russia
Argentina	Denmark	Kuwait[1]	Saint Kitts and Nevis
Aruba	Dominica	Latvia	Saint Lucia
Australia	Estonia	Lebanon[1]	Saint Vincent and the Grenadines
Austria	Faroe Islands	Liechtenstein	Samoa
The Bahamas	Finland	Lithuania	San Marino
Bahrain[1]	France	Luxembourg	Saudi Arabia
Barbados	Germany	Macau	Seychelles
Belgium	Ghana[1]	Malaysia	Singapore
Belize	Gibraltar	Malta	Sint Maarten
Bermuda	Greece	Marshall Islands	Slovak Republic
Brazil	Greenland	Mauritius	Slovenia
British Virgin Islands	Grenada	Mexico	South Africa
Brunei Darussalam	Guernsey	Monaco	Spain
Bulgaria	Hong Kong	Montserrat	Sweden
Canada	Hungary	Nauru[1]	Switzerland
Cayman Islands	Iceland	Netherlands (including Bonaire, Sint Eustatius and Saba)	Trinidad and Tobago
Chile	India	New Zealand (not including Tokelau)	Turkey
China	Indonesia	Niue	Turks and Caicos Islands
Colombia	Ireland	Norway	United Arab Emirates
Cook Islands[1]	Isle of Man	Panama[1]	Uruguay
Costa Rica	Israel	Poland	Vanuatu[1]
Croatia	Italy	Portugal	

[1]   Added from 3.11.17 when Albania and USA (excluding overseas territories and possessions) removed.

Deliberate enablers of offshore evasion or non-compliance

Applies to	Commencement date	Penalty details
A person who has enabled another person (Q) to commit a relevant offence in relation to IT, CGT or IHT, or to engage in conduct which makes Q liable to a penalty under FA 2007 Sch 24 para 1, FA 2008 Sch 41, FA 2009 Sch 55, or FA 2015 Sch 21 above, provided certain other conditions are met (FA 2016 Sch 20; SI 2016/1249).	1 January 2017	For penalties other than under FA 2015 Sch 21, the higher of— (a) 100% of potential lost revenue; and (b) £3,000 For penalties under FA 2015 Sch 21, the higher of— (a) 50% of potential lost revenue in respect of the original tax non-compliance; and (b) £3,000 Reductions available for disclosure

Asset-based penalty for offshore inaccuracies and failures

Applies to	Commencement date	Penalty details
A person to whom a CGT, IHT or asset-based IT penalty under FA 2007 Sch 24 para 1, FA 2008 Sch 41, or FA 2009 Sch 55 above already applies for a deliberate failure in relation to an offshore matter or transfer for a tax year in which the potential lost revenue exceeds £25,000 (FA 2016 Sch 22; SI 2017/277).	2016–17 onwards for CGT and IT Transfers of value on or after 1 April 2017 for IHT	The lower of— (a) 10% of the value of the asset; and (b) 10 times the offshore potential lost revenue (as defined) Reductions available for disclosure

Personal tax and corporation tax

Offence	Penalty	
Failure to render return for corporation tax (FA 1998 Sch 18 paras 17, 18).	(a)	£100 if up to three months late (£500 if previous two returns also late);
	(b)	£200 if over three months late (£1,000 if previous two returns also late);
	(c)	if failure continues, on final day for delivery of return or, if later, 18 months after return period, 10% of tax unpaid 18 months after return period (20% of tax unpaid at that date if return not made within two years of return period).
Failure to maintain records supporting personal and trustees' returns of partnership returns (TMA 1970 s 12B).	Up to £3,000.	
Fraudulently or negligently making an incorrect statement in connection with a claim to reduce payments on account (TMA 1970 s 59A(6)).	Up to the amount (or additional amount) payable on account if a correct statement had been made.	
Deliberately or recklessly failing to pay corporation tax due in respect of total liability of company for accounting period, or fraudulently or negligently making claim for repayment (TMA 1970 s 59E(4); SI 1998/3175 reg 13).	Penalty not exceeding twice amount of interest charged under SI 1998/3175 reg 7.	

PAYE

Offence	Penalty	
Failure to submit return P9D or P11D (benefits in kind) by due date (6 July following subsequent tax years) (TMA 1970 s 98(1)).	(a)	Initial penalty up to £300; and
	(b)	continuing penalty up to £60 for each day on which the failure continues.
Failure to submit information in connection with mandatory e-filing from 2004–05 onwards (SI 2003/2682 as amended by 2009/2029 reg 14).	Penalty based on number of employees not exceeding £3,000 for 1,000 or more employees.	
Failure to submit returns P11D(b) (Class 1A NIC returns) by due date (6 July following tax year, but by concession until 31 March 2013, 19 July applied) (SI 2001/1004 reg 81(2)).	(a)	First 12 months: penalty of £100 for each 50 employees (or part thereof) for each month the failure continues (but total penalty not to exceed total Class 1A NIC due);
	(b)	failures exceeding 12 months: a penalty not exceeding the amount of Class 1A NIC due and unpaid after 19 July following tax year.

Inheritance tax returns and information[1]

Offence	Penalty
Failure to deliver an account within 12 months of death (unless tax is less than £100 or there is a reasonable excuse) (IHTA 1984 s 245).	(*a*) Initial penalty of £100 (or the amount of tax payable if less); (*b*) further penalty up to £60 (where penalty determined by court or tribunal) for each day on which the failure continues; (*c*) if failure continues after six months after the date on which account is due, and proceedings not commenced, a further penalty of £100 (or amount of tax payable if less); and (*d*) if failure continues one year after end of the period in which account is due, and IHT is payable, a penalty not exceeding £3,000.
Failure to submit account or notify HMRC under IHTA 1984 s 218A if a disposition on a death is varied within six months of the variation and additional tax is payable (IHTA 1984 s 245A(1A), (1B)).	(*a*) Initial penalty up to £100; (*b*) further penalty up to £60 (if determined by court or tribunal) for each day on which the failure continues; (*c*) up to £3,000 if failure continues after 12 months from date notification is due.
Failure to provide information etc under IHTA 1984 s 218 concerning a settlement by a UK-domiciled settlor with non-resident trustees (IHTA 1984 s 245A(1)).	(*a*) Initial penalty up to £300; and (*b*) further penalty up to £60 (where penalty determined by court or tribunal) for each day on which the failure continues.
Person other than the taxpayer fraudulently or negligently delivering, furnishing or producing incorrect accounts, information or documents (IHTA 1984 s 247(3); FA 2004 s 295(4), (9)).	Up to £3,000.

[1] Appointed Day Orders will be made in due course to align the treatment of interest and penalties for inheritance tax purposes with other taxes.

Special returns of information

Offence	Penalty
Failure to comply with a notice to deliver a return or other document, furnish particulars or make anything available for inspection under any of the provisions listed in column 1 of the table in TMA 1970 s 98.	(*a*) Initial penalty up to £300; (*b*) further penalty up to £60 for each day on which the failure continues.
Failure to furnish information, give certificates or produce documents or records under any of the provisions listed in column 2 of the table in TMA 1970 s 98.	(*a*) Initial penalty up to £300; and (*b*) further penalty up to £60 for each day on which the failure continues.
Failure to deduct income tax at source from payments of interest or royalties under ITA 2007 Part 15 where the exemption does not apply and the company did not believe or could not reasonably have believed that it would apply (TMA 1970 s 98(4A)–(4E)).	(*a*) Initial penalty up to £3,000; and (*b*) further penalty up to £600 for each day on which the failure continues.
Failure of an employment intermediary to furnish information or produce documents or records (TMA 1970 s 98(4F)).	(*a*) Initial penalty up to £3,000; and (*b*) further penalty up to £600 for each day on which the failure continues.
Advance pricing agreements: Fraudulently or negligently making a false or misleading statement in the preparation of, or application to enter into, any advance pricing agreement (TIOPA 2010 s 227).	Penalty up to £10,000.
Declaration of non-UK residence: Fraudulently or negligently making a false or misleading declaration of non-UK residence to a deposit-taker or building society under ITA 2007 ss 858-861 (TMA 1970 s 99B).	Penalty up to £3,000.

Other offences by taxpayers, agents etc

Offence	Penalty
GAAR. Applies to arrangements entered into after 15 September 2016 if a taxpayer (or in some cases another person) submits a return, claim, or other document on the basis that a tax advantage arises from the tax arrangements and all or part of that tax advantage is later counteracted under the GAAR (FA 2013 s 212A).	60% of the value of the counteracted advantage.
Serial tax avoiders. Use of any avoidance schemes in the warning period after the defeat of a relevant scheme. Applies to defeats incurred after 15 September 2016 (FA 2016 Sch 18).	(*a*) 20% of the tax understated or overclaimed for the first defeat of a scheme used during the warning period; (*b*) 40% for the second such defeat; and (*c*) 60% for any subsequent defeats.
Falsification of documents. Intentionally falsifying, concealing or destroying documents required under TMA 1970 ss 20A (repealed with effect from 1 April 2013) or 20BA (TMA 1970 s 20BB).	On summary conviction, a fine up to the statutory maximum (£5,000); on conviction on indictment, imprisonment for a term not exceeding two years or a fine or both.
European Economic Interest Groupings– Offences in connection with the supply of information:	
(i) failure to supply information	Initial penalty up to £300 per member of the Grouping at the time of failure and after direction by the tribunal: continuing penalty up to £60 per member of the Grouping at the end of the day for each day on which the failure continues.
(ii) fraudulent or negligent delivery of an incorrect return, accounts or statement (TMA 1970 s 98B).	Up to £3,000 for each member of the Grouping at the time of delivery.
Certificates of non-liability to income tax: Fraudulently or negligently giving such a certificate for the purposes of receiving interest gross on a bank or building society account, or failing to comply with an undertaking given in such a certificate (TMA 1970 s 99A).	Penalty up to £3,000.
Refusal to allow a deduction of income tax at source (TMA 1970 s 106).	£50.
Construction Industry Scheme: (post 31 March 2007 scheme) Making false statements etc for the purpose of obtaining a gross payment certificate (FA 2004 s 72).	Up to £3,000.
Fraudulent evasion of income tax (TMA 1970 s 106A).	On summary conviction, imprisonment for up to six months or a fine up to the statutory maximum (£5,000) or both; on conviction on indictment, imprisonment for up to seven years or a fine or both.
Enterprise investment scheme relief: Issue by a company of a certificate of approval for such relief fraudulently or negligently or without the authority of HMRC (ITA 2007 s 207).	Not exceeding £3,000.
Failure of a company to maintain records (other than those only required for claims, etc, or dividend vouchers and certificates of income tax deducted where other evidence is available) (FA 1998 Sch 18 para 23).	Penalty not exceeding £3,000.
Failure to notify notifiable proposals or notifiable arrangements, or failure to notify the client of the relevant scheme reference number under the provisions of FA 2004 ss 306–319 (TMA 1970 s 98C).	(*a*) Up to 31 December 2010 an initial penalty not exceeding £5,000; (i) From 1 January 2011 in the case of provisions under FA 2004 ss 308(1) and (3), 309(1) and 310 up to £600 per day in 'initial period' (but a tribunal can determine a higher penalty up to £1 million); (ii) From 1 January 2011 in the case of provisions in FA 2004 ss 312(2), 312A(2), 313ZA, 313A, 313B, 313C, from 17 July 2013 in the case of provisions in ss 312B and 313ZB, and from 26 March 2015 in the case of ss 310C, 312A(2A), 313ZC, and 316A, an initial penalty up to £5,000. Where a disclosure order is made the amount in (i) above is increased up to £5,000 per day that failure continues from ten days after the order is made. (*b*) a continuing penalty not exceeding £600 for each day on which the failure continues after imposition of initial penalty. Where a disclosure order is made the amount is increased up to £5,000 per day that failure continues from ten days after the order is made.

Offence	Penalty
Failure to notify scheme reference number etc under FA 2004 s 313(1);	Penalty not exceeding £5,000 in respect of each scheme to which the failure relates;
for second failure, occurring within three years from the date on which the first failure began;	penalty not exceeding £7,500 in respect of each scheme to which the failure relates;
for subsequent failures, occurring within three years from the date on which the previous failure began.	penalty not exceeding £10,000 in respect of each scheme to which the failure relates.
(TMA 1970 s 98C; FA 2004 s 315(1)).	
Failure to comply with HMRC investigatory powers under FA 2008 Sch 36.	(*a*) an initial penalty of £300;
Failure to comply with an information notice within FA 2008 Sch 36 Pt 1 or deliberately obstructing an HMRC officer in the course of an inspection of business premises under FA 2008 Sch 36 Pt 2 which has been approved by the First-tier Tribunal. Applies to IT (including PAYE and CIS), CT, CGT, VAT and certain foreign taxes with effect from 1 April 2009. Extended to IHT, SDLT and other taxes from 1 April 2010, to ATED from 17 July 2013; to pension scheme registration applications from 17 July 2014; to Diverted Profits Tax from 1 April 2015, and to Digital Services Tax from 1 April 2020.	(*b*) if failure/obstruction continues, a further penalty up to £60 per day; (*c*) if failure/obstruction continues after penalty under (*a*) imposed, a tax-related amount determined by the Upper Tribunal.
Carelessly or deliberately providing inaccurate information or an inaccurate document in response to an information notice.	Up to £3,000 per inaccuracy.
Failure of a senior accounting officer to ensure a company maintains appropriate tax accounting arrangements (FA 2009 Sch 46).	£5,000.
Failure of a senior accounting officer to provide a certificate stating whether the company had appropriate tax accounting arrangements (FA 2009 Sch 46).	£5,000.
Failure to notify Commissioners of name of senior accounting officer (FA 2009 Sch 46).	£5,000.
Failure of a third party to notify the contact details of a debtor (FA 2009 Sch 49).	£300.
Failure to comply with data-holder notice (FA 2011 Sch 23).	(*a*) an initial penalty of £300. (*b*) if failure continues, a further penalty up to £60 per day. (*c*) increased daily penalty of up to £1,000 to be set by Tribunal if notice still not complied with within 30 days of a daily penalty being notified.
Tax agent failure to comply with file access notice (FA 2012 Sch 38).	(*a*) an initial penalty of £300. (*b*) if failure continues, a further penalty up to £60 per day.
Tax agent engaging in dishonest conduct (FA 2012 Sch 38).	£5,000 minimum to £50,0000 maximum subject to the quality of disclosure and compliance with any access notice, with possible special reduction of £5,000 penalty to nil at HMRC's discretion.
Failure to keep records for the purposes of the annual tax on enveloped dwellings (FA 2013 Sch 33).	Up to £3,000
Corrective action not taken in response to follower notice (FA 2014 s 208).	50% of value of the denied advantage (20% for relevant partners). May be reduced for co-operation.
Failure to pay accelerated payment (FA 2014 s 226).	(*a*) Initial penalty of 5% of any amount unpaid at end of payment period (or where the accelerated payment relates to an instalment of IHT, 5% of any amount unpaid by the later due date of that instalment if applicable). (*b*) Further penalty of 5% of any amount unpaid after 5 months. (*c*) Further penalty of 5% of any amount unpaid after 11 months.
Failure of monitored promoter of a tax avoidance scheme, or their intermediary, to comply with various duties to notify clients, provide information or produce documents (FA 2014 Sch 35 para 2).	(*a*) Initial maximum penalty of £5,000, £7,500, £10,000, or £1,000,000 depending on failure. (*b*) Further daily penalty for each day on which failure continues of up to £10,000 where the maximum penalty could have been £1,000,000, or otherwise, £600.
Provision of inaccurate information or document by a monitored promoter of a tax avoidance scheme when complying with an information duty (FA 2014 Sch 35 para 4).	Maximum penalty of £5,000, £10,000, or £1,000,000 depending on duty being complied with.
Concealing, destroying etc documents required to be produced in connection with a monitored promoter of a tax avoidance scheme (FA 2014 s 280).	On summary conviction, a fine; on conviction on indictment, imprisonment for up to two years or a fine or both.

Offence	Penalty
Failure of a company to provide a return in respect of a SIP, SAYE option, CSOP, EMI or other employee share scheme (ITEPA 2003 Sch 2 para 81C; Sch 3 para 40C; Sch 4 para 28C; Sch 5 para 57B; s 421JC).	(a) Initial penalty of £100. (b) Further penalty of £300 if failure continues for 3 months. (c) Further penalty of £300 if failure continues for 6 months. (d) Further penalty of £10 for each day that failure continues beyond 9 months (with notice).
Inaccurate return provided by a company, or return not filed electronically as required in respect of a SIP, SAYE option, CSOP, EMI or other employee share scheme (ITEPA 2003 Sch 2 para 81E; Sch 3 para 40E; Sch 4 para 28E; Sch 5 para 57C; s 421JD).	Up to £5,000.
Failure to comply with the rules in respect of a SIP, SAYE option, or CSOP scheme (ITEPA 2003 Sch 2 para 81H–81I; Sch 3 para 40H–41I; Sch 4 para 28H–28I).	If scheme does not comply at all, penalty not exceeding twice the tax and NIC HMRC estimate has been 'saved'. Otherwise, up to £5,000.
Failure of a company to provide to HMRC a declaration under ITEPA 2003 Sch 5 para 44(6) by individual to whom an EMI option is granted (ITEPA 2003 Sch 5 para 57A).	£500.
A social enterprise fraudulently or negligently issuing a compliance certificate or statement (ITA 2007 s 257PD).	Up to £3,000.
Failure by a qualifying company or partnership, or by the head of a UK group of companies or by the head of a UK sub-group of a foreign group of companies to publish the company's, partnership's, group's or sub-group's tax strategy or to make it freely available after publication. Applies to financial years beginning on or after 15 September 2016 (FA 2016 Sch 19).	(a) Initial penalty of up to £7,500. (b) further penalty of £7,500 if failure continues for 6 months; and (c) further penalty of £7,500 for every subsequent month that failure continues.
Enablers of defeated tax avoidance. Penalty applies to persons who enable the use of abusive tax avoidance arrangements which are later defeated (F(No 2)A 2017 Sch 16).	The amount of consideration received or receivable by enabler for enabling the tax avoidance arrangements.
Failure to correct on or by 30 September 2018 irregularities in relation to undeclared past UK IT, CGT and IHT liabilities involving offshore interests which exist at 5 April 2017 (F(No 2)A 2017 Sch 18).	200% of the offshore potential lost revenue (PLR). Reductions apply for disclosure but minimum penalty will be 100% of PLR.
Failure to provide loan charge information for income provided through third parties (F(No 2) A 2017 Schs 11 and 12).	(a) an initial penalty of £300. (b) if failure continues, a further penalty up to £60 per day up to a maximum of 90 days.
Inaccuracy in information or document relating to loan charge for income provided through third parties (F(No 2)A 2017 Schs 11 and 12).	Up to £3,000 per inaccuracy.
Failure to amend a company tax return in relation to corporate interest restriction (TIOPA 2010 Sch 7A).	£500.
Failure by the lead trustee to register a trust before the trust deadline, or to tell HMRC about any changes to the registration.	(a) £100 if registered within up to 3 months of deadline[1]. (b) £200 if registered between 3 to 6 months of deadline. (c) higher of £300 or 5% of total tax liability in relevant year if registered more than 6 months after deadline.
Failure by a fund manager to notify a participant of certain deemed disposals of UK land (TCGA 1992 Sch 5AAA).	Up to £3,000
Failure to deliver a Digital Services Tax (DST) return subject to Royal Assent to Finance Bill 2020.	(a) £100 if delivered within 3 months of the filing date. (b) £200 in any other case. (c) increased to £500 and £1,000 respectively for a third successive failure. (d) if not delivered within 18 months of end of accounting period, tax-geared penalties apply of (i) 10% of the unpaid tax if delivered within 2 years (ii) 20% in any other case.
Failure to preserve records to enable delivery of a DST return, subject to Royal Assent to Finance Bill 2020.	Up to £3,000

[1] Penalties not issued automatically and to be reviewed on a case by case basis. Penalties relating to notification of changes will only apply once facility to notify has been set up.

Mitigation of penalties

HMRC have discretion to mitigate or entirely remit any penalty or to stay or compound any penalty proceedings (TMA 1970 s 102).

Interest on penalties

Penalties under TMA 1970 Parts II (ss 7–12B), IV (ss 28A–43B), VA (ss 59A–59D) and X (ss 93–107), and FA 1998 Sch 18 carry interest at the prescribed rate (see p 5): TMA 1970 s 103A. This applies to penalties in relation to promoters of tax avoidance schemes from 17 July 2014. For interest which applies to penalties under the **harmonised interest regime** see p 4.

Publishing details of deliberate tax defaulters

From 1 April 2010 HMRC have the power to publish the names and details of taxpayers who are penalised for deliberate defaults leading to a loss of tax of more than £25,000. From 1 April 2017 the power applies to certain individuals who control a body corporate or a partnership, or who are trustees of a settlement, which is penalised for such deliberate defaults relating to an offshore matter or transfer, but only where the individual would obtain a tax advantage from the default. From the same date, only taxpayers who make full unprompted disclosures are protected (FA 2009 s 94; SI 2017/261).

Publishing details of deliberate enablers of offshore evasion or non-compliance

From 1 January 2017 HMRC have the power to publish the names and details of enablers of offshore tax evasion or non-compliance who are found liable for a penalty and the potential lost revenue involved exceeds £25,000. They may also publish information about a person who has been found to have incurred 5 or more penalties in any 5-year period (FA 2016 Sch 20; SI 2016/1249).

Publishing details of serial tax avoiders

Broadly from 15 September 2016 HMRC have the power to publish the names and details of serial tax avoiders if they are given three warning notices in respect of schemes used while in a warning period and which are defeated (FA 2016 Sch 18).

Publishing details of persistently uncooperative large businesses

HMRC have the power to publish the names and details of a large company, partnership, UK group of companies, or UK sub-group of a foreign group of companies which is subject to a confirmed special measures notice. The provisions apply in relation to the body or entity's first financial year and subsequent years following 15 September 2016 (FA 2016 Sch 19).

Publishing details of enablers of defeated abusive tax avoidance arrangements

HMRC have the power to publish the names and details of persons who have been assessed to a penalty which has become final in relation to enabling defeated tax avoidance arrangements, provided they have incurred at least 50 other such penalties, or total penalties incurred including the current one will exceed £25,000 (F(No 2)A 2017 Sch 16).

Criminal offence for offshore matters

From 7 October 2017 a criminal offence which does not require the need to prove intent will apply for failing to accurately declare taxable offshore income and gains. The specific offences are failure to notify, failure to deliver a return and making an inaccurate return. It will apply where the loss of tax exceeds £25,000 (TMA 1970 ss 106B–106H; SI 2017/970; SI 2017/988).

Corporate offence of failure to prevent criminal facilitation of tax evasion

From 30 September 2017 an offence will be committed where a body corporate or partnership fails to prevent an associated person (broadly an employee, agent or other person who performs services for them) criminally facilitating the evasion of a tax in the UK or abroad (Criminal Finances Act 2017 ss 44–52; SI 2017/739).

Tax agent dishonest conduct

From 1 April 2013, in addition to the penalties listed above, HMRC have the power to publish names and details of tax agents who incur penalties for dishonest conduct over £5,000 (FA 2012 Sch 38; SI 2013/279).

Failure to provide security

A person who fails to comply with a requirement imposed under the PAYE regulations to give security or further security is liable on summary conviction to a fine (not exceeding level 5 on the standard scale (£5,000) in Scotland or Northern Ireland). Also applies to construction industry scheme deductions and corporation tax payments from 6 April 2019 (FA 1998 Sch 18 para 88A(5); ITEPA 2003 s 684(4A); FA 2004 s 70A(5)).

Time limits for claims and elections

Whenever possible, a claim or election must be made on the tax return or by an amendment to the return (TMA 1970 s 42 and FA 1998 Sch 18 paras 9, 10, 67 and 79). Exceptions to this general rule are dealt with in TMA 1970 Sch 1A. Except where another period is expressly prescribed, a claim for relief in respect of income tax and capital gains tax must be made within four years after the end of the tax year. (TMA 1970 s 43(1); FA 2008

Sch 39 para 12.) The time limit for claims by companies is four years from the end of the accounting period to which it relates (FA 1998 Sch 18 para 55; FA 2008 Sch 39 para 45). The tables below set out some of the main exceptions to the general limits.

Income tax

Claim	Time limit
Trading losses: Loss sustained in a trade, profession or vocation to be set against other income of the year or the last preceding year. Extended to certain pre-trading expenditure by ITTOIA 2005 s 57 (ITA 2007 s 64). SEE TOLLEY'S TAX COMPUTATIONS 26.2.	One year after 31 January next following tax year in which loss arose.
Unrelieved trading losses to be set against capital gains (TCGA 1992 ss 261B, 261C). SEE TOLLEY'S TAX COMPUTATIONS 15.2.	One year after 31 January next following tax year in which loss arose.
Losses of new trade etc: Loss sustained in the first four years of a new trade, profession or vocation to be offset against other income arising in the three years immediately preceding the year of loss. Extended to certain pre-trading expenditure by ITTOIA 2005 s 57 (ITA 2007 s 72). SEE TOLLEY'S TAX COMPUTATIONS 15.3.	One year after 31 January next following tax year in which loss arose.
Property business losses: Claim for relief against total income (ITA 2007 s 124).	One year after 31 January next following tax year specified in claim.
Simplified cash basis for unincorporated property businesses: Cash basis *not* to apply (ITTOIA 2005 s 271A).	One year after 31 January next following tax year specified in claim.
Loss on disposal of unlisted shares: Loss on disposal of shares in an EIS company or a qualifying trading company to be offset against other income of the year of loss or the last preceding year (ITA 2007 s 132). SEE TOLLEY'S TAX COMPUTATIONS 15.5.	One year after 31 January next following tax year in which loss arose.
Gift aid: Election to treat donations to charity under gift aid made after 5 April 2003 as made in the previous tax year (ITA 2007 s 426).	On or before date on which donor delivers tax return for the previous tax year and not later than 31 January after that year.
Enterprise investment scheme relief: Income tax relief of 30% on amount invested within specified limits (ITA 2007 s 202).	5 years after 31 January next following tax year in which shares are issued.
Seed enterprise investment scheme relief: Income tax relief of 50% on amount invested within specified limits (ITA 2007 s 257EA). SEE TOLLEY'S TAX COMPUTATIONS 227.3.	5 years after 31 January next following tax year in which shares are issued.
Social investment tax relief: Income tax relief of 30% on amount invested within specified limits (ITA 2007 s 257P).	5 years after 31 January next following tax year in which investment is made.
Rent-a-room relief: Relief not to apply; to apply to gross income in excess of limit; withdrawal of claim (ITTOIA 2005 ss 799, 800).	One year after 31 January next following tax year specified in claim.
Trading or property allowance: Full relief not to apply; partial relief to apply (ITTOIA 2005 ss 783AL, 783AM, 783BJ, 783BK).	One year after 31 January next following tax year specified in claim.

Capital gains

Claim	Time limit
Assets of negligible value: Loss to be allowed where the value of an asset has become negligible (TCGA 1992 s 24(2)). SEE TOLLEY'S TAX COMPUTATIONS 217.1.	Two years after end of chargeable period of deemed sale (and reacquisition).
Assets held on 31 March 1982 for corporation tax purposes only: Events occurring prior to 31 March 1982 to be ignored in computing gains arising after 5 April 1988 (TCGA 1992 s 35(5), (6) as amended). SEE TOLLEY'S TAX COMPUTATIONS 205.2, 214.1 ONWARDS.	Two years after end of accounting period in which first relevant disposal made after 31.3.88; or such further time as HMRC may allow.
Main residence: Determination of main residence for principal private residence exemption (TCGA 1992 s 222(5)(*a*)). SEE TOLLEY'S TAX COMPUTATIONS 223.2.	Two years after acquisition of second residence.
Relief for loans to traders: Losses on certain loans to traders to be allowed as capital losses at the time of claim or 'earlier time' (TCGA 1992 s 253(3A)).	Two years after the end of the tax year or accounting period of loss.
Relief for loans to traders (payments by guarantor): Losses arising from payments by guarantor of certain irrecoverable loans to traders to be allowed as capital losses at time of claim or 'earlier time' (TCGA 1992 s 253(4), (4A)).	Four years after the end of the tax year or accounting period in which payment made (for claims before 1 April 2010, five years after 31 January following tax year in which payment made (capital gains tax); six years after end of accounting period in which payment made (corporation tax)).
Election for valuation at 6 April 1965 for corporation tax purposes only: Gain on a disposal of an asset held at 6 April 1965 to be computed as if the asset had been acquired on that date. An election once made is irrevocable (TCGA 1992 Sch 2 para 17).	Two years after end of accounting period in which disposal made; or such further time as HMRC may allow.
Entrepreneurs' relief / business asset disposal relief: Gain to be taxed at reduced rate of 10% (TCGA 1992 s 169M). SEE TOLLEY'S TAX COMPUTATIONS 211.1.	One year after 31 January next following tax year of qualifying business disposal.

Corporation tax

Claim	Time limit
Trading losses: Loss sustained by a company in a trade in an accounting period to be offset against profits of that accounting period and profits of the preceding year. Extended to certain pre-trading expenditure by CTA 2009 s 61 (CTA 2010 s 37(7)).	Two years after end of loss-making period; or such further period as HMRC may allow.
Trading losses: Post-1 April 2017 loss to be offset against *total* profits of a later accounting period (CTA 2010 s 45A(7)).	Two years after end of loss-making period; or such further period as HMRC may allow.
Trading losses: Post-1 April 2017 loss *not* to be carried forward against *trade* profits of next accounting period (CTA 2010 s 45B(6)).	Two years after end of loss-making period; or such further period as HMRC may allow.
Property losses: Carry forward of post-1 April 2017 losses (CTA 2010 s 62(5C)).	Two years after end of loss-making period; or such further period as HMRC may allow.
Group relief and Group relief for carried forward losses: Group relief to be given for accounting periods ending after 30 June 1999. The surrendering company must consent to the claim (FA 1998 Sch 18 paras 66–77A).	The last of: (*a*) one year from filing date of claimant company's return for accounting period for which claim is made; (*b*) 30 days after end of an enquiry into return; (*c*) if HMRC amend return after an enquiry, 30 days after issue of notice of amendment; (*d*) if an appeal is made against amendment, 30 days after determination of appeal; (or such later time as HMRC may allow).
Non-trading deficit on loan relationship: Claim for non-trading deficits on loan relationships (including non-trading debits on derivative contracts) in an accounting period to be: SEE TOLLEY'S TAX COMPUTATIONS 113.1 ONWARDS.	
(*a*) offset against profits of same period or carried back (CTA 2009 s 460);	Two years after end of accounting period in which deficit arose (or such later time as HMRC may allow).
(*b*) not treated as non-trading deficit of subsequent accounting period but to be carried forward to succeeding accounting periods (CTA 2009 ss 458, 463B).	Two years after end of that subsequent accounting period.
(*c*) for post-1 April 2017 deficits only, carried forward against *total* profits of succeeding accounting periods (CTA 2009 s 463G).	Two years after end of that subsequent accounting period.
Intangible assets: Election to replace accounts depreciation with fixed writing-down allowance of 4% (CTA 2009 s 730). SEE TOLLEY'S TAX COMPUTATIONS 108.1.	Two years after end of the accounting period in which asset was created or acquired.
Research and development: Claim for tax relief to be made, amended or withdrawn in company tax return (or amended return) (FA 1998 Sch 18 para 83E).	One year from the filing date for return or such later time as HMRC may allow.

Capital allowances

Claim	Time limit
Corporation tax claims: Claims, amended claims and withdrawals of claims in respect of corporation tax capital allowances (CAA 2001 s 3(2), (3)(*b*); FA 1998 Sch 18 para 82).	The last of: (*a*) one year after filing date of claimant company's return for accounting period for which claim is made; (*b*) 30 days after end of enquiry into return; (*c*) if HMRC amend the return after an enquiry, 30 days after issue of notice of amendment; (*d*) if appeal is made against amendment, 30 days after determination of appeal; (or such later time as HMRC may allow).
Short life assets: Plant or machinery to be treated as a short life asset (CAA 2001 s 85(2)). SEE TOLLEY'S TAX COMPUTATIONS 4.4.	One year after 31 January after tax year in which chargeable period ends (income tax); two years after end of chargeable period (corporation tax).
Connected persons: Succession to a trade between connected persons to be ignored in computing capital allowances (CAA 2001 s 266). SEE TOLLEY'S TAX COMPUTATIONS 4.2.	Two years after date of the succession.
Sales between persons under common control treated as made at the lower of open market value and tax written down value (CAA 2001 s 570(5)).	Two years after date of the disposal.

Exchanges

Recognised stock exchanges

The following is a list of countries with exchanges which have been designated as recognised stock exchanges under ITA 2007 s 1005; CTA 2010 s 1137. Unless otherwise specified, any stock exchange (or options exchange) in a country listed below is a recognised stock exchange provided it is recognised under the law of the country concerned relating to stock exchanges.

HMRC may make an order designating a market in the UK as a recognised stock exchange.

Country	Date of recognition
Astana International Exchange	25 January 2019
Australian Stock Exchange and its stock exchange subsidiaries	22 September 1988
National Stock Exchange of Australia	19 June 2014
Austria[3]	22 October 1970
Bahamas	
Bahamas International Securities Exchange	19 April 2010
Belgium[3]	22 October 1970
Bermuda	4 December 2007
Botswana	8 October 2018
Brazil	
Rio De Janeiro Stock Exchange	17 August 1995
São Paulo Stock Exchange	11 December 1995
Canada	
Any stock exchange prescribed for the purposes of the Canadian Income Tax Act	22 October 1970
Caribbean	
Dutch Caribbean Securities Exchange	8 December 2014
The Barbados Stock Exchange	2 April 2019
Cayman Islands Stock Exchange	4 March 2004
Channel Islands Securities Exchange Authority[3]	20 December 2013
China	
Hong Kong – Any stock exchange recognised under Section 2A(1) of the Hong Kong Companies Ordinance[3]	26 February 1971
Cyprus	
Cyprus Stock Exchange	22 June 2009
Denmark	
Copenhagen Stock Exchange	22 October 1970
Estonia	
NASDAQ OMX Tallinn	5 May 2010
European Wholesale Securities Market	17 January 2013
Finland	
Helsinki Stock Exchange	22 October 1970
France[3]	22 October 1970
Germany[3]	5 August 1971
Gibraltar	16 August 2016
Global Board of Trade	30 July 2013
Greece	
Athens Stock Exchange	14 June 1993
Guernsey[3]	10 December 2002
GXG Main Quote	23 September 2013
GXG Official List	16 May 2013
Iceland	31 March 2006
IPSX UK Limited	25 January 2019
Irish Republic[3]	22 October 1970
Israel	
The Tel-Aviv Stock Exchange	8 January 2019
Italy[3]	3 May 1972
Japan[3]	22 October 1970
Korea	10 October 1994
Latvia	
NASDAQ Riga	8 January 2019
Lithuania	
NASDAQ OMX Vilnius	12 March 2012
Luxembourg[3]	21 February 1972
Malaysia	
Kuala Lumpur Stock Exchange	10 October 1994
Malta Stock Exchange	29 December 2005
Mauritius Stock Exchange	31 January 2011
Mexico	10 October 1994

Country	Date of recognition
Netherlands[3]	22 October 1970
New Zealand	22 September 1988
Norway[3]	22 October 1970
Poland	
Warsaw Stock Exchange	25 February 2010
Portugal[3]	21 February 1972
Russia	
MICEX Stock Exchange	5 January 2011
Singapore	30 June 1977
Singapore Exchange Securities Trading Limited (SGX-ST)[4]	7 October 2014
Singapore Exchange Derivatives Trading Limited (SGX-DT)[4]	7 October 2014
South Africa	
Bond Exchange of South Africa	16 April 2008
Johannesburg Stock Exchange	22 October 1970
Spain[3] .	5 August 1971
Sri Lanka	
Colombo Stock Exchange	21 February 1972
Sweden	
Stockholm Stock Exchange	16 July 1985
Swiss Stock Exchange	12 May 1997
Thailand	10 October 1994
United Kingdom	
London Stock Exchange	19 July 2007
PLUS-listed Market	19 July 2007
ICAP Securities & Derivatives Exchange Ltd	25 April 2013
LIFFE Administration and Management	26 September 2011
Euronext London	4 February 2015
United States	
Any stock exchange registered with the SEC as a national securities exchange[1]	22 October 1970
Nasdaq Stock Market[2]	10 March 1992

[1] 'National securities exchange' does not include any local exchanges registered with Securities and Exchange Commission.

[2] As maintained through the facilities of the National Association of Securities Dealers Inc and its subsidiaries.

[3] i.e., a stock exchange according to the law of the country concerned relating to stock exchanges.

[4] The original Singapore Stock Exchange merged with two other exchanges and is now known as SGX. The SGX-ST market was identified as representing the originally designated exchange.

Recognised futures exchanges

The following is a list of exchanges which have been designated as recognised futures exchanges under TCGA 1992 s 288(6). By concession, those exchanges were recognised futures exchanges for the tax year of recognition onwards.

Recognised futures exchanges	Date of recognition
International Petroleum Exchange of London	6 August 1985
London Metal Exchange	6 August 1985
London Gold Market	12 December 1985
London Silver Market	12 December 1985
CME Group (formerly Chicago Mercantile Exchange and Chicago Board of Trade)	19 December 1986
New York Mercantile Exchange	19 December 1986
Philadelphia Board of Trade	19 December 1986
Mid America Commodity Exchange	29 July 1987
Montreal Exchange	29 July 1987
Hong Kong Futures Exchange	15 December 1987
Commodity Exchange (Comex)	25 August 1988
Sydney Futures Exchange	13 October 1988
Euronext (London International Financial Futures and Options Exchange)	22 March 1992
OM Stockholm	18 March 1992
OMLX (formerly OM London)	18 March 1992
New York Board of Trade	10 June 2004
Eurex Deutschland	13 March 2015

Recognised investment exchanges and clearing houses

The following is a list of investment exchanges and clearing houses recognised as investment exchanges under the Financial Services and Markets Act 2000 and able to carry out investment business in the UK.

Recognised investment exchanges	Date of recognition
London Stock Exchange plc	22 November 2001
The London Metal Exchange Ltd	22 November 2001
ICE Futures Europe	22 November 2001
NEX Exchange Ltd (formerly ICAP Securities & Derivatives Exchange Ltd)	19 July 2007
Cboe Europe Ltd (formerly BATS Trading Ltd)	20 May 2013
Euronext UK Markets Ltd	2 June 2014
IPSX UK Limited	8 January 2019

[1] List as at 30 March 2020 on Financial Conduct Authority website.

Recognised clearing houses[2]	Date of recognition
LCH Ltd[1]	22 November 2001
Euroclear UK & Ireland Ltd	23 November 2001
ICE Clear Europe Ltd[1]	15 May 2008
LME Clear Ltd[1]	3 September 2014

[1] These clearing houses are recognised central counterparties. LCH Ltd was recognised as such on 12 June 2014. CME Clearing Europe Ltd was recognised as such on 4 August 2014. LME Clear Ltd was recognised as such on 3 September 2014. ICE Clear Europe Ltd was recognised as such on 19 September 2016.

[2] List as at 30 March 2020 on Bank of England website.

Recognised overseas investment exchanges

The following is a list of overseas investment exchanges and clearing houses recognised under the Financial Services and Markets Act 2000 and able to conduct investment business in the UK.

Recognised overseas investment exchange	Date of recognition
National Association of Securities Dealers Automated Quotations (NASDAQ)	23 November 2001
Australian Securities Exchange Ltd	30 January 2002
The Chicago Mercantile Exchange (CME)	23 November 2001
Chicago Board of Trade (CBOT)	23 November 2001
New York Mercantile Exchange Inc (NYMEX Inc)	23 November 2001
SIX Swiss Exchange AG	23 November 2001
ICE Futures US Inc	17 May 2007
European Energy Exchange AG	21 February 2019
ICE Endex Markets B.V.	21 February 2019
Börse Frankfurt Zertifikate AG	21 February 2019
Deutsche Börse AG	21 February 2019
Eurex Frankfurt AG	21 February 2019
Singapore Exchange Derivatives Trading Ltd	5 March 2019
Singapore Exchange Securities Trading Ltd	5 March 2019
Commodity Exchange, Inc.	26 March 2019
Euronext Amsterdam N.V.	26 March 2019
Powernext SAS	26 March 2019
Euronext Paris SA	26 March 2019
Cboe Europe B.V.	16 April 2019
BORSA ITALIANA SpA	16 October 2019
Nasdaq Oslo ASA	17 October 2019
MTS S.p.A.	22 January 2020

[1] List as at 30 March 2020 on Financial Conduct Authority website.

Alternative finance investment bonds

List of recognised stock exchanges designated solely for the purposes of ITA 2007 s 564G, TCGA 1992 s 151N, CTA 2009 s 507.

Recognised stock exchanges	Date of recognition
Abu Dhabi Securities Market	1 April 2007
Bahrain Stock Exchange	1 April 2007
Dubai Financial Market	1 April 2007
NASDAQ Dubai (formerly Dubai International Financial Exchange)	1 April 2007
Labuan International Financial Exchange	1 April 2007

Recognised stock exchanges	Date of recognition
Saudi Stock Exchange (Tadawul)	1 April 2007
Surabaya Stock Exchange	1 April 2007

Applications for clearances and approvals

Note that during the COVID–19 (coronavirus) pandemic HMRC is only accepting non-statutory clearance applications via email and not via post.

Statutory clearance applications and approvals	Address
Demergers (CTA 2010 s 1091); Company purchase of own shares (CTA 2010 s 1044); Transactions in securities (CTA 2010 s 748; ITA 2007 s 701); Enterprise Investment Scheme – acquisition of shares by new company (ITA 2007 s 247(1)(f)); Share exchanges (TCGA 1992 s 138); Reconstruction regarding transfer of a business (TCGA 1992 s 139); Transfer of a UK trade between EU member states (TCGA 1992 ss 140B, 140D); Intangible fixed assets (CTA 2009 s 831); Loan relationships transfers/mergers (CTA 2009 ss 426, 427, 437); Derivative contracts transfers/mergers (CTA 2009 ss 677, 686); Schemes converting income to capital (TCGA 1992 ss 184G–H); Assignment of lease granted at undervalue (CTA 2009 s 237; ITTOIA 2005 s 300); Transactions in land (CTA 2010 s 831; ITA 2007 s 770); Collective investment schemes (TCGA 1992 s 103K)	HM Revenue & Customs, BAI Clearance, BX9 1JL (Applications should be marked "market sensitive" or "non-market sensitive" as appropriate.)[1]
Employee share schemes (ITEPA 2003 Schs 2, 3, 4)	Self-certification applies and can be made through HMRC Online services; see www.gov.uk/guidance/self-certify-your-tax-advantaged-employment-related-securities
Pensions	Registration of a pension scheme from 6 April 2006 must be done online, but HMRC can be contacted at Pension Schemes Services, HM Revenue & Customs, BX9 1GH, United Kingdom
Transfers of long-term business (FA 2012 s 132)	HM Revenue & Customs, CS&TD Business, Assets and International, BAI Financial Services Team, 4th Floor, Meldrum House, 15 Drumsheugh Gardens, Edinburgh EH3 7UL
Transactions in shares or debentures (TA 1988 ss 765 and 765A)	The recommendation is that businesses should address the reports directly to the customer relationship manager dealing with their affairs

Non-statutory clearance applications	Address
Controlled foreign companies (TIOPA 2010 Part 9A; TA 1988 ss 747–756, Schs 24–26)	HM Revenue & Customs, Business, Assets and International, Base Protection Policy Team, NE98 1ZZ
Company migration (TMA 1970 s 109B–100F)	HM Revenue & Customs, Business, Assets and International, Base Protection Policy Team, NE98 1ZZ
Inward investment (in Statement of Practice 02/07)	Inward Investment Support, HM Revenue & Customs, CTIAA Business International, 100 Parliament Street, London SW1A 2BQ
Creative industries (CTA 2009 Pts 15, 15A, 15B)	Creative Industries Unit (Film, Television/Animation and Video Games Tax Reliefs), HM Revenue & Customs - Local Compliance, Manchester Incentives and Reliefs Team S0733, Newcastle upon Tyne NE98 1ZZ, United Kingdom
Enterprise Investment Scheme (EIS), Seed Enterprise Investment Scheme (SEIS) and Venture Capital Trust (VCT) scheme (ITA 2007 Pts 5, 5A, 6)	Venture Capital Reliefs Team, HM Revenue & Customs, WMBC, BX9 1BN Telephone: 0300 123 3440[3]
Business investment relief (ITA 2007 s 809VC)	Wealthy and Mid-sized Business Compliance, HM Revenue & Customs, BX9 1BN
IHT business property relief (IHTA 1984 Pt 5 Ch 1)	Inheritance Tax, HM Revenue & Customs, BX9 1HT, United Kingdom
Social investment tax relief (ITA 2007 Pt 5B)	Venture Capital Reliefs Team, HM Revenue & Customs, WMBC, BX9 1BN Telephone: 0300 123 3440[3]
Other non-statutory clearances including VAT	Large businesses should contact their client relationship manager. All other businesses and their agents should send applications to HM Revenue & Customs Non-statutory Clearances Team SO563, 5th Floor, Saxon House, 1 Causeway Lane, Leicester LE1 4AA[2] or email nonstatutoryclearanceteam.hmrc@hmrc.gov.uk. Regarding emails see[1]

Confirmation or pre-transaction or general advice	Address
General enquiries on IR35	HM Revenue & Customs, IR35 Customer Service Unit, S0733, Newcastle Upon Tyne, NE98 1ZZ Telephone 0300 123 2326
Advance thin capitalisation agreements (Statement of Practice 1/12)	The first contact for information about advance thin capitalisation agreements under the Statement of Practice should be the Customer Relationship Manager (CRM) or Customer Contact (CC) of the business concerned, and they will engage the assistance of a transfer pricing specialist. If there is no known CRM or CC, the application may be sent to the local Transfer Pricing team leader
CGT post-transaction value checks	Completed form CG34 which must be received by HMRC at least two months before the relevant filing deadline
Professional bodies (relief for subscriptions) (ITEPA 2003 s 343)	A list of approved professional bodies and learned societies is available on the HMRC website (at www.gov.uk/government/publications/professional-bodies-approved-for-tax-relief-list-3)
General advice on specialist technical issues	See www.gov.uk/contact-hmrc
SDLT transactions	See www.gov.uk/stamp-duty-land-tax
Post-transaction clearances connected to an offshore disclosure	HM Revenue & Customs, WDF Clearance Team, Individual & Small Business Compliance, Compliance Centres, Digital Disclosure Service Room BP3002, Benton Park View, S1250 Newcastle upon Tyne, NE98 1YX Email isbc.disclosureposttransactionclearance@hmrc.gsi.gov.uk

[1]   Where clearance is sought under any one or more of the sections handled by the Clearance and Counteraction Team, clearance applications may be sent in a single letter to the above Newcastle address for clearances under those sections. The letter should make clear what clearance(s) is required. HMRC acknowledge only those applications that request acknowledgement. An email acknowledgement may be requested. E-mail applications can be sent to nonstatutoryclearanceteam.hmrc@hmrc.gov.uk. Attachments to emails should be no larger than 2MB. Self-extracting zip files should not be sent as HMRC software will block them. Security of emails is not guaranteed. Information about market or price sensitive matters, or well known individuals, should not be sent by email.

[2]   Non-statutory clearances: Taxpayers may apply for a non-statutory clearance where they require clarification on guidance or legislation for other circumstances after having checked that the transaction is not covered by a more appropriate clearance or approval route. Taxpayers must provide all the necessary information requested in the relevant checklist. HMRC will not give clearances or advice in respect of the application of the 'settlements legislation' in ITTOIA 2005 Pt 5 Ch 5, the tax consequences of executing non-charitable trust deeds or settlements, or the venture capital schemes. See www.gov.uk/non-statutory-clearance-service-guidance.

[3]   See Agent update 68 for details of the name change for the Small Company Enterprise Centre to the Venture Capital Reliefs Team.

Capital allowances

Rates of capital allowances

Cars

SEE TOLLEY'S TAX COMPUTATIONS 4.3.

Cars qualify for plant and machinery capital allowances at a rate based on their CO_2 emissions — see table on p 30.

New low-emission cars qualify for first-year allowances — see note 5 on p 31.

Otherwise for **expenditure on or after 1 April 2009 (corporation tax) or 6 April 2009 (income tax)** cars qualify for writing-down allowances and are allocated to the special rate pool if the car's CO_2 emissions exceed 110g/km for expenditure incurred on or after 1 April 2018 (130g/km for expenditure incurred before 1 April 2018, 160g/km for expenditure incurred before 1 April 2013 (corporation tax) or 6 April 2013 (income tax)) and otherwise to the general pool. **Threshold to be reduced to 50g/km of CO_2 for expenditure incurred from April 2021**. See notes 8 and 11 on pp 31–32. Cars with non-business use are allocated to a single asset pool, but rate of WDA depends on emissions (CAA 2001 ss 104AA, 104F, 208A, 268A–268D; SI 2016/984.)

Dredging

SEE TOLLEY'S TAX COMPUTATIONS 3.2.

	Expenditure incurred after	% Rate
Writing-down allowance	5 November 1962	4

Know-how

Expenditure incurred after 31 March 1986: **annual 25% writing-down allowance** (reducing balance basis).

Mineral extraction

SEE TOLLEY'S TAX COMPUTATIONS 3.3.

First-year allowance: **100% FYA** is available for certain expenditure incurred after 16 April 2002 wholly for the purposes of a North Sea Oil ring-fence trade or on plant and machinery used in such a trade.

Writing-down allowance: for expenditure incurred after 31 March 1986, **10%** for expenditure on the acquisition of a mineral asset and certain pre-trading expenditure, otherwise **25%** (on reducing balance basis) (CAA 2001 s 418.)

Patent rights

SEE TOLLEY'S TAX COMPUTATIONS 3.4.

Writing-down allowance

Expenditure incurred after 31 March 1986: **annual 25% writing-down allowance** (reducing balance basis) (CAA 2001 s 472.)

Plant and machinery

	Expenditure incurred after	Expenditure incurred before	Up to pa
Annual investment allowance[1]			
for income tax purposes	31 December 2020		£200,000
	31 December 2018	**1 January 2021**	**£1,000,000**
	31 December 2015	1 January 2019	£200,000
	5 April 2014	1 January 2016	£500,000
for corporation tax purposes	31 December 2020		£200,000
	31 December 2018	**1 January 2021**	**£1,000,000**
	31 December 2015	1 January 2019	£200,000
	31 March 2014	1 January 2016	£500,000

	Expenditure incurred after	Expenditure incurred before	% Rate
First-year allowance (FYA)[12, 13]			
Energy-saving plant or machinery[2]			
for income tax purposes	31 March 2001	6 April 2020	100
for corporation tax purposes	31 March 2001	1 April 2020	100
New low-emission cars[3]	**16 April 2002**	**1 April 2025**	**100**
Certain refuelling equipment[3]	**16 April 2002**	**1 April 2025**	**100**
Environmentally beneficial plant or machinery[4]			
for income tax purposes	31 March 2003	6 April 2020	100
for corporation tax purposes	31 March 2003	1 April 2020	100
Zero-emission goods vehicles[5]			
for income tax purposes	**5 April 2010**	**6 April 2025**	**100**
for corporation tax purposes	**31 March 2010**	**1 April 2025**	**100**
Enterprise zones[6]	**31 March 2012**		**100**
Electric charge-point equipment[7]			
for income tax purposes	**22 November 2016**	**6 April 2023**	**100**
for corporation tax purposes	**22 November 2016**	**1 April 2023**	**100**

	Chargeable period beginning on or after	Chargeable period ending before	
Writing-down allowance (WDA)			
General pool[8]			
for income tax purposes	**6 April 2012**		**18**
for corporation tax purposes	**1 April 2012**		**18**
Special rate pool[8]			
Long-life assets[8, 9]			
for income tax purposes	**6 April 2019**		**6**
for corporation tax purposes	**1 April 2019**		**6**
for income tax purposes	6 April 2012	6 April 2019	8
for corporation tax purposes	1 April 2012	1 April 2019	8
Integral features[8, 10]			
for income tax purposes	**6 April 2019**		**6**
for corporation tax purposes	**1 April 2019**		**6**
for income tax purposes	6 April 2012	6 April 2019	8
for corporation tax purposes	1 April 2012	1 April 2019	8
Thermal insulation[8, 15]			
for income tax purposes	**6 April 2019**		**6**
for corporation tax purposes	**1 April 2019**		**6**
for income tax purposes	6 April 2012	6 April 2019	8
for corporation tax purposes	1 April 2012	1 April 2019	8
Certain cars[8, 11]			
for income tax purposes	**6 April 2019**		**6**
for corporation tax purposes	**1 April 2019**		**6**
for income tax purposes	6 April 2012	6 April 2019	8
for corporation tax purposes	1 April 2012	1 April 2019	8
Solar panels[8, 14]			
for income tax purposes	**6 April 2019**		**6**
for corporation tax purposes	**1 April 2019**		**6**
for income tax purposes	6 April 2012	6 April 2019	8
for corporation tax purposes	1 April 2012	1 April 2019	8
Cushion gas[8, 16]			
for income tax purposes	**6 April 2019**		**6**
for corporation tax purposes	**1 April 2019**		**6**
for income tax purposes	6 April 2012	6 April 2019	8
for corporation tax purposes	1 April 2012	1 April 2019	8

[1] **Annual investment allowance:** The first £1,000,000 (for expenditure on or after 1 January 2019 and before 1 January 2021) of qualifying expenditure incurred in a chargeable period qualifies for the annual investment allowance at 100%. Reduced back to £200,000 for expenditure on or after 1 January 2021; see table for earlier amounts. Where a chargeable period spans the date of an increase or decrease, transitional rules apply. The limit is proportionately increased or decreased where the chargeable period is longer or shorter than a year. A group of companies (defined as for company law purposes) can only receive a single allowance. This restriction also applies to certain related businesses or companies. Expenditure on cars and that qualifying for structures and buildings allowance does not qualify (CAA 2001 ss 38A, 38B, 51A–51N; FA 2019 s 32, Sch 13).
SEE TOLLEY'S TAX COMPUTATIONS 4.6.

[2] **Energy-saving plant or machinery:** The allowance is withdrawn for expenditure on or after 1 April 2020 (corporation tax) and 6 April 2020 (income tax). The allowances were available for investment by *any* business in designated energy-saving plant and machinery in accordance with the Government's Energy Technology Product List. 100% first-year allowances were not available for expenditure incurred on or after 1 April 2012 (corporation tax) or 6 April 2012 (income tax) on plant or machinery to generate renewable electricity or heat where tariff payments are received under either of the renewable energy schemes introduced by the Department of Energy and Climate Change. The restriction applied from April 2014 for combined heat and power equipment (CAA 2001 ss 45A–45C, 46; SI 2018/268; SI 2019/501). The product lists are available at www.gov.uk/energy-technology-list.

[3] **Low-emission cars:** The allowance is given on (*a*) new cars which are either electrically propelled or emit not more than 50g/km of CO_2 for expenditure incurred on or after 1 April 2018 (75g/km for expenditure incurred before 1 April 2018, 95g/km for expenditure incurred before 1 April 2015, 110g/km for expenditure incurred before 1 April 2013, 120g/km for expenditure incurred before 1 April 2008), registered after 16 April 2002 and (*b*) new plant and machinery to refuel vehicles in a gas refuelling station with natural gas, hydrogen fuels, or (for expenditure on or after 1 April 2008) biogas. For expenditure incurred after 31 March 2013 cars provided for leasing no longer qualify for the FYA (CAA 2001 ss 45D, 45E, 46; SI 2016/984; SI 2017/1304). **Threshold to be reduced to 0g/km of CO_2 for expenditure incurred from April 2021.**
SEE TOLLEY'S TAX COMPUTATIONS 4.3.

[4] **Environmentally beneficial plant or machinery:** The allowance is withdrawn for expenditure on or after 1 April 2020 (corporation tax) and 6 April 2020 (income tax). The allowances were available for expenditure by *any* business on new and unused designated technologies and products which satisfy the relevant environmental criteria in accordance with the Government's technologies or products lists (CAA 2001 ss 45H–45J, 46; SI 2003/2076; SI 2019/499). The product lists are available at www.gov.uk/government/publications/water-efficient-enhanced-capital-allowances.

[5] **Zero-emission goods vehicles:** The allowance is given on new (and not second hand) vehicles which cannot under any circumstances produce CO_2 emissions when driven and which are of a design primarily suited to the conveyance of goods or burden. The expenditure is limited to €85 million per undertaking (as defined) over the period for which the provisions apply. The allowance is not available where another State aid has been or will be received towards the qualifying expenditure. Other exclusions apply (CAA 2001 ss 45DA–45DB, 212T; SI 2017/1304).

[6] **Enterprise zones:** For expenditure incurred for the purpose of a qualifying activity in the period ending on the later of 31 March 2021 or eight years from the date the area is (or is treated as) designated, 100% first-year allowances are available for companies chargeable to corporation tax which invest in unused (not second hand) plant or machinery for use primarily in designated assisted areas within certain enterprise zones. Expenditure must be incurred for the purposes of broadly a new or expanding business carried on by the company, must not be replacement expenditure and is limited to €125 million per single investment project (as defined) over the eight years. Exclusions apply. See SI 2014/3183, SI 2015/2047, SI 2016/751 and SI 2018/485 for details of the current enterprise zones. The Northern Ireland Executive proposes to establish a pilot enterprise zone in Northern Ireland which, if implemented, will benefit from the enhanced capital allowances (CAA 2001 ss 45K–N, 212U; SI 2020/260).

[7] **Electric charge-point equipment:** 100% first-year allowance is available for expenditure on new (not second hand), unused electric vehicle charging point equipment installed solely for the purpose of charging electric vehicles (CAA 2001 s 45EA).

[8] **WDAs** are calculated either at the general rate or the special rate on a reducing balance basis. For special rate expenditure for chargeable periods beginning before 1 April 2019 (corporation tax) or 6 April 2019 (income tax) and ending on or after that date a hybrid rate applies, calculated by time apportionment of the 8% and 6% rates. The special rate for ring fence trades is 10%. For chargeable periods beginning on or after 6 April 2008 (income tax) or 1 April 2008 (corporation tax), a WDA of up to £1,000 can be claimed in respect of the main pool and/or the special rate pool where the unrelieved expenditure in the pool concerned is £1,000 or less.

[9] **Long-life assets:** Applies to plant or machinery with an expected working life, when new, of 25 years or more where expenditure on long-life assets in a year is more than £100,000 (in the case of companies the de minimis limit is £100,000 divided by one plus the number of related 51% group companies). It does not apply to plant or machinery in a building used wholly or mainly as, or for purposes ancillary to, a dwelling-house, retail shop, showroom, hotel or office; cars; or sea-going ships and railway assets acquired before 1 January 2011. Expenditure qualifies as special rate expenditure, see note 8 above regarding the hybrid rate applying for periods spanning a change of rate (CAA 2001 ss 90–104E, Sch 3 para 20).
SEE TOLLEY'S TAX COMPUTATIONS 4.5.

[10] **Integral features** of a building are electrical systems (including lighting systems); cold water systems; space or water heating systems, powered ventilation systems, air cooling or purification and any floor or ceiling comprised in such systems; lifts, escalators and moving walkways and external solar shading. Expenditure qualifies as special rate expenditure, see note 8 above regarding the hybrid rate applying for periods spanning a change of rate (CAA 2001 ss 33A, 104A–104E).
SEE TOLLEY'S TAX COMPUTATIONS 4.5.

11 **Cars:** For expenditure on and after 1 April 2009 (corporation tax), 6 April 2009 (income tax), cars with CO_2 emissions exceeding 110g/km for expenditure incurred on or after 1 April 2018 (130g/km for expenditure incurred before 1 April 2018, 160g/km for expenditure incurred before 1 April 2013 (corporation tax) or 6 April 2013 (income tax)) are allocated to the special rate pool. All other cars will go into the general pool. See note 8 above regarding the hybrid rate applying for periods spanning a change of rate (CAA 2001 ss 104A–104E; SI 2016/984). **Threshold to be reduced to 50g/km of CO_2 for expenditure incurred from April 2021**.
SEE TOLLEY'S TAX COMPUTATIONS 4.3.

12 **First-year tax credits:** For expenditure incurred on or after 1 April 2008 and before 1 April 2020, a company can surrender a tax loss attributable to first-year allowances for energy-saving or environmentally beneficial equipment (see notes 2 and 4 above) in exchange for a cash payment from the Government. The cash payment is equal to a percentage of the loss surrendered, subject to an upper limit of the greater of £250,000 and the company's PAYE and NIC liability for the period concerned. For chargeable periods beginning before 1 April 2018 the percentage was fixed at 19%. For chargeable periods beginning on or after 1 April 2018 the percentage is 2/3 of the corporation tax rate chargeable (CAA 2001 Sch A1; SI 2013/464).

13 **First year allowances,** where applicable, are available on expenditure over the annual investment allowance level or on which annual investment allowance has not been claimed, which would otherwise qualify for writing down allowance at 18% in the general plant and machinery pool.

14 **Solar panels**: Expenditure on solar panels qualifies as special rate expenditure, see note 8 above regarding the hybrid rate applying for periods spanning a change of rate (CAA 2001 s 104A–104E).

15 **Thermal insulation**: Expenditure on thermal insulation qualifies as special rate expenditure, see note 8 above regarding the hybrid rate applying for periods spanning a change of rate (CAA 2001 ss 28, 104A–104E).

16 **Cushion gas:** Expenditure on cushion gas qualifies as special rate expenditure, see note 8 above regarding the hybrid rate applying for periods spanning a change of rate (CAA 2001 ss 70J, 104A–104E).

Cars: Car hire p 85.

Renovation of business premises *for periods before April 2017*
SEE TOLLEY'S TAX COMPUTATIONS 3.1.

	Expenditure incurred between	% Rate
First-year allowance	11 April 2007 and 1 or 6 April 2017	100

The relief is withdrawn for expenditure incurred on or after 1 April 2017 (corporation tax) and 6 April 2017 (income tax) (SI 2012/868)

Expenditure had to be incurred on renovating or converting vacant business properties in Northern Ireland or the designated disadvantaged areas in the UK that had been vacant for at least a year, to bring the property back into business use. Premises refurbished by or used by businesses in certain trades were excluded from the scheme. For qualifying expenditure incurred on or after 1 April 2014 (corporation tax) and on or after 6 April 2014 (income tax), allowances were not available if another form of State aid had been, or would be, received. A writing-down allowance was given at 25% (on a straight-line basis) on unrelieved expenditure (FA 2005 s 92, Sch 6; SI 2012/868)

Research and development
SEE TOLLEY'S TAX COMPUTATIONS 3.5.

	Expenditure incurred after	% Rate
Allowance in year 1	**5 November 1962**	**100**

Note: Land and houses are excluded.

Structures and buildings allowance

	Annual rate on or after	Annual rate before	% Rate
for income tax purposes	**6 April 2020**		**3**
	28 October 2018	6 April 2020	2
for corporation tax purposes	**1 April 2020**		**3**
	28 October 2018	1 April 2020	2

Applies on a straight-line basis to qualifying construction expenditure on new non-residential structures and buildings (but not land) where contract for construction is entered into after 28 October 2018. Relief applies to UK and overseas structures and buildings, including new conversions or renovations, where the business is within the charge to UK tax. Where a chargeable period spans 1 or 6 April 2020 the rate of 2% will apply for days before the relevant date and 3% for the days after (CAA 2001 Part 2A; SI 2019/1087).

Capital gains

Annual exempt amount

(TCGA 1992, s 1K, Sch 1C)

Individuals[a], personal representatives[b] and certain trusts[c]

SEE TOLLEY'S TAX COMPUTATIONS 225.1.

[a] An individual who claims to use the remittance basis for a tax year is not entitled to the capital gains tax annual exempt amount for that year. This does not apply if the individual's unremitted foreign income and gains for the year are less than £2,000 (TCGA 1992 s 1K(6); ITA 2007 s 809D).

[b] Year of death and following two years (maximum) (TCGA 1992 s 1K(7)).

[c] Trusts for disabled persons as defined. Exemption divided by number of qualifying settlements created (after 9 March 1981) by one settlor, subject to a minimum of one-tenth (TCGA 1992 Sch 1C; FA 2005 Sch 1A).

Exempt amount of net gains	2015–16	2016–17	2017–18	2018–19	2019–20	2020–21
	£11,100	£11,100	£11,300	£11,700	£12,000	£12,300

Trusts[a] generally

SEE TOLLEY'S TAX COMPUTATIONS 228.1.

Exempt amount of net gains	2015–16	2016–17	2017–18	2018–19	2019–20	2020–21
	£5,550	£5,550	£5,650	£5,850	£6,000	£6,150

[a] Exemption divided by number of qualifying settlements created (after 6 June 1978) by one settlor, subject to a minimum of one-fifth (TCGA 1992 Sch 1C).

Chattel exemption

SEE TOLLEY'S TAX COMPUTATIONS 212.1.
(TCGA 1992 s 262)

	Disposals exemption	Marginal relief: Maximum chargeable gain
From 1989–90 onwards	£6,000	5/3 excess over £6,000

Rates of tax

SEE TOLLEY'S TAX COMPUTATIONS 201.1.
(TCGA 1992 s 1H)

2020–21*	**Gains accruing on the disposal of interests in residential properties (where not exempt), and gains arising in respect of carried interest**		
	Individuals	• to income tax basic rate limit £37,500 (see note)	**18%**
		• above income tax basic rate limit £37,500	**28%**
	Trusts and personal representatives		**28%**
	Other gains		
	Individuals	• to income tax basic rate limit £37,500 (see note)	**10%**
		• above income tax basic rate limit £37,500	**20%**
	Trusts and personal representatives		**20%**
2019–20*	**Gains accruing on the disposal of interests in residential properties (where not exempt), and gains arising in respect of carried interest**		
	Individuals	• to income tax basic rate limit £37,500 (see note)	18%
		• above income tax basic rate limit £37,500	28%
	Trusts and personal representatives		28%
	Other gains		
	Individuals	• to income tax basic rate limit £37,500 (see note)	10%
		• above income tax basic rate limit £37,500	20%
	Trusts and personal representatives		20%
2018–19*	**Gains accruing on the disposal of interests in residential properties (where not exempt), and gains arising in respect of carried interest**		
	Individuals	• to income tax basic rate limit £34,500 (see note)	18%
		• above income tax basic rate limit £34,500	28%
	Trusts and personal representatives		28%
	Other gains		
	Individuals	• to income tax basic rate limit £34,500 (see note)	10%
		• above income tax basic rate limit £34,500	20%
	Trusts and personal representatives		20%
2017–18*	**Gains accruing on the disposal of interests in residential properties (where not exempt), and gains arising in respect of carried interest**		
	Individuals	• to income tax basic rate limit £33,500 (see note)	18%
		• above income tax basic rate limit £33,500	28%
	Trusts and personal representatives		28%
	Other gains		
	Individuals	• to income tax basic rate limit £33,500 (see note)	10%
		• above income tax basic rate limit £33,500	20%
	Trusts and personal representatives		20%
2016–17*	**Gains accruing on the disposal of interests in residential properties (where not exempt), and gains arising in respect of carried interest**		
	Individuals	• to income tax basic rate limit £32,000	18%
		• above income tax basic rate limit £32,000	28%
	Trusts and personal representatives		28%
	Other gains		
	Individuals	• to income tax basic rate limit £32,000	10%
		• above income tax basic rate limit £32,000	20%
	Trusts and personal representatives		20%
2015–16*	*Individuals* • to income tax basic rate limit £31,785		18%
	• above income tax basic rate limit £31,785		28%
	Trusts and personal representatives		28%

Share identification rules

SEE TOLLEY'S TAX COMPUTATIONS **230.1, 230.2**.

(TCGA 1992 ss 104–106A)

For disposals on or after 6 April 2008 by individuals, trustees or personal representatives, shares and securities of the same class in the same company are identified with acquisitions in the following order[2]:
- acquisitions on the same day as the disposal;
- acquisitions within 30 days after the day of disposal on a first in/first out basis[1];
- shares comprised in a single pool incorporating all other shares of the same class, whenever acquired.

For the purposes of corporation tax on chargeable gains, disposals of shares etc are identified with acquisitions in the following order:
- same day acquisitions;
- acquisitions within the previous nine days on a first in/first out basis;
- the pool of shares acquired after 31 March 1982;
- any shares held at 31 March 1982;
- any shares acquired on or before 6 April 1965 on a last in/first out basis;
- (if shares disposed of still not fully matched) subsequent acquisitions.

[1] The 30-day matching rule does not apply in relation to acquisitions after 21 March 2006 where the individual making the disposal is not (or is not treated as) resident (or before 6 April 2013, ordinarily resident) in the UK at the time of the acquisition.
[2] Different rules apply for SIP shares, exempt employee shareholder shares, BES shares, community investment tax relief shares, relevant EMI shares, EIS shares, VCT shares, SEIS shares, EOT exempt shares and social investment tax relief shares.

Business asset disposal relief (formerly known as entrepreneurs' relief)

SEE TOLLEY'S TAX COMPUTATIONS **211.6**.

(TCGA 1992 ss 169H–169V; FA 2019 s 39, Sch 16)

The relief applies to disposals by an individual on or after 6 April 2008 of:
- all or part of a trade carried on alone or in partnership;
- assets of such a trade following cessation; or
- shares or securities in the individual's personal trading company.

Personal trading company is broadly one in which the individual holds at least 5% of ordinary share capital, 5% of voting rights, and, additionally for disposals after 28 October 2018, by virtue of their shareholding, at least 5% of the distributable profits and 5% of assets available for distribution to equity holders on a winding up, and/or is beneficially entitled to at least 5% of the proceeds on the disposal of all the company's ordinary share capital. Where the shareholding is diluted below 5% as a result of a new share issue after 5 April 2019, an election can be made to allow relief for gains up to that time, subject to conditions.

Where a disposal of shares or of an interest in the assets of a partnership qualifies for relief, an associated disposal of assets owned by the individual and used by the company or partnership also qualifies for relief. For disposals on or after 18 March 2015, to qualify the claimant must generally reduce his participation in the business by also disposing of a minimum 5% of the shares of the company carrying on the business, or (where the business is carried on in partnership) of a minimum 5% share in the assets of the partnership carrying on the business. However, the disposal may be of less than a 5% share in the assets of the partnership providing the claimant disposes of the whole of his interest and owned 5% or more of the assets for a continuous period of three years in the eight years preceding the disposal. In addition, for assets acquired on or after 13 June 2016, the asset must have been held for three years before disposal.

Where a qualifying disposal is not of shares or securities in the individual's personal trading company, the relief is given only in respect of 'relevant business assets' comprised in the qualifying business disposal (ie assets used for purpose of the business but excluding shares and securities and other assets held as investments).

Relief is not available for disposals of goodwill on or after 3 December 2014 to a close company to which the seller is related unless the business is transferred to a company controlled by 5 or fewer persons or by its directors and the claimant holds less than 5% of the shares, and less than 5% of the voting power, in the acquiring company. Relief will still also be due where the claimant does hold 5% or more of the shares or voting power provided the transfer of the business to the company is part of arrangements for the company to be sold to a new, independent owner.

Trustees can claim relief where a qualifying beneficiary has an interest in the business concerned.

Relief is extended to a disposal by an employee or officer of a trading company (or one or more companies in same trading group) of relevant EMI shares (as defined). Relief applies from 6 April 2013 where the shares were acquired on or after 6 April 2012.

The relief is available where the relevant conditions are met throughout a period of two years (one year for disposals before 6 April 2019, and for cessations of a business or trading company status before 29 October 2018). The relief operates by charging qualifying net gains to CGT at **10% and is subject to a lifetime limit of gains of £1 million for qualifying disposals made on or after 11 March 2020, though specific rules may apply for contracts exchanged before 11 March but not completed until after that date and for certain reorganisations and share exchanges made before 11 March** (£10 million for disposals before 11 March 2020; £5 million for disposals before 6 April 2011; £2 million for disposals before 23 June 2010; £1 million for disposals before 6 April 2010). Disposals before 6 April 2008 do not count towards the limit. Relief given to trustees counts towards the limit of the qualifying beneficiary.

Transitional rules apply to allow relief to be claimed in certain circumstances where a gain made before 6 April 2008 is deferred and becomes chargeable on or after that date. In addition, gains which would have originally accrued on or after 3 December 2014 but which are deferred into the Enterprise Investment Scheme (see p 39) or Social Investment Tax Relief (see p 40) remain eligible for relief when the deferred gain becomes chargeable.

Investors' relief

SEE TOLLEY'S TAX COMPUTATIONS 215.1.
(TCGA 1992 ss 169VA–169VY, Sch 7ZB)

Relief is available for gains accruing on the disposal of ordinary shares in an unlisted trading company, held for a period of at least three years starting on or after 6 April 2016, which are newly issued to the claimant and acquired for new consideration on or after 17 March 2016. Generally neither the investor nor a person connected to them can be an employee or officer of the company or a connected company, though some exceptions apply. The relief operates by charging relevant gains to CGT at **10% and is subject to a lifetime limit of £10 million**. Relief can be claimed by trustees where an eligible beneficiary has an interest in settled property which includes the qualifying shares.

Other reliefs

The following is a summary of the other main capital gains tax reliefs and exemptions.

Charities and CASCs

Gains accruing to charities and Community Amateur Sports Clubs which are both applicable and applied for charitable purposes are exempt.

Individuals

Business asset disposal relief (formerly known as entrepreneurs' relief) (see p 37) SEE TOLLEY'S TAX COMPUTATIONS 211.1 ONWARDS.	Gains on specified assets chargeable at 10% rate up to lifetime limit.
Companies owned by employee-ownership trusts	Relief from capital gains tax is available for disposals by a person other than a company of shares in either a trading company which is not a member of a group, or a parent company of a trading group, where the disposal is to a trust with specified characteristics. The disposal is treated as being made at no gain/no loss if the settlement is for the benefit of all eligible employees of the company or group and the settlement acquires a controlling interest in the company during the tax year in which the disposal is made. Further conditions apply.
Compensation (injury to person, profession or vocation)	Exempt.
Decorations for valour (acquired otherwise than for money or money's worth)	Gain exempt.
Employee shareholder shares (see p 102) SEE TOLLEY'S TAX COMPUTATIONS 218.2.	Gains on disposals of shares which were worth up to £50,000 on acquisition are exempt, provided the Employee Shareholder Agreement was entered into before 1 December 2016 (or 2 December 2016 where professional advice was given in relation to the share offer on 23 November 2016 before 1.30pm). A lifetime limit of £100,000 applies to exempt gains on disposal of shares acquired under Employee Shareholder Agreements entered into after 16 March 2016.

Enterprise Investment Scheme (see p 100) **SEE TOLLEY'S TAX COMPUTATIONS 210.1 ONWARDS.**	Gain on disposal after relevant three-year period exempt to extent full relief given on shares. Deferral relief is available on gains on assets where the disposal proceeds are reinvested in EIS shares within one year before and three years after the disposal.
Entrepreneurs' relief (now known as business asset disposal relief) (see p 39) **SEE TOLLEY'S TAX COMPUTATIONS 211.1 ONWARDS.**	Gains on specified assets chargeable at 10% rate up to lifetime limit.
Foreign currency acquired for personal expenditure	Gain exempt.
Gifts for public benefit, works of art, historic buildings etc	No chargeable gain/allowable loss.
Gifts of pre-eminent objects	Donors who gift pre-eminent objects to the nation will receive a reduction in their UK tax liability of 30% of the value of the object they are donating. The tax reduction can be against income or capital gains tax and can be spread forward across a period of up to five years starting with the tax year in which the object is offered. The gift must be accepted as pre-eminent by the Arts Council under the Cultural Gifts Scheme. See p 64 for relief applying to companies.
Gilt-edged stock	No chargeable gain/allowable loss.
Hold-over relief for gifts **SEE TOLLEY'S TAX COMPUTATIONS 213.1 ONWARDS.**	Restricted to: (1) gifts of business assets (including unquoted shares in trading companies and holding companies of trading groups). Relief is not available on the transfer of shares or securities to a company; (2) gifts of heritage property; (3) gifts to heritage maintenance funds; (4) gifts to political parties; and (5) gifts which are chargeable transfers for inheritance tax. Where available, transferee's acquisition cost treated as reduced by held-over gain.
Investors' relief (see p 39) **SEE TOLLEY'S TAX COMPUTATIONS 215.1 ONWARDS.**	Gains on qualifying ordinary shares in an unlisted trading company chargeable at 10% rate up to lifetime limit.
Married persons or civil partners living together **SEE TOLLEY'S TAX COMPUTATIONS 218.1 ONWARDS.**	No chargeable gain/allowable loss on transfers between spouses or civil partners.
Motor vehicles	Gain exempt.
Principal private residence **SEE TOLLEY'S TAX COMPUTATIONS 223.1 ONWARDS.**	Gain exempt if property is main residence throughout period of ownership, or throughout the period of ownership except for all or any part of the last 9 months of that period (18 months for disposals before 6 April 2020; 36 months for disposals before 6 April 2014). The 36-month period continues to apply where property is disposed of by an individual who is, or whose spouse or civil partner is, a disabled person or long-term resident of a care home, provided that neither holds an interest in any other dwelling on which private residence relief can be claimed. For disposals after 5 April 2015 property is treated as not being occupied as a residence for tax years when neither the taxpayer nor their spouse or civil partner is tax-resident in the territory in which the property is situated, and they do not stay overnight at the property at least 90 times during the year (pro-rated for part tax years). Period of ownership does not include any period before 31 March 1982. Certain other periods of absence qualify for exemption.
If residence is partly let, exemption for the let part is limited to the smaller of–	(1) exemption on owner-occupied part; and (2) £40,000*. *From April 2020 the relief is only available if owner is in shared-occupancy with the tenant.
Qualifying corporate bonds **SEE TOLLEY'S TAX COMPUTATIONS 224.1 ONWARDS.**	No chargeable gain (for loans made before 17 March 1998, allowable loss in certain cases if all or part of loss is irrecoverable).

Seed enterprise investment scheme (see p 100) **SEE TOLLEY'S TAX COMPUTATIONS 227.1 ONWARDS.**	Reinvestment relief may be claimed where an individual realises capital gains on disposals of assets in a tax year and in the same year makes investments that qualify for, and he claims, the main seed enterprise investment scheme (SEIS) relief from income tax. For disposals of assets in 2012–13 the relief applies to the full qualifying re-invested amount. From 2013–14 the relief applies to half the qualifying re-invested amount. SEIS shares can be treated as issued in the previous tax year as a result of a SEIS income tax relief carry-back claim. SEIS re-investment relief then also has effect as if those shares had been issued on a day in the previous tax year. The maximum exemption is £100,000 of gains for 2012–13 and £50,000 thereafter. A disposal of shares on which SEIS income tax relief has been given and not withdrawn is exempt.
Social investment tax relief (see p 101) **SEE TOLLEY'S TAX COMPUTATIONS 231.1 ONWARDS.**	Deferral relief is available for gains arising on assets in the period 6 April 2014 to 5 April 2021 where the disposal proceeds are reinvested in shares or debt investments which qualify for the social investment tax relief (SITR) income tax relief and investor is UK-resident. The qualifying investment must be made in the period from one year before to three years after the disposal. Limit of £1 million of gains which can be relieved in a tax year. A gain on a disposal of shares on which SITR income tax relief has been given and not withdrawn is exempt from capital gains tax where shares held for at least 3 years.
Venture capital trusts (see p 101) **SEE TOLLEY'S TAX COMPUTATIONS 32.3.**	Gain on disposal of shares by original investor exempt if company still a venture capital trust. Exemption applies only to shares acquired up to the permitted maximum of £200,000 per year of assessment. Deferral relief was available on gains on assets where the disposal proceeds were reinvested in VCT shares issued before 6 April 2004 and within one year before or after the disposal. This relief is withdrawn for shares issued after that date.

Businesses

Roll-over relief for replacement of business assets

SEE TOLLEY'S TAX COMPUTATIONS 103.3, 226.1 ONWARDS.

(TCGA 1992 s 155)

Qualifying assets:
Buildings and land both occupied and used for the purposes of the trade.
Fixed plant and machinery.
Ships, aircraft and hovercraft.
Satellites, space stations and spacecraft.
Goodwill[1].
Milk and potato quotas[1].
Ewe and suckler cow premium quotas[1].
Fish quotas[1].
Payment entitlement under farmers' single payment scheme[1].
Payment entitlement under farmers' basic payment scheme[1].
Lloyd's syndicate rights.

[1] From 1 April 2002 onwards, subject to transitional rules, these items are removed from the list for companies only (as they fall within the intangible assets regime from that date).

[2] The 'replacement' assets must be acquired within 12 months before or three years after the disposal of the old asset. Both assets must be within any of the above classes. Holdover relief is available where the new asset is a depreciating asset (having a predictable useful life not exceeding 60 years).

Roll-over relief on the transfer of a business ('incorporation relief')

SEE TOLLEY'S TAX COMPUTATIONS 213.3.

(TCGA 1992 s 162)

On incorporation of a business, the assets of the business are transferred to a company which then carries on the business in succession to the former proprietor. Gains realised on the transfer can be rolled over where the transfer is wholly or partly in consideration for the issue of shares. Relief is automatic (no claim is required).

See p 63 for disincorporation relief for companies. See p 40 for gifts of business assets.

Personal representatives

Allowable expenses

(SP 2/04)

Expenses allowable for the costs of establishing title in computing chargeable gains on disposal of assets in a deceased person's estate: deaths occurring after 5 April 2004. (HMRC accepts computations based either on the scale or on the actual allowable expenditure incurred.)

Gross value of estate	Allowable expenditure
Up to £50,000	1.8% of the probate value of the assets sold by the personal representatives.
Between £50,001 and £90,000	£900, to be divided between all the assets of the estate in proportion to the probate values and allowed in those proportions on assets sold by the personal representatives.
Between £90,001 and £400,000	1% of the probate value of the assets sold.
Between £400,001 and £500,000	£4,000, to be divided between all the assets of the estate in proportion to the probate values and allowed in those proportions on assets sold by the personal representatives.
Between £500,001 and £1,000,000	0.8% of the probate value of the assets sold.
Between £1,000,001 and £5,000,000	£8,000 to be divided between all the assets of the estate in proportion to the probate values and allowed in those proportions on assets sold by the personal representatives.
Exceeding £5,000,000	0.16% of the probate value of the assets sold subject to a maximum of £10,000.

Trustees

Allowable expenses

(SP 2/04)

Expenses allowable in computing chargeable gains of corporate trustees in the administration of trusts and estates: acquisition, disposals and deemed disposals after 5 April 2004. (HMRC accepts computations based either on the scale or on the actual allowable expenditure incurred.)

Transfers of assets to beneficiaries etc	
(a) Quoted stocks and shares	
(i) One beneficiary	£25 per holding.
(ii) More than one beneficiary	£25 per holding, divided equally between the beneficiaries.
(b) Unquoted shares	As (a) above, plus any exceptional expenditure.
(c) Other assets	As (a) above, plus any exceptional expenditure.
Actual disposals and acquisitions	
(a) Quoted stocks and shares	Investment fee as charged by the trustees (where a comprehensive annual management fee is charged, the investment fee is taken to be £0.25 per £100 of the sale or purchase moneys).
(b) Unquoted shares	As (a) above, plus actual valuation costs.
(c) Other assets	Investment fee (as (a) above), subject to a maximum of £75, plus actual valuation costs.
Deemed disposals by trustees	
(a) Quoted stocks and shares	£8 per holding.
(b) Unquoted shares	Actual valuation costs.
(c) Other assets	Actual valuation costs.

Indexation allowance – corporation tax on chargeable gains

SEE TOLLEY'S TAX COMPUTATIONS 214.1.

(TCGA 1992 ss 53–57, 109)

For corporation tax purposes, an indexation allowance is given as a deduction in calculating gains on disposals from the amount realised (or deemed to be realised) on disposal. Indexation allowance is 'frozen' from 1 January 2018, so for disposals on or after this date the allowance is calculated up to December 2017. Indexation allowance is calculated by multiplying each item of allowable expenditure by:

$$\frac{RD - RI}{RI}$$

Where:

RD is the retail prices index figure for month of disposal (or December 2017 if earlier);

RI is the retail prices index for month of expenditure (or March 1982 if later).

Indexation allowance can only be used to reduce or extinguish a gain. It cannot be used to create or increase a capital loss. It is not available to individuals, trustees and personal representatives. See p 60 for RPI values. The factors below can be used to calculate the indexation allowance for corporation tax purposes.

MONTH OF DISPOSAL

	2015						2016								
1982	July	Aug	Sep	Oct	Nov	Dec	Jan	Feb	Mar	Apr	May	June	July	Aug	Sep
Mar	2.255	2.270	2.268	2.267	2.270	2.280	2.258	2.273	2.287	2.290	2.299	2.312	2.316	2.328	2.334
Apr	2.191	2.206	2.203	2.202	2.206	2.216	2.194	2.208	2.222	2.226	2.234	2.247	2.250	2.263	2.269
May	2.168	2.183	2.181	2.179	2.183	2.193	2.171	2.185	2.199	2.203	2.211	2.223	2.227	2.239	2.245
June	2.159	2.174	2.172	2.170	2.174	2.184	2.162	2.177	2.190	2.194	2.202	2.214	2.218	2.230	2.236
July	2.158	2.173	2.171	2.169	2.173	2.183	2.161	2.176	2.189	2.193	2.201	2.213	2.217	2.229	2.235
Aug	2.157	2.172	2.170	2.168	2.172	2.182	2.160	2.175	2.188	2.192	2.200	2.212	2.216	2.228	2.234
Sept	2.159	2.174	2.172	2.170	2.174	2.184	2.162	2.177	2.190	2.194	2.202	2.214	2.218	2.230	2.236
Oct	2.144	2.158	2.156	2.155	2.158	2.168	2.146	2.161	2.174	2.178	2.186	2.199	2.202	2.214	2.220
Nov	2.128	2.143	2.141	2.139	2.143	2.153	2.131	2.145	2.159	2.162	2.171	2.183	2.186	2.199	2.205
Dec	2.134	2.149	2.146	2.145	2.149	2.158	2.137	2.151	2.164	2.168	2.177	2.189	2.192	2.204	2.211
1983	July	Aug	Sep	Oct	Nov	Dec	Jan	Feb	Mar	Apr	May	June	July	Aug	Sep
Jan	2.130	2.145	2.142	2.141	2.145	2.155	2.133	2.147	2.161	2.164	2.173	2.185	2.188	2.201	2.207
Feb	2.117	2.131	2.129	2.128	2.131	2.141	2.119	2.134	2.147	2.151	2.159	2.171	2.175	2.187	2.193
Mar	2.111	2.126	2.123	2.122	2.126	2.135	2.114	2.128	2.141	2.145	2.153	2.165	2.169	2.181	2.187
Apr	2.068	2.082	2.080	2.079	2.082	2.092	2.071	2.085	2.098	2.101	2.110	2.122	2.125	2.137	2.143
May	2.055	2.070	2.067	2.066	2.070	2.079	2.058	2.072	2.085	2.088	2.097	2.109	2.112	2.124	2.130
June	2.048	2.062	2.060	2.059	2.062	2.072	2.050	2.065	2.078	2.081	2.089	2.101	2.105	2.116	2.122
July	2.032	2.046	2.043	2.042	2.046	2.055	2.034	2.048	2.061	2.065	2.073	2.084	2.088	2.100	2.106
Aug	2.018	2.032	2.030	2.029	2.032	2.042	2.021	2.035	2.047	2.051	2.059	2.071	2.074	2.086	2.092
Sept	2.005	2.019	2.017	2.015	2.019	2.028	2.007	2.021	2.034	2.037	2.046	2.057	2.061	2.072	2.078
Oct	1.994	2.008	2.006	2.005	2.008	2.018	1.997	2.011	2.023	2.027	2.035	2.046	2.050	2.062	2.067
Nov	1.984	1.998	1.995	1.994	1.998	2.007	1.986	2.000	2.013	2.016	2.024	2.036	2.039	2.051	2.057
Dec	1.976	1.990	1.988	1.986	1.990	1.999	1.978	1.992	2.005	2.008	2.016	2.028	2.031	2.043	2.049
1984	July	Aug	Sep	Oct	Nov	Dec	Jan	Feb	Mar	Apr	May	June	July	Aug	Sep
Jan	1.978	1.992	1.989	1.988	1.992	2.001	1.980	1.994	2.007	2.010	2.018	2.030	2.033	2.045	2.050
Feb	1.968	1.979	1.977	1.976	1.979	1.989	1.968	1.982	1.994	1.998	2.006	2.017	2.021	2.032	2.038
Mar	1.956	1.970	1.968	1.966	1.970	1.979	1.958	1.972	1.985	1.988	1.996	2.008	2.011	2.022	2.028
Apr	1.927	1.931	1.929	1.927	1.931	1.940	1.920	1.933	1.945	1.949	1.957	1.968	1.971	1.983	1.988
May	1.906	1.920	1.918	1.917	1.920	1.929	1.909	1.922	1.935	1.938	1.946	1.957	1.960	1.972	1.977
June	1.899	1.913	1.910	1.909	1.913	1.921	1.901	1.915	1.927	1.930	1.938	1.950	1.953	1.964	1.970
July	1.902	1.916	1.914	1.912	1.916	1.925	1.905	1.918	1.930	1.934	1.942	1.953	1.956	1.967	1.973
Aug	1.875	1.889	1.886	1.885	1.889	1.898	1.878	1.891	1.903	1.906	1.914	1.925	1.929	1.940	1.945
Sept	1.870	1.883	1.881	1.880	1.883	1.892	1.872	1.885	1.897	1.901	1.909	1.920	1.923	1.934	1.940
Oct	1.852	1.865	1.863	1.862	1.865	1.874	1.854	1.867	1.880	1.883	1.891	1.902	1.905	1.916	1.922
Nov	1.843	1.856	1.854	1.853	1.856	1.865	1.846	1.859	1.871	1.874	1.882	1.893	1.896	1.907	1.913
Dec	1.856	1.859	1.857	1.856	1.859	1.868	1.848	1.861	1.873	1.876	1.884	1.895	1.899	1.910	1.915
1985	July	Aug	Sep	Oct	Nov	Dec	Jan	Feb	Mar	Apr	May	June	July	Aug	Sep
Jan	1.835	1.849	1.846	1.845	1.849	1.857	1.838	1.851	1.863	1.866	1.874	1.885	1.888	1.899	1.904
Feb	1.813	1.826	1.824	1.823	1.826	1.834	1.815	1.828	1.840	1.843	1.851	1.862	1.865	1.876	1.881
Mar	1.787	1.800	1.797	1.796	1.800	1.808	1.789	1.802	1.814	1.817	1.824	1.835	1.838	1.849	1.854
Apr	1.728	1.741	1.739	1.738	1.741	1.750	1.731	1.743	1.755	1.758	1.765	1.776	1.779	1.790	1.795
May	1.716	1.729	1.727	1.726	1.729	1.737	1.718	1.731	1.742	1.746	1.753	1.763	1.767	1.777	1.782
June	1.710	1.723	1.721	1.720	1.723	1.731	1.712	1.725	1.737	1.740	1.747	1.758	1.761	1.771	1.776
July	1.715	1.728	1.726	1.725	1.728	1.736	1.718	1.730	1.742	1.745	1.752	1.763	1.766	1.776	1.782
Aug	1.708	1.721	1.719	1.718	1.721	1.729	1.710	1.723	1.734	1.738	1.745	1.755	1.758	1.769	1.774
Sept	1.710	1.722	1.720	1.719	1.722	1.731	1.712	1.724	1.736	1.739	1.746	1.757	1.760	1.770	1.776
Oct	1.705	1.718	1.716	1.715	1.718	1.726	1.707	1.720	1.731	1.735	1.742	1.752	1.756	1.766	1.771
Nov	1.696	1.709	1.706	1.705	1.709	1.717	1.698	1.711	1.722	1.725	1.733	1.743	1.746	1.756	1.762
Dec	1.692	1.705	1.703	1.702	1.705	1.713	1.695	1.707	1.718	1.722	1.729	1.739	1.742	1.753	1.758

MONTH OF DISPOSAL

	2016			2017											
1982	Oct	Nov	Dec	Jan	Feb	Mar	Apr	May	June	July	Aug	Sep	Oct	Nov	Dec
Mar	2.333	2.342	2.362	2.342	2.379	2.390	2.406	2.420	2.428	2.435	2.458	2.463	2.465	2.472	2.501
Apr	2.268	2.276	2.296	2.276	2.312	2.323	2.339	2.353	2.360	2.368	2.390	2.395	2.397	2.403	2.432
May	2.244	2.253	2.272	2.253	2.288	2.299	2.315	2.329	2.336	2.343	2.366	2.370	2.373	2.379	2.407
June	2.235	2.244	2.263	2.244	2.279	2.290	2.306	2.319	2.327	2.334	2.356	2.361	2.363	2.370	2.398
July	2.234	2.243	2.262	2.243	2.278	2.289	2.305	2.318	2.326	2.333	2.355	2.360	2.362	2.369	2.397
Aug	2.233	2.242	2.261	2.242	2.277	2.288	2.304	2.317	2.325	2.332	2.354	2.359	2.361	2.367	2.396
Sept	2.235	2.244	2.263	2.244	2.279	2.290	2.306	2.319	2.327	2.334	2.356	2.361	2.363	2.370	2.398
Oct	2.219	2.228	2.247	2.228	2.263	2.274	2.290	2.303	2.310	2.318	2.340	2.344	2.347	2.353	2.381
Nov	2.203	2.212	2.231	2.212	2.247	2.258	2.274	2.287	2.294	2.301	2.323	2.328	2.330	2.336	2.364
Dec	2.209	2.218	2.237	2.218	2.253	2.264	2.280	2.293	2.300	2.307	2.329	2.334	2.337	2.343	2.371
1983	Oct	Nov	Dec	Jan	Feb	Mar	Apr	May	June	July	Aug	Sep	Oct	Nov	Dec
Jan	2.205	2.214	2.233	2.214	2.249	2.260	2.276	2.289	2.296	2.303	2.325	2.330	2.332	2.339	2.366
Feb	2.192	2.200	2.219	2.200	2.235	2.246	2.262	2.275	2.282	2.289	2.311	2.316	2.318	2.324	2.352
Mar	2.186	2.194	2.214	2.194	2.229	2.240	2.256	2.269	2.276	2.283	2.305	2.310	2.312	2.318	2.346
Apr	2.142	2.150	2.169	2.150	2.184	2.195	2.211	2.224	2.231	2.238	2.259	2.264	2.266	2.272	2.300
May	2.129	2.137	2.156	2.137	2.171	2.182	2.197	2.210	2.217	2.224	2.246	2.250	2.253	2.259	2.286
June	2.121	2.129	2.148	2.129	2.164	2.174	2.189	2.202	2.210	2.217	2.238	2.243	2.245	2.251	2.278
July	2.104	2.113	2.131	2.113	2.147	2.157	2.172	2.185	2.192	2.199	2.220	2.225	2.228	2.233	2.260
Aug	2.091	2.099	2.117	2.099	2.133	2.143	2.158	2.171	2.178	2.185	2.206	2.211	2.213	2.219	2.246
Sept	2.077	2.085	2.104	2.085	2.119	2.129	2.144	2.157	2.164	2.171	2.192	2.197	2.199	2.205	2.232
Oct	2.066	2.074	2.093	2.074	2.108	2.118	2.133	2.146	2.153	2.160	2.181	2.185	2.188	2.194	2.220
Nov	2.055	2.063	2.082	2.063	2.097	2.107	2.122	2.135	2.142	2.149	2.170	2.174	2.177	2.182	2.209
Dec	2.047	2.055	2.074	2.055	2.089	2.099	2.114	2.127	2.134	2.141	2.161	2.166	2.168	2.174	2.200
1984	Oct	Nov	Dec	Jan	Feb	Mar	Apr	May	June	July	Aug	Sep	Oct	Nov	Dec
Jan	2.049	2.057	2.076	2.057	2.091	2.101	2.116	2.129	2.136	2.142	2.163	2.168	2.170	2.176	2.202
Feb	2.037	2.045	2.063	2.045	2.078	2.088	2.103	2.116	2.123	2.130	2.150	2.155	2.157	2.163	2.189
Mar	2.027	2.035	2.053	2.035	2.068	2.078	2.093	2.106	2.113	2.120	2.140	2.145	2.147	2.153	2.179
Apr	1.987	1.995	2.013	1.995	2.028	2.038	2.053	2.065	2.072	2.079	2.099	2.103	2.106	2.111	2.137
May	1.976	1.984	2.002	1.984	2.017	2.027	2.041	2.054	2.060	2.067	2.087	2.092	2.094	2.100	2.126
June	1.969	1.976	1.994	1.976	2.009	2.019	2.034	2.046	2.053	2.059	2.080	2.084	2.086	2.092	2.118
July	1.972	1.980	1.998	1.980	2.012	2.022	2.037	2.049	2.056	2.063	2.083	2.088	2.090	2.095	2.121
Aug	1.944	1.952	1.970	1.952	1.984	1.994	2.009	2.021	2.028	2.034	2.054	2.059	2.061	2.067	2.092
Sept	1.938	1.946	1.964	1.946	1.978	1.988	2.003	2.015	2.022	2.028	2.048	2.053	2.055	2.061	2.086
Oct	1.920	1.928	1.946	1.928	1.960	1.970	1.984	1.997	2.003	2.010	2.030	2.034	2.036	2.042	2.067
Nov	1.911	1.919	1.937	1.919	1.951	1.961	1.975	1.987	1.994	2.001	2.020	2.025	2.027	2.032	2.058
Dec	1.914	1.922	1.939	1.922	1.954	1.963	1.978	1.990	1.996	2.003	2.023	2.027	2.029	2.035	2.060
1985	Oct	Nov	Dec	Jan	Feb	Mar	Apr	May	June	July	Aug	Sep	Oct	Nov	Dec
Jan	1.903	1.911	1.929	1.911	1.943	1.953	1.967	1.979	1.986	1.992	2.012	2.016	2.019	2.024	2.049
Feb	1.880	1.888	1.905	1.888	1.919	1.929	1.943	1.955	1.962	1.968	1.988	1.992	1.994	2.000	2.025
Mar	1.853	1.861	1.878	1.861	1.892	1.902	1.916	1.928	1.934	1.941	1.960	1.964	1.967	1.972	1.997
Apr	1.794	1.801	1.818	1.801	1.832	1.841	1.855	1.867	1.873	1.879	1.898	1.903	1.905	1.910	1.934
May	1.781	1.789	1.805	1.789	1.819	1.829	1.842	1.854	1.860	1.866	1.885	1.889	1.892	1.897	1.921
June	1.775	1.783	1.799	1.783	1.813	1.822	1.836	1.848	1.854	1.860	1.879	1.883	1.885	1.891	1.915
July	1.781	1.788	1.805	1.788	1.818	1.828	1.841	1.853	1.859	1.866	1.884	1.889	1.891	1.896	1.920
Aug	1.773	1.780	1.797	1.780	1.811	1.820	1.834	1.845	1.852	1.858	1.877	1.881	1.883	1.888	1.912
Sept	1.775	1.782	1.799	1.782	1.812	1.822	1.835	1.847	1.853	1.859	1.878	1.883	1.885	1.890	1.914
Oct	1.770	1.778	1.794	1.778	1.808	1.817	1.831	1.842	1.849	1.855	1.874	1.878	1.880	1.885	1.909
Nov	1.761	1.768	1.785	1.768	1.798	1.808	1.821	1.833	1.839	1.845	1.864	1.868	1.870	1.875	1.899
Dec	1.757	1.764	1.781	1.764	1.795	1.804	1.817	1.829	1.835	1.841	1.860	1.864	1.866	1.872	1.895

MONTH OF DISPOSAL

	2015						2016								
1986	July	Aug	Sep	Oct	Nov	Dec	Jan	Feb	Mar	Apr	May	June	July	Aug	Sep
Jan	1.687	1.699	1.697	1.696	1.699	1.708	1.689	1.701	1.713	1.716	1.723	1.734	1.737	1.747	1.752
Feb	1.677	1.689	1.687	1.686	1.689	1.698	1.679	1.691	1.703	1.706	1.713	1.724	1.727	1.737	1.742
Mar	1.673	1.686	1.684	1.683	1.686	1.694	1.675	1.688	1.699	1.702	1.710	1.720	1.723	1.733	1.739
Apr	1.648	1.660	1.658	1.657	1.660	1.668	1.650	1.662	1.673	1.676	1.684	1.694	1.697	1.707	1.712
May	1.643	1.655	1.653	1.652	1.655	1.663	1.645	1.657	1.668	1.672	1.679	1.689	1.692	1.702	1.707
June	1.644	1.657	1.655	1.654	1.657	1.665	1.646	1.659	1.670	1.673	1.680	1.690	1.693	1.704	1.709
July	1.652	1.664	1.662	1.661	1.664	1.672	1.654	1.666	1.678	1.681	1.688	1.698	1.701	1.711	1.716
Aug	1.644	1.656	1.654	1.653	1.656	1.664	1.646	1.658	1.669	1.672	1.679	1.690	1.693	1.703	1.708
Sept	1.631	1.643	1.641	1.640	1.643	1.651	1.633	1.645	1.656	1.659	1.666	1.676	1.680	1.690	1.695
Oct	1.627	1.639	1.637	1.636	1.639	1.647	1.629	1.641	1.652	1.655	1.662	1.672	1.675	1.686	1.691
Nov	1.604	1.617	1.615	1.614	1.617	1.625	1.606	1.619	1.630	1.633	1.640	1.650	1.653	1.663	1.668
Dec	1.596	1.608	1.606	1.605	1.608	1.616	1.598	1.610	1.621	1.624	1.631	1.641	1.644	1.654	1.659
1987	July	Aug	Sep	Oct	Nov	Dec	Jan	Feb	Mar	Apr	May	June	July	Aug	Sep
Jan	1.586	1.598	1.596	1.595	1.598	1.606	1.588	1.600	1.611	1.614	1.621	1.631	1.634	1.644	1.649
Feb	1.576	1.588	1.586	1.585	1.588	1.596	1.578	1.590	1.601	1.604	1.611	1.621	1.624	1.633	1.638
Mar	1.571	1.583	1.581	1.580	1.583	1.590	1.573	1.584	1.595	1.598	1.605	1.615	1.618	1.628	1.633
Apr	1.540	1.552	1.550	1.549	1.552	1.560	1.542	1.554	1.565	1.568	1.575	1.584	1.587	1.597	1.602
May	1.538	1.550	1.548	1.547	1.550	1.557	1.540	1.552	1.562	1.565	1.572	1.582	1.585	1.595	1.600
June	1.538	1.550	1.548	1.547	1.550	1.557	1.540	1.552	1.562	1.565	1.572	1.582	1.585	1.595	1.600
July	1.540	1.552	1.550	1.549	1.552	1.560	1.542	1.554	1.565	1.568	1.575	1.584	1.587	1.597	1.602
Aug	1.533	1.545	1.543	1.542	1.545	1.552	1.535	1.547	1.557	1.560	1.567	1.577	1.580	1.590	1.595
Sept	1.525	1.537	1.535	1.534	1.537	1.545	1.527	1.539	1.550	1.553	1.560	1.569	1.572	1.582	1.587
Oct	1.513	1.525	1.523	1.522	1.525	1.533	1.515	1.527	1.537	1.540	1.547	1.557	1.560	1.569	1.574
Nov	1.501	1.513	1.511	1.510	1.513	1.520	1.503	1.515	1.525	1.528	1.535	1.544	1.547	1.557	1.562
Dec	1.503	1.515	1.513	1.512	1.515	1.523	1.505	1.517	1.528	1.530	1.537	1.547	1.550	1.560	1.564
1988	July	Aug	Sep	Oct	Nov	Dec	Jan	Feb	Mar	Apr	May	June	July	Aug	Sep
Jan	1.503	1.515	1.513	1.512	1.515	1.523	1.505	1.517	1.528	1.530	1.537	1.547	1.550	1.560	1.564
Feb	1.494	1.505	1.503	1.502	1.505	1.513	1.496	1.507	1.518	1.521	1.527	1.537	1.540	1.550	1.554
Mar	1.484	1.496	1.494	1.493	1.496	1.503	1.486	1.498	1.508	1.511	1.518	1.527	1.530	1.540	1.545
Apr	1.444	1.456	1.454	1.453	1.456	1.463	1.446	1.457	1.468	1.471	1.477	1.487	1.490	1.499	1.504
May	1.435	1.446	1.444	1.444	1.446	1.454	1.437	1.448	1.459	1.461	1.468	1.477	1.480	1.490	1.494
June	1.426	1.437	1.435	1.434	1.437	1.445	1.428	1.439	1.449	1.452	1.459	1.468	1.471	1.480	1.485
July	1.424	1.435	1.433	1.432	1.435	1.442	1.425	1.437	1.447	1.450	1.456	1.466	1.469	1.478	1.483
Aug	1.397	1.408	1.406	1.405	1.408	1.415	1.399	1.410	1.420	1.423	1.429	1.438	1.441	1.450	1.455
Sept	1.386	1.397	1.395	1.394	1.397	1.404	1.387	1.399	1.409	1.411	1.418	1.427	1.430	1.439	1.444
Oct	1.362	1.373	1.371	1.370	1.373	1.380	1.363	1.374	1.384	1.387	1.394	1.403	1.405	1.415	1.419
Nov	1.351	1.362	1.360	1.359	1.362	1.369	1.353	1.364	1.374	1.376	1.383	1.392	1.395	1.404	1.408
Dec	1.345	1.355	1.354	1.353	1.355	1.363	1.346	1.357	1.367	1.370	1.376	1.385	1.388	1.397	1.402
1989	July	Aug	Sep	Oct	Nov	Dec	Jan	Feb	Mar	Apr	May	June	July	Aug	Sep
Jan	1.330	1.341	1.339	1.338	1.341	1.348	1.332	1.342	1.352	1.355	1.361	1.370	1.373	1.382	1.386
Feb	1.313	1.324	1.322	1.321	1.324	1.331	1.315	1.326	1.335	1.338	1.344	1.353	1.356	1.365	1.369
Mar	1.303	1.313	1.312	1.311	1.313	1.321	1.305	1.315	1.325	1.328	1.334	1.343	1.346	1.354	1.359
Apr	1.262	1.273	1.271	1.270	1.273	1.280	1.264	1.275	1.284	1.287	1.293	1.302	1.304	1.313	1.318
May	1.249	1.259	1.257	1.257	1.259	1.266	1.250	1.261	1.270	1.273	1.279	1.288	1.290	1.299	1.303
June	1.241	1.251	1.250	1.249	1.251	1.258	1.243	1.253	1.263	1.265	1.271	1.280	1.282	1.291	1.295
July	1.239	1.249	1.248	1.247	1.249	1.256	1.241	1.251	1.261	1.263	1.269	1.278	1.281	1.289	1.294
Aug	1.233	1.244	1.242	1.241	1.244	1.250	1.235	1.245	1.255	1.257	1.263	1.272	1.275	1.283	1.288
Sept	1.218	1.228	1.226	1.226	1.228	1.235	1.220	1.230	1.239	1.242	1.248	1.256	1.259	1.268	1.272
Oct	1.201	1.211	1.209	1.209	1.211	1.218	1.203	1.213	1.222	1.225	1.231	1.239	1.242	1.250	1.254
Nov	1.182	1.192	1.191	1.190	1.192	1.199	1.184	1.194	1.203	1.206	1.212	1.220	1.223	1.231	1.235
Dec	1.177	1.187	1.185	1.184	1.187	1.194	1.178	1.189	1.198	1.200	1.206	1.215	1.217	1.226	1.230

MONTH OF DISPOSAL

1986	2016 Oct	Nov	Dec	2017 Jan	Feb	Mar	Apr	May	June	July	Aug	Sep	Oct	Nov	Dec
Jan	1.751	1.758	1.775	1.758	1.789	1.798	1.811	1.823	1.829	1.835	1.854	1.858	1.860	1.866	1.889
Feb	1.741	1.748	1.765	1.748	1.778	1.788	1.801	1.813	1.819	1.825	1.844	1.848	1.850	1.855	1.879
Mar	1.738	1.745	1.761	1.745	1.775	1.784	1.797	1.809	1.815	1.821	1.840	1.844	1.846	1.851	1.875
Apr	1.711	1.718	1.735	1.718	1.748	1.757	1.771	1.782	1.788	1.794	1.813	1.817	1.819	1.824	1.847
May	1.706	1.713	1.730	1.713	1.743	1.752	1.766	1.777	1.783	1.789	1.807	1.812	1.814	1.819	1.842
June	1.708	1.715	1.731	1.715	1.745	1.754	1.767	1.778	1.784	1.791	1.809	1.813	1.815	1.820	1.844
July	1.715	1.723	1.739	1.723	1.752	1.762	1.775	1.786	1.792	1.799	1.817	1.821	1.823	1.828	1.852
Aug	1.707	1.714	1.731	1.714	1.744	1.753	1.766	1.778	1.784	1.790	1.808	1.812	1.814	1.819	1.843
Sept	1.694	1.701	1.717	1.701	1.730	1.740	1.753	1.764	1.770	1.776	1.794	1.799	1.801	1.806	1.829
Oct	1.690	1.697	1.713	1.697	1.726	1.735	1.748	1.760	1.766	1.772	1.790	1.794	1.796	1.801	1.825
Nov	1.667	1.674	1.690	1.674	1.703	1.712	1.725	1.736	1.742	1.749	1.767	1.771	1.773	1.778	1.801
Dec	1.658	1.665	1.681	1.665	1.694	1.703	1.716	1.727	1.733	1.739	1.757	1.762	1.764	1.769	1.792

1987	Oct	Nov	Dec	Jan	Feb	Mar	Apr	May	June	July	Aug	Sep	Oct	Nov	Dec
Jan	1.648	1.655	1.671	1.655	1.684	1.693	1.706	1.717	1.723	1.729	1.747	1.751	1.753	1.758	1.781
Feb	1.637	1.644	1.660	1.644	1.673	1.682	1.695	1.706	1.712	1.718	1.736	1.740	1.742	1.747	1.770
Mar	1.632	1.639	1.655	1.639	1.668	1.677	1.690	1.701	1.707	1.713	1.731	1.735	1.737	1.742	1.764
Apr	1.601	1.608	1.624	1.608	1.637	1.645	1.658	1.669	1.675	1.681	1.698	1.702	1.704	1.709	1.732
May	1.599	1.605	1.621	1.605	1.634	1.643	1.656	1.666	1.672	1.678	1.696	1.700	1.702	1.707	1.729
June	1.599	1.605	1.621	1.605	1.634	1.643	1.656	1.666	1.672	1.678	1.696	1.700	1.702	1.707	1.729
July	1.601	1.608	1.624	1.608	1.637	1.645	1.658	1.669	1.675	1.681	1.698	1.702	1.704	1.709	1.732
Aug	1.594	1.600	1.616	1.600	1.629	1.638	1.650	1.661	1.667	1.673	1.690	1.694	1.696	1.701	1.724
Sept	1.586	1.593	1.608	1.593	1.621	1.630	1.643	1.653	1.659	1.665	1.683	1.687	1.688	1.693	1.716
Oct	1.573	1.580	1.596	1.580	1.608	1.617	1.630	1.640	1.646	1.652	1.670	1.673	1.675	1.680	1.703
Nov	1.561	1.568	1.583	1.568	1.596	1.604	1.617	1.628	1.633	1.639	1.657	1.661	1.662	1.667	1.690
Dec	1.563	1.570	1.586	1.570	1.598	1.607	1.620	1.630	1.636	1.642	1.659	1.663	1.665	1.670	1.692

1988	Oct	Nov	Dec	Jan	Feb	Mar	Apr	May	June	July	Aug	Sep	Oct	Nov	Dec
Jan	1.563	1.570	1.586	1.570	1.598	1.607	1.620	1.630	1.636	1.642	1.659	1.663	1.665	1.670	1.692
Feb	1.554	1.560	1.576	1.560	1.588	1.597	1.609	1.620	1.626	1.632	1.649	1.653	1.655	1.660	1.682
Mar	1.544	1.550	1.566	1.550	1.578	1.587	1.599	1.610	1.616	1.622	1.639	1.643	1.645	1.649	1.671
Apr	1.503	1.509	1.525	1.509	1.537	1.545	1.558	1.568	1.574	1.579	1.596	1.600	1.602	1.607	1.629
May	1.493	1.500	1.515	1.500	1.527	1.536	1.548	1.558	1.564	1.570	1.587	1.590	1.592	1.597	1.619
June	1.484	1.491	1.506	1.491	1.518	1.526	1.538	1.549	1.554	1.560	1.577	1.581	1.583	1.587	1.609
July	1.482	1.488	1.503	1.488	1.515	1.524	1.536	1.546	1.552	1.558	1.575	1.578	1.580	1.585	1.606
Aug	1.454	1.461	1.475	1.461	1.487	1.496	1.508	1.518	1.524	1.529	1.546	1.550	1.551	1.556	1.577
Sept	1.443	1.449	1.464	1.449	1.476	1.484	1.496	1.506	1.512	1.518	1.534	1.538	1.540	1.544	1.565
Oct	1.418	1.425	1.439	1.425	1.451	1.459	1.471	1.481	1.487	1.492	1.509	1.512	1.514	1.519	1.540
Nov	1.407	1.414	1.428	1.414	1.440	1.448	1.460	1.470	1.475	1.481	1.497	1.501	1.503	1.507	1.528
Dec	1.401	1.407	1.422	1.407	1.433	1.442	1.453	1.463	1.469	1.474	1.490	1.494	1.496	1.500	1.521

1989	Oct	Nov	Dec	Jan	Feb	Mar	Apr	May	June	July	Aug	Sep	Oct	Nov	Dec
Jan	1.386	1.392	1.406	1.392	1.418	1.426	1.438	1.448	1.453	1.459	1.475	1.478	1.480	1.485	1.505
Feb	1.369	1.375	1.389	1.375	1.401	1.409	1.420	1.430	1.436	1.441	1.457	1.461	1.462	1.467	1.487
Mar	1.358	1.364	1.378	1.364	1.390	1.398	1.410	1.419	1.425	1.430	1.446	1.450	1.451	1.456	1.476
Apr	1.317	1.323	1.337	1.323	1.348	1.356	1.367	1.377	1.382	1.388	1.403	1.407	1.409	1.413	1.433
May	1.303	1.309	1.323	1.309	1.334	1.342	1.353	1.363	1.368	1.373	1.389	1.392	1.394	1.398	1.418
June	1.295	1.301	1.315	1.301	1.326	1.334	1.345	1.354	1.360	1.365	1.380	1.384	1.386	1.390	1.410
July	1.293	1.299	1.313	1.299	1.324	1.332	1.343	1.352	1.358	1.363	1.378	1.382	1.384	1.388	1.408
Aug	1.287	1.293	1.307	1.293	1.318	1.326	1.337	1.346	1.351	1.357	1.372	1.376	1.377	1.382	1.402
Sept	1.271	1.277	1.291	1.277	1.302	1.310	1.321	1.330	1.335	1.340	1.356	1.359	1.361	1.365	1.385
Oct	1.254	1.260	1.273	1.260	1.284	1.292	1.303	1.312	1.317	1.323	1.338	1.341	1.343	1.347	1.367
Nov	1.235	1.241	1.254	1.241	1.265	1.273	1.284	1.293	1.298	1.303	1.318	1.322	1.323	1.327	1.347
Dec	1.229	1.235	1.248	1.235	1.259	1.267	1.278	1.287	1.292	1.297	1.312	1.316	1.317	1.322	1.341

MONTH OF DISPOSAL

	2015						2016								
1990	July	Aug	Sep	Oct	Nov	Dec	Jan	Feb	Mar	Apr	May	June	July	Aug	Sep
Jan	1.164	1.174	1.172	1.172	1.174	1.181	1.166	1.176	1.185	1.187	1.193	1.202	1.204	1.213	1.217
Feb	1.151	1.161	1.160	1.159	1.161	1.168	1.153	1.163	1.172	1.175	1.181	1.189	1.191	1.200	1.204
Mar	1.130	1.140	1.138	1.138	1.140	1.147	1.132	1.142	1.151	1.153	1.159	1.167	1.170	1.178	1.182
Apr	1.067	1.077	1.075	1.074	1.077	1.083	1.069	1.078	1.087	1.090	1.095	1.103	1.106	1.114	1.118
May	1.049	1.059	1.057	1.056	1.059	1.065	1.051	1.060	1.069	1.071	1.077	1.085	1.087	1.095	1.099
June	1.041	1.051	1.049	1.048	1.051	1.057	1.043	1.052	1.061	1.063	1.069	1.077	1.079	1.087	1.091
July	1.039	1.049	1.047	1.047	1.049	1.055	1.041	1.050	1.059	1.062	1.067	1.075	1.077	1.085	1.089
Aug	1.019	1.028	1.027	1.026	1.028	1.034	1.020	1.030	1.038	1.041	1.046	1.054	1.056	1.064	1.068
Sept	1.000	1.009	1.008	1.007	1.009	1.015	1.002	1.011	1.019	1.022	1.027	1.035	1.037	1.045	1.049
Oct	.985	.994	.992	.992	.994	1.000	.986	.995	1.004	1.006	1.012	1.019	1.021	1.029	1.033
Nov	.989	.998	.997	.996	.998	1.005	.991	1.000	1.008	1.011	1.016	1.024	1.026	1.034	1.038
Dec	.991	1.000	.998	.998	1.000	1.006	.992	1.002	1.010	1.012	1.018	1.025	1.028	1.035	1.039
1991	July	Aug	Sep	Oct	Nov	Dec	Jan	Feb	Mar	Apr	May	June	July	Aug	Sep
Jan	.986	.995	.994	.993	.995	1.002	.988	.997	1.005	1.008	1.013	1.021	1.023	1.031	1.035
Feb	.976	.985	.983	.982	.985	.991	.977	.986	.995	.997	1.002	1.010	1.012	1.020	1.024
Mar	.968	.977	.976	.975	.977	.983	.970	.979	.987	.989	.995	1.002	1.005	1.012	1.016
Apr	.943	.952	.950	.950	.952	.958	.944	.953	.962	.964	.969	.977	.979	.986	.990
May	.937	.946	.945	.944	.946	.952	.939	.948	.956	.958	.963	.971	.973	.981	.984
June	.928	.937	.936	.935	.937	.943	.930	.939	.947	.949	.955	.962	.964	.972	.975
July	.933	.942	.940	.939	.942	.948	.934	.943	.951	.954	.959	.966	.969	.976	.980
Aug	.928	.937	.936	.935	.937	.943	.930	.939	.947	.949	.955	.962	.964	.972	.975
Sept	.921	.930	.929	.928	.930	.936	.923	.932	.940	.942	.947	.955	.957	.964	.968
Oct	.914	.923	.922	.921	.923	.929	.916	.925	.933	.935	.940	.947	.950	.957	.961
Nov	.907	.916	.914	.914	.916	.922	.909	.917	.926	.928	.933	.940	.942	.950	.954
Dec	.906	.915	.913	.912	.915	.920	.907	.916	.924	.926	.931	.939	.941	.948	.952
1992	July	Aug	Sep	Oct	Nov	Dec	Jan	Feb	Mar	Apr	May	June	July	Aug	Sep
Jan	.907	.916	.914	.914	.916	.922	.909	.917	.926	.928	.933	.940	.942	.950	.954
Feb	.897	.906	.905	.904	.906	.912	.899	.908	.916	.918	.923	.930	.933	.940	.944
Mar	.892	.901	.899	.898	.901	.906	.893	.902	.910	.912	.917	.925	.927	.934	.938
Apr	.863	.872	.870	.870	.872	.878	.865	.873	.881	.883	.888	.896	.898	.905	.909
May	.856	.865	.864	.863	.865	.871	.858	.866	.874	.877	.882	.889	.891	.898	.902
June	.856	.865	.864	.863	.865	.871	.858	.866	.874	.877	.882	.889	.891	.898	.902
July	.863	.872	.870	.870	.872	.878	.865	.873	.881	.883	.888	.896	.898	.905	.909
Aug	.862	.870	.869	.868	.870	.876	.863	.872	.880	.882	.887	.894	.896	.904	.907
Sept	.855	.864	.862	.862	.864	.869	.857	.865	.873	.875	.880	.887	.890	.897	.900
Oct	.848	.857	.856	.855	.857	.863	.850	.858	.866	.868	.873	.881	.883	.890	.893
Nov	.851	.860	.858	.858	.860	.865	.853	.861	.869	.871	.876	.883	.885	.893	.896
Dec	.858	.866	.865	.864	.866	.872	.859	.868	.876	.878	.883	.890	.892	.899	.903
1993	July	Aug	Sep	Oct	Nov	Dec	Jan	Feb	Mar	Apr	May	June	July	Aug	Sep
Jan	.875	.884	.883	.882	.884	.890	.877	.885	.893	.896	.901	.908	.910	.917	.921
Feb	.863	.872	.870	.870	.872	.878	.865	.873	.881	.883	.888	.896	.898	.905	.909
Mar	.856	.865	.864	.863	.865	.871	.858	.866	.874	.877	.882	.889	.891	.898	.902
Apr	.839	.848	.846	.846	.848	.853	.841	.849	.857	.859	.864	.871	.873	.881	.884
May	.833	.841	.840	.839	.841	.847	.834	.843	.850	.853	.858	.865	.867	.874	.877
June	.834	.843	.841	.840	.843	.848	.835	.844	.852	.854	.859	.866	.868	.875	.879
July	.838	.846	.845	.844	.846	.852	.839	.848	.856	.858	.863	.870	.872	.879	.883
Aug	.830	.839	.837	.837	.839	.844	.832	.840	.848	.850	.855	.862	.864	.871	.875
Sept	.822	.831	.829	.829	.831	.837	.824	.832	.840	.842	.847	.854	.856	.863	.867
Oct	.824	.832	.831	.830	.832	.838	.825	.834	.841	.843	.848	.855	.858	.865	.868
Nov	.826	.835	.833	.833	.835	.840	.828	.836	.844	.846	.851	.858	.860	.867	.871
Dec	.822	.831	.829	.829	.831	.837	.824	.832	.840	.842	.847	.854	.856	.863	.867

MONTH OF DISPOSAL

	2016			2017											
1990	Oct	Nov	Dec	Jan	Feb	Mar	Apr	May	June	July	Aug	Sep	Oct	Nov	Dec
Jan	1.216	1.222	1.235	1.222	1.246	1.254	1.264	1.274	1.279	1.284	1.299	1.302	1.304	1.308	1.327
Feb	1.203	1.209	1.222	1.209	1.233	1.240	1.251	1.260	1.265	1.270	1.285	1.289	1.290	1.295	1.314
Mar	1.181	1.187	1.200	1.187	1.211	1.218	1.229	1.238	1.243	1.248	1.263	1.266	1.268	1.272	1.291
Apr	1.117	1.122	1.135	1.122	1.145	1.153	1.163	1.172	1.177	1.181	1.196	1.199	1.201	1.205	1.223
May	1.098	1.104	1.116	1.104	1.127	1.134	1.144	1.153	1.158	1.162	1.177	1.180	1.181	1.185	1.204
June	1.090	1.096	1.108	1.096	1.118	1.125	1.136	1.144	1.149	1.154	1.168	1.171	1.173	1.177	1.195
July	1.088	1.094	1.106	1.094	1.117	1.124	1.134	1.143	1.147	1.152	1.166	1.170	1.171	1.175	1.193
Aug	1.067	1.073	1.085	1.073	1.095	1.102	1.112	1.121	1.126	1.130	1.144	1.148	1.149	1.153	1.171
Sept	1.048	1.053	1.066	1.053	1.076	1.083	1.093	1.101	1.106	1.111	1.125	1.128	1.129	1.133	1.151
Oct	1.032	1.038	1.050	1.038	1.060	1.067	1.077	1.085	1.090	1.094	1.108	1.111	1.113	1.117	1.134
Nov	1.037	1.042	1.055	1.042	1.065	1.072	1.082	1.090	1.095	1.099	1.113	1.116	1.118	1.122	1.139
Dec	1.038	1.044	1.056	1.044	1.066	1.073	1.083	1.092	1.096	1.101	1.115	1.118	1.119	1.123	1.141
1991	Oct	Nov	Dec	Jan	Feb	Mar	Apr	May	June	July	Aug	Sep	Oct	Nov	Dec
Jan	1.034	1.039	1.051	1.039	1.061	1.068	1.078	1.087	1.091	1.096	1.110	1.113	1.114	1.118	1.136
Feb	1.023	1.028	1.040	1.028	1.050	1.057	1.067	1.076	1.080	1.085	1.099	1.102	1.103	1.107	1.125
Mar	1.015	1.021	1.033	1.021	1.043	1.049	1.059	1.068	1.072	1.077	1.091	1.094	1.095	1.099	1.116
Apr	.989	.995	1.007	.995	1.017	1.023	1.033	1.041	1.046	1.050	1.064	1.067	1.068	1.072	1.089
May	.984	.989	1.001	.989	1.010	1.017	1.027	1.035	1.040	1.044	1.058	1.061	1.062	1.066	1.083
June	.975	.980	.992	.980	1.001	1.008	1.018	1.026	1.031	1.035	1.048	1.051	1.053	1.057	1.074
July	.979	.984	.996	.984	1.006	1.013	1.022	1.031	1.035	1.040	1.053	1.056	1.058	1.061	1.078
Aug	.975	.980	.992	.980	1.001	1.008	1.018	1.026	1.031	1.035	1.048	1.051	1.053	1.057	1.074
Sept	.967	.973	.984	.973	.994	1.001	1.010	1.019	1.023	1.027	1.041	1.044	1.045	1.049	1.066
Oct	.960	.965	.977	.965	.987	.993	1.003	1.011	1.016	1.020	1.033	1.036	1.038	1.041	1.058
Nov	.953	.958	.970	.958	.979	.986	.996	1.004	1.008	1.013	1.026	1.029	1.030	1.034	1.051
Dec	.951	.957	.968	.957	.978	.985	.994	1.002	1.007	1.011	1.024	1.027	1.029	1.032	1.049
1992	Oct	Nov	Dec	Jan	Feb	Mar	Apr	May	June	July	Aug	Sep	Oct	Nov	Dec
Jan	.953	.958	.970	.958	.979	.986	.996	1.004	1.008	1.013	1.026	1.029	1.030	1.034	1.051
Feb	.943	.948	.960	.948	.969	.976	.985	.993	.998	1.002	1.015	1.018	1.020	1.023	1.040
Mar	.937	.942	.954	.942	.963	.970	.980	.988	.992	.996	1.010	1.012	1.014	1.018	1.034
Apr	.908	.913	.924	.913	.934	.940	.950	.957	.962	.966	.979	.982	.983	.987	1.004
May	.901	.906	.917	.906	.927	.933	.943	.950	.955	.959	.972	.975	.976	.980	.996
June	.901	.906	.917	.906	.927	.933	.943	.950	.955	.959	.972	.975	.976	.980	.996
July	.908	.913	.924	.913	.934	.940	.950	.957	.962	.966	.979	.982	.983	.987	1.004
Aug	.906	.911	.923	.911	.932	.939	.948	.956	.960	.965	.978	.981	.982	.986	1.002
Sept	.900	.905	.916	.905	.925	.932	.941	.949	.953	.958	.971	.973	.975	.978	.995
Oct	.893	.898	.909	.898	.919	.925	.934	.942	.946	.951	.964	.966	.968	.971	.988
Nov	.895	.901	.912	.901	.921	.928	.937	.945	.949	.953	.966	.969	.971	.974	.991
Dec	.902	.907	.919	.907	.928	.935	.944	.952	.956	.960	.973	.976	.978	.981	.998
1993	Oct	Nov	Dec	Jan	Feb	Mar	Apr	May	June	July	Aug	Sep	Oct	Nov	Dec
Jan	.920	.925	.937	.925	.946	.953	.962	.970	.975	.979	.992	.995	.996	1.000	1.017
Feb	.908	.913	.924	.913	.934	.940	.950	.957	.962	.966	.979	.982	.983	.987	1.004
Mar	.901	.906	.917	.906	.927	.933	.943	.950	.955	.959	.972	.975	.976	.980	.996
Apr	.883	.888	.900	.888	.909	.915	.925	.932	.937	.941	.954	.957	.958	.962	.978
May	.877	.882	.893	.882	.902	.909	.918	.926	.930	.934	.947	.950	.951	.955	.971
June	.878	.883	.894	.883	.904	.910	.919	.927	.931	.935	.948	.951	.952	.956	.972
July	.882	.887	.898	.887	.908	.914	.923	.931	.935	.940	.952	.955	.957	.960	.977
Aug	.874	.879	.890	.879	.900	.906	.915	.923	.927	.931	.944	.947	.948	.952	.968
Sept	.866	.871	.882	.871	.891	.898	.907	.915	.919	.923	.936	.939	.940	.944	.960
Oct	.867	.872	.884	.872	.893	.899	.908	.916	.920	.925	.937	.940	.941	.945	.961
Nov	.870	.875	.886	.875	.895	.902	.911	.919	.923	.927	.940	.943	.944	.948	.964
Dec	.866	.871	.882	.871	.891	.898	.907	.915	.919	.923	.936	.939	.940	.944	.960

MONTH OF DISPOSAL

	2015						2016								
1994	July	Aug	Sep	Oct	Nov	Dec	Jan	Feb	Mar	Apr	May	June	July	Aug	Sep
Jan	.830	.839	.837	.837	.839	.844	.832	.840	.848	.850	.855	.862	.864	.871	.875
Feb	.820	.828	.827	.826	.828	.834	.821	.830	.837	.840	.844	.852	.854	.861	.864
Mar	.815	.823	.822	.821	.823	.829	.816	.825	.832	.834	.839	.846	.848	.855	.859
Apr	.793	.802	.800	.800	.802	.807	.795	.803	.811	.813	.818	.825	.827	.834	.837
May	.787	.795	.794	.793	.795	.801	.789	.797	.804	.806	.811	.818	.820	.827	.831
June	.787	.795	.794	.793	.795	.801	.789	.797	.804	.806	.811	.818	.820	.827	.831
July	.796	.804	.803	.802	.804	.810	.797	.806	.813	.815	.820	.827	.829	.836	.840
Aug	.787	.795	.794	.793	.795	.801	.789	.797	.804	.806	.811	.818	.820	.827	.831
Sept	.783	.792	.790	.790	.792	.797	.785	.793	.801	.803	.808	.814	.817	.823	.827
Oct	.781	.789	.788	.787	.789	.795	.782	.791	.798	.800	.805	.812	.814	.821	.824
Nov	.780	.788	.787	.786	.788	.794	.781	.789	.797	.799	.804	.811	.813	.820	.823
Dec	.771	.779	.778	.777	.779	.785	.773	.781	.788	.790	.795	.802	.804	.811	.814
1995	July	Aug	Sep	Oct	Nov	Dec	Jan	Feb	Mar	Apr	May	June	July	Aug	Sep
Jan	.771	.779	.778	.777	.779	.785	.773	.781	.788	.790	.795	.802	.804	.811	.814
Feb	.760	.769	.767	.767	.769	.774	.762	.770	.777	.779	.784	.791	.793	.800	.803
Mar	.753	.761	.760	.759	.761	.767	.755	.763	.770	.772	.777	.784	.786	.793	.796
Apr	.736	.744	.742	.742	.744	.749	.737	.745	.752	.754	.759	.766	.768	.774	.778
May	.729	.737	.735	.735	.737	.742	.730	.738	.745	.747	.752	.759	.761	.767	.771
June	.726	.734	.733	.732	.734	.740	.728	.736	.743	.745	.750	.756	.758	.765	.768
July	.734	.742	.741	.740	.742	.748	.736	.744	.751	.753	.758	.765	.767	.773	.777
Aug	.725	.733	.732	.731	.733	.738	.726	.734	.742	.744	.748	.755	.757	.764	.767
Sept	.717	.725	.724	.723	.725	.730	.718	.726	.734	.736	.740	.747	.749	.756	.759
Oct	.726	.734	.733	.732	.734	.740	.728	.736	.743	.745	.750	.756	.758	.765	.768
Nov	.726	.734	.733	.732	.734	.740	.728	.736	.743	.745	.750	.756	.758	.765	.768
Dec	.716	.724	.723	.722	.724	.729	.717	.725	.733	.735	.739	.746	.748	.754	.758
1996	July	Aug	Sep	Oct	Nov	Dec	Jan	Feb	Mar	Apr	May	June	July	Aug	Sep
Jan	.722	.730	.728	.728	.730	.735	.723	.731	.738	.740	.745	.752	.754	.760	.764
Feb	.714	.722	.720	.720	.722	.727	.715	.723	.730	.732	.737	.744	.746	.752	.755
Mar	.707	.715	.714	.713	.715	.720	.708	.716	.723	.725	.730	.737	.739	.745	.749
Apr	.695	.702	.701	.701	.702	.708	.696	.704	.711	.713	.718	.724	.726	.733	.736
May	.691	.699	.698	.697	.699	.704	.693	.700	.708	.710	.714	.721	.723	.729	.733
June	.690	.698	.697	.696	.698	.703	.692	.699	.707	.708	.713	.720	.722	.728	.731
July	.697	.705	.703	.703	.705	.710	.698	.706	.713	.715	.720	.726	.728	.735	.738
Aug	.689	.697	.696	.695	.697	.702	.690	.698	.705	.707	.712	.718	.720	.727	.730
Sept	.681	.689	.688	.687	.689	.694	.683	.691	.698	.700	.704	.711	.713	.719	.722
Oct	.681	.689	.688	.687	.689	.694	.683	.691	.698	.700	.704	.711	.713	.719	.722
Nov	.680	.688	.687	.686	.688	.693	.682	.689	.697	.699	.703	.710	.712	.718	.721
Dec	.675	.683	.681	.681	.683	.688	.676	.684	.691	.693	.698	.704	.706	.712	.716
1997	July	Aug	Sep	Oct	Nov	Dec	Jan	Feb	Mar	Apr	May	June	July	Aug	Sep
Jan	.675	.683	.681	.681	.683	.688	.676	.684	.691	.693	.698	.704	.706	.712	.716
Feb	.668	.676	.675	.674	.676	.681	.670	.677	.685	.686	.691	.697	.699	.706	.709
Mar	.664	.672	.671	.670	.672	.677	.665	.673	.680	.682	.687	.693	.695	.701	.705
Apr	.655	.662	.661	.660	.662	.667	.656	.663	.671	.672	.677	.683	.685	.692	.695
May	.648	.656	.655	.654	.656	.661	.649	.657	.664	.666	.670	.677	.679	.685	.688
June	.642	.650	.648	.648	.650	.655	.643	.651	.658	.660	.664	.670	.672	.679	.682
July	.642	.650	.648	.648	.650	.655	.643	.651	.658	.660	.664	.670	.672	.679	.682
Aug	.632	.639	.638	.637	.639	.644	.633	.640	.647	.649	.654	.660	.662	.668	.671
Sept	.623	.631	.630	.629	.631	.636	.625	.632	.639	.641	.645	.652	.653	.660	.663
Oct	.621	.629	.628	.627	.629	.634	.623	.630	.637	.639	.643	.650	.651	.658	.661
Nov	.620	.628	.627	.626	.628	.633	.622	.629	.636	.638	.642	.648	.650	.657	.660
Dec	.616	.624	.623	.622	.624	.629	.618	.625	.632	.634	.638	.644	.646	.653	.656

MONTH OF DISPOSAL

	2016			2017											
1994	Oct	Nov	Dec	Jan	Feb	Mar	Apr	May	June	July	Aug	Sep	Oct	Nov	Dec
Jan	.874	.879	.890	.879	.900	.906	.915	.923	.927	.931	.944	.947	.948	.952	.968
Feb	.863	.868	.880	.868	.889	.895	.904	.912	.916	.920	.933	.936	.937	.941	.957
Mar	.858	.863	.874	.863	.884	.890	.899	.907	.911	.915	.928	.931	.932	.935	.952
Apr	.836	.841	.852	.841	.861	.868	.877	.884	.888	.893	.905	.908	.909	.913	.929
May	.830	.835	.846	.835	.855	.861	.870	.878	.882	.886	.898	.901	.903	.906	.922
June	.830	.835	.846	.835	.855	.861	.870	.878	.882	.886	.898	.901	.903	.906	.922
July	.839	.844	.855	.844	.864	.870	.879	.887	.891	.895	.908	.910	.912	.915	.931
Aug	.830	.835	.846	.835	.855	.861	.870	.878	.882	.886	.898	.901	.903	.906	.922
Sept	.826	.831	.842	.831	.851	.857	.866	.874	.878	.882	.894	.897	.899	.902	.918
Oct	.824	.829	.840	.829	.848	.855	.864	.871	.875	.879	.892	.895	.896	.899	.915
Nov	.822	.827	.838	.827	.847	.853	.862	.870	.874	.878	.891	.893	.895	.898	.914
Dec	.814	.818	.829	.818	.838	.845	.853	.861	.865	.869	.882	.884	.886	.889	.905
1995	Oct	Nov	Dec	Jan	Feb	Mar	Apr	May	June	July	Aug	Sep	Oct	Nov	Dec
Jan	.814	.818	.829	.818	.838	.845	.853	.861	,865	.869	.882	.884	.886	.889	.905
Feb	.803	.807	.818	.807	.827	.833	.842	.850	.854	.858	.870	.873	.874	.877	.893
Mar	.795	.800	.811	.800	.820	.826	.835	.842	.846	.850	.862	.865	.866	.870	.885
Apr	.777	.782	.793	.782	.801	.807	.816	.823	.828	.832	.844	.846	.848	.851	.866
May	.770	.775	.785	.775	.794	.800	.809	.816	.820	.824	.836	.839	.840	.844	.859
June	.768	.772	.783	.772	.792	.798	.806	.814	.818	.822	.834	.836	.838	.841	.856
July	.776	.781	.791	.781	.800	.806	.815	.822	.826	.830	.842	.845	.846	.850	.865
Aug	.767	.772	.782	.771	.791	.797	.805	.813	.817	.821	.833	.835	.837	.840	.855
Sept	.758	.763	.774	.763	.782	.788	.797	.804	.808	.812	.824	.827	.828	.831	.847
Oct	.768	.772	.783	.772	.792	.798	.806	.814	.818	.822	.834	.836	.838	.841	.856
Nov	.768	.772	.783	.772	.792	.798	.806	.814	.818	.822	.834	.836	.838	.841	.856
Dec	.757	.762	.772	.762	.781	.787	.796	.803	.807	.811	.823	.825	.827	.830	.845
1996	Oct	Nov	Dec	Jan	Feb	Mar	Apr	May	June	July	Aug	Sep	Oct	Nov	Dec
Jan	.763	.768	.778	.768	.787	.793	.802	.809	.813	.817	.829	.832	.833	.836	.852
Feb	.755	.759	.770	.759	.779	.785	.793	.801	.805	.808	.820	.823	.824	.828	.843
Mar	.748	.752	.763	.752	.772	.778	.786	.793	.797	.801	.813	.816	.817	.820	.836
Apr	.735	.740	.750	.740	.759	.765	.773	.780	.784	.788	.800	.803	.804	.807	.822
May	.732	.736	.747	.736	.755	.761	.770	.777	.781	.785	.797	.799	.801	.804	.819
June	.731	.735	.746	.735	.754	.760	.769	.776	.780	.784	.795	.798	.799	.803	.818
July	.738	.742	.753	.742	.761	.767	.776	.783	.787	.791	.802	.805	.806	.810	.825
Aug	.730	.734	.745	.734	.753	.759	.767	.775	.779	.782	.794	.797	.798	.801	.816
Sept	.722	.726	.737	.726	.745	.751	.759	.767	.770	.774	.786	.789	.790	.793	.808
Oct	.722	.726	.737	.726	.745	.751	.759	.767	.770	.774	.786	.789	.790	.793	.808
Nov	.721	.725	.736	.725	.744	.750	.758	.765	.769	.773	.785	.788	.789	.792	.807
Dec	.715	.720	.730	.720	.738	.744	.753	.760	.764	.767	.779	.782	.783	.786	.801
1997	Oct	Nov	Dec	Jan	Feb	Mar	Apr	May	June	July	Aug	Sep	Oct	Nov	Dec
Jan	.715	.720	.730	.720	.738	.744	.753	.760	.764	.767	.779	.782	.783	.786	.801
Feb	.708	.713	.723	.713	.732	.737	.746	.753	.757	.761	.772	.775	.776	.779	.794
Mar	.704	.708	.719	.708	.727	.733	.741	.748	.752	.756	.768	.770	.772	.775	.790
Apr	.694	.699	.709	.699	.717	.723	.731	.738	.742	.746	.758	.760	.761	.765	.779
May	.688	.692	.702	.692	.711	.716	.725	.732	.736	.739	.751	.753	.755	.758	.772
June	.681	.686	.696	.686	.704	.710	.718	.725	.729	.733	.744	.747	.748	.751	.766
July	.681	.686	.696	.686	.704	.710	.718	.725	.729	.733	.744	.747	.748	.751	.766
Aug	.671	.675	.685	.675	.693	.699	.707	.714	.718	.722	.733	.736	.737	.740	.755
Sept	.662	.667	.677	.667	.685	.691	.699	.706	.709	.713	.724	.727	.728	.731	.746
Oct	.660	.665	.675	.665	.683	.688	.697	.703	.707	.711	.722	.725	.726	.729	.744
Nov	.659	.664	.674	.664	.682	.687	.695	.702	.706	.710	.721	.724	.725	.728	.742
Dec	.655	.659	.669	.659	.678	.683	.691	.698	.702	.706	.717	.719	.721	.724	.738

MONTH OF DISPOSAL

	2015						2016								
1998	July	Aug	Sep	Oct	Nov	Dec	Jan	Feb	Mar	Apr	May	June	July	Aug	Sep
Jan	.621	.629	.628	.627	.629	.634	.623	.630	.637	.639	.643	.650	.651	.658	.661
Feb	.613	.621	.619	.619	.621	.626	.614	.622	.629	.631	.635	.641	.643	.649	.653
Mar	.608	.616	.614	.614	.616	.621	.609	.617	.624	.626	.630	.636	.638	.644	.647
Apr	.590	.598	.597	.596	.598	.603	.592	.599	.606	.608	.612	.618	.620	.626	.629
May	.582	.589	.588	.587	.589	.594	.583	.590	.597	.599	.603	.609	.611	.617	.620
June	.583	.590	.589	.588	.590	.595	.584	.591	.598	.600	.604	.610	.612	.618	.621
July	.587	.594	.593	.592	.594	.599	.588	.595	.602	.604	.608	.614	.616	.622	.625
Aug	.580	.587	.586	.585	.587	.592	.581	.588	.595	.597	.601	.607	.609	.615	.618
Sept	.573	.580	.579	.578	.580	.585	.574	.582	.588	.590	.594	.600	.602	.608	.611
Oct	.572	.579	.578	.578	.579	.584	.573	.581	.587	.589	.593	.599	.601	.607	.610
Nov	.573	.580	.579	.578	.580	.585	.574	.582	.588	.590	.594	.600	.602	.608	.611
Dec	.573	.580	.579	.578	.580	.585	.574	.582	.588	.590	.594	.600	.602	.608	.611
1999	July	Aug	Sep	Oct	Nov	Dec	Jan	Feb	Mar	Apr	May	June	July	Aug	Sep
Jan	.583	.590	.589	.588	.590	.595	.584	.591	.598	.600	.604	.610	.612	.618	.621
Feb	.580	.587	.586	.585	.587	.592	.581	.588	.595	.597	.601	.607	.609	.615	.618
Mar	.576	.583	.582	.581	.583	.588	.577	.584	.591	.593	.597	.603	.605	.611	.614
Apr	.565	.573	.571	.571	.573	.577	.567	.574	.581	.582	.587	.593	.594	.600	.604
May	.562	.569	.568	.567	.569	.574	.563	.570	.577	.579	.583	.589	.591	.597	.600
June	.562	.569	.568	.567	.569	.574	.563	.570	.577	.579	.583	.589	.591	.597	.600
July	.566	.574	.572	.572	.574	.578	.568	.575	.581	.583	.588	.594	.595	.601	.604
Aug	.563	.570	.569	.568	.570	.575	.564	.571	.578	.579	.584	.590	.592	.598	.601
Sept	.556	.563	.562	.561	.563	.568	.557	.564	.571	.573	.577	.583	.585	.591	.594
Oct	.553	.560	.559	.559	.560	.565	.554	.562	.568	.570	.574	.580	.582	.588	.591
Nov	.551	.558	.557	.557	.558	.563	.552	.560	.566	.568	.572	.578	.580	.586	.589
Dec	.546	.553	.552	.551	.553	.558	.547	.554	.561	.562	.567	.573	.574	.580	.583
2000	July	Aug	Sep	Oct	Nov	Dec	Jan	Feb	Mar	Apr	May	June	July	Aug	Sep
Jan	.552	.559	.558	.558	.559	.564	.553	.561	.567	.569	.573	.579	.581	.587	.590
Feb	.544	.551	.550	.549	.551	.556	.545	.552	.559	.561	.565	.571	.573	.579	.581
Mar	.536	.543	.542	.541	.543	.548	.537	.544	.550	.552	.556	.562	.564	.570	.573
Apr	.520	.527	.526	.526	.527	.532	.521	.529	.535	.537	.541	.547	.549	.554	.557
May	.515	.522	.521	.520	.522	.527	.516	.523	.530	.531	.535	.541	.543	.549	.552
June	.511	.518	.517	.517	.518	.523	.513	.520	.526	.528	.532	.538	.539	.545	.548
July	.517	.524	.523	.522	.524	.528	.518	.525	.531	.533	.537	.543	.545	.551	.554
Aug	.517	.524	.523	.522	.524	.528	.518	.525	.531	.533	.537	.543	.545	.551	.554
Sept	.506	.513	.512	.511	.513	.518	.507	.514	.521	.522	.526	.532	.534	.540	.543
Oct	.507	.514	.513	.512	.514	.519	.508	.515	.522	.523	.527	.533	.535	.541	.544
Nov	.503	.510	.508	.508	.510	.514	.504	.511	.517	.519	.523	.529	.531	.536	.539
Dec	.502	.509	.508	.507	.509	.513	.503	.510	.516	.518	.522	.528	.530	.535	.538
2001	July	Aug	Sep	Oct	Nov	Dec	Jan	Feb	Mar	Apr	May	June	July	Aug	Sep
Jan	.511	.518	.517	.517	.518	.523	.513	.520	.526	.528	.532	.538	.539	.545	.548
Feb	.503	.510	.509	.509	.510	.515	.505	.512	.518	.520	.524	.530	.531	.537	.540
Mar	.502	.509	.508	.507	.509	.513	.503	.510	.516	.518	.522	.528	.530	.535	.538
Apr	.494	.501	.500	.499	.501	.505	.495	.502	.508	.510	.514	.520	.522	.527	.530
May	.485	.491	.490	.490	.491	.496	.486	.493	.499	.501	.505	.510	.512	.518	.521
June	.483	.490	.489	.488	.490	.494	.484	.491	.497	.499	.503	.509	.510	.516	.519
July	.492	.499	.498	.497	.499	.504	.493	.500	.507	.508	.512	.518	.520	.526	.529
Aug	.486	.493	.492	.491	.493	.498	.487	.494	.501	.502	.506	.512	.514	.520	.522
Sept	.481	.488	.487	.486	.488	.493	.482	.489	.495	.497	.501	.507	.509	.514	.517
Oct	.484	.491	.489	.489	.491	.495	.485	.492	.498	.500	.504	.509	.511	.517	.520
Nov	.490	.497	.495	.495	.497	.501	.491	.498	.504	.506	.510	.516	.517	.523	.526
Dec	.491	.498	.497	.497	.498	.503	.493	.499	.506	.507	.512	.517	.519	.525	.528

MONTH OF DISPOSAL

	2016			2017											
1998	Oct	Nov	Dec	Jan	Feb	Mar	Apr	May	June	July	Aug	Sep	Oct	Nov	Dec
Jan	.660	.665	.675	.665	.683	.688	.697	.703	.707	.711	.722	.725	.726	.729	.744
Feb	.652	.656	.666	.656	.674	.680	.688	.695	.699	.702	.714	.716	.717	.721	.735
Mar	.647	.651	.661	.651	.669	.675	.683	.690	.693	.697	.708	.711	.712	.715	.729
Apr	.629	.633	.643	.633	.651	.656	.664	.671	.675	.678	.689	.692	.693	.696	.710
May	.620	.624	.634	.624	.642	.647	.655	.662	.665	.669	.680	.683	.684	.687	.701
June	.621	.625	.635	.625	.643	.648	.656	.663	.666	.670	.681	.684	.685	.688	.702
July	.625	.629	.639	.629	.647	.652	.660	.667	.671	.674	.685	.688	.689	.692	.706
Aug	.618	.622	.632	.622	.640	.645	.653	.660	.663	.667	.678	.681	.682	.685	.699
Sept	.611	.615	.625	.615	.633	.638	.646	.653	.656	.660	.671	.673	.675	.678	.692
Oct	.610	.614	.624	.614	.632	.637	.645	.652	.655	.659	.670	.672	.674	.677	.691
Nov	.611	.615	.625	.615	.633	.638	.646	.653	.656	.660	.671	.673	.675	.678	.692
Dec	.611	.615	.625	.615	.633	.638	.646	.653	.656	.660	.671	.673	.675	.678	.692
1999	Oct	Nov	Dec	Jan	Feb	Mar	Apr	May	June	July	Aug	Sep	Oct	Nov	Dec
Jan	.621	.625	.635	.625	.643	.648	.656	.663	.666	.670	.681	.684	.685	.688	.702
Feb	.618	.622	.632	.622	.640	.645	.653	.660	.663	.667	.678	.681	.682	.685	.699
Mar	.614	.618	.628	.618	.636	.641	.649	.656	.659	.663	.674	.676	.678	.681	.695
Apr	.603	.607	.617	.607	.625	.630	.638	.645	.648	.652	.663	.665	.666	.669	.683
May	.599	.603	.613	.603	.621	.626	.634	.641	.644	.648	.659	.661	.662	.665	.679
June	.599	.603	.613	.603	.621	.626	.634	.641	.644	.648	.659	.661	.661	.665	.679
July	.604	.608	.618	.608	.626	.631	.639	.646	.649	.653	.664	.666	.667	.671	.684
Aug	.600	.604	.614	.604	.622	.627	.635	.642	.645	.649	.660	.662	.663	.666	.680
Sept	.593	.597	.607	.597	.615	.620	.628	.635	.638	.642	.653	.655	.656	.659	.673
Oct	.590	.595	.604	.595	.612	.617	.625	.632	.635	.639	.650	.652	.653	.656	.670
Nov	.588	.593	.602	.593	.610	.615	.623	.630	.633	.637	.648	.650	.651	.654	.668
Dec	.583	.587	.597	.587	.604	.610	.617	.624	.628	.631	.642	.644	.646	.649	.662
2000	Oct	Nov	Dec	Jan	Feb	Mar	Apr	May	June	July	Aug	Sep	Oct	Nov	Dec
Jan	.589	.594	.603	.594	.611	.616	.624	.631	.634	.638	.649	.651	.652	.655	.669
Feb	.581	.585	.595	.585	.602	.608	.616	.622	.626	.629	.640	.642	.644	.647	.660
Mar	.572	.577	.586	.577	.594	.599	.607	.613	.617	.621	.631	.634	.635	.638	.651
Apr	.557	.561	.570	.561	.578	.583	.591	.597	.601	.604	.615	.617	.618	.621	.635
May	.551	.555	.565	.555	.572	.578	.585	.592	.595	.599	.609	.612	.613	.616	.629
June	.548	.552	.561	.552	.569	.574	.582	.588	.591	.595	.605	.608	.609	.612	.625
July	.553	.557	.567	.557	.574	.579	.587	.594	.597	.601	.611	.613	.615	.618	.631
Aug	.553	.557	.567	.557	.574	.579	.587	.594	.597	.601	.611	.613	.615	.618	.631
Sept	.542	.546	.556	.546	.563	.568	.576	.582	.586	.589	.600	.602	.603	.606	.620
Oct	.543	.547	.557	.547	.564	.569	.577	.583	.587	.590	.601	.603	.604	.607	.621
Nov	.539	.543	.552	.543	.560	.565	.572	.579	.582	.586	.596	.598	.600	.603	.616
Dec	.538	.542	.551	.542	.559	.564	.571	.578	.581	.585	.595	.598	.599	.602	.615
2001	Oct	Nov	Dec	Jan	Feb	Mar	Apr	May	June	July	Aug	Sep	Oct	Nov	Dec
Jan	.548	.552	.561	.552	.569	.574	.582	.588	.591	.595	.605	.608	.609	.612	.625
Feb	.540	.544	.553	.544	.560	.566	.573	.580	.583	.587	.597	.599	.601	.603	.617
Mar	.538	.542	.551	.542	.559	.564	.571	.578	.581	.585	.595	.598	.599	.602	.615
Apr	.530	.534	.543	.534	.551	.556	.563	.570	.573	.577	.587	.589	.590	.593	.607
May	.520	.524	.533	.524	.541	.546	.553	.560	.563	.567	.577	.579	.580	.583	.596
June	.518	.522	.532	.522	.539	.544	.552	.558	.561	.565	.575	.577	.577	.581	.595
July	.528	.532	.541	.532	.549	.554	.561	.568	.571	.575	.585	.587	.589	.591	.605
Aug	.522	.526	.535	.526	.543	.548	.555	.561	.565	.568	.579	.581	.582	.585	.598
Sept	.517	.521	.530	.521	.537	.542	.550	.556	.560	.563	.573	.576	.577	.580	.593
Oct	.519	.523	.532	.523	.540	.545	.552	.559	.562	.566	.576	.578	.579	.582	.596
Nov	.525	.529	.539	.529	.546	.551	.559	.565	.569	.572	.582	.585	.586	.589	.602
Dec	.527	.531	.540	.531	.548	.553	.561	.567	.570	.574	.584	.587	.588	.591	.604

MONTH OF DISPOSAL

	2015						2016								
2002	July	Aug	Sep	Oct	Nov	Dec	Jan	Feb	Mar	Apr	May	June	July	Aug	Sep
Jan	.492	.499	.498	.497	.499	.504	.493	.500	.507	.508	.512	.518	.520	.526	.529
Feb	.488	.495	.494	.493	.495	.499	.489	.496	.502	.504	.508	.514	.516	.521	.524
Mar	.482	.489	.488	.487	.489	.493	.483	.490	.496	.498	.502	.508	.509	.515	.518
Apr	.472	.479	.478	.477	.479	.483	.473	.480	.486	.488	.492	.497	.499	.505	.508
May	.468	.474	.473	.473	.474	.479	.469	.476	.482	.484	.488	.493	.495	.501	.503
June	.468	.474	.473	.473	.474	.479	.469	.476	.482	.484	.488	.493	.495	.501	.503
July	.470	.477	.476	.475	.477	.482	.471	.478	.484	.486	.490	.496	.497	.503	.506
Aug	.466	.473	.472	.471	.473	.477	.467	.474	.480	.482	.486	.491	.493	.499	.502
Sept	.456	.463	.462	.461	.463	.467	.457	.464	.470	.472	.476	.481	.483	.489	.492
Oct	.454	.460	.459	.459	.460	.465	.455	.461	.468	.469	.473	.479	.481	.486	.489
Nov	.451	.458	.457	.456	.458	.462	.452	.459	.465	.467	.471	.476	.478	.484	.487
Dec	.449	.455	.454	.454	.455	.460	.450	.457	.463	.464	.468	.474	.476	.481	.484
2003	July	Aug	Sep	Oct	Nov	Dec	Jan	Feb	Mar	Apr	May	June	July	Aug	Sep
Jan	.450	.456	.455	.455	.456	.461	.451	.457	.464	.465	.469	.475	.476	.482	.485
Feb	.442	.449	.448	.447	.449	.453	.443	.450	.456	.458	.462	.467	.469	.475	.477
Mar	.437	.444	.443	.442	.444	.449	.439	.445	.451	.453	.457	.462	.464	.470	.472
Apr	.427	.434	.433	.432	.434	.438	.428	.435	.441	.443	.446	.452	.454	.459	.462
May	.425	.431	.430	.430	.431	.436	.426	.433	.439	.440	.444	.450	.451	.457	.460
June	.426	.433	.432	.431	.433	.437	.427	.434	.440	.442	.446	.451	.453	.458	.461
July	.426	.433	.432	.431	.433	.437	.427	.434	.440	.442	.446	.451	.453	.458	.461
Aug	.424	.431	.430	.429	.431	.435	.425	.432	.438	.439	.443	.449	.450	.456	.459
Sept	.416	.424	.422	.422	.424	.428	.418	.425	.431	.432	.436	.442	.443	.449	.452
Oct	.416	.423	.422	.421	.423	.427	.417	.424	.430	.432	.435	.441	.442	.448	.451
Nov	.415	.422	.421	.420	.422	.426	.417	.423	.429	.431	.435	.440	.442	.447	.450
Dec	.409	.416	.415	.414	.416	.420	.410	.417	.423	.425	.428	.434	.435	.441	.444
2004	July	Aug	Sep	Oct	Nov	Dec	Jan	Feb	Mar	Apr	May	June	July	Aug	Sep
Jan	.412	.419	.418	.417	.419	.423	.413	.420	.426	.428	.431	.437	.439	.444	.447
Feb	.407	.413	.412	.412	.413	.418	.408	.415	.421	.422	.426	.431	.433	.439	.441
Mar	.401	.407	.406	.406	.407	.412	.402	.408	.414	.416	.420	.425	.427	.432	.435
Apr	.393	.399	.398	.397	.399	.403	.394	.400	.406	.408	.411	.417	.418	.424	.426
May	.387	.393	.392	.391	.393	.397	.388	.394	.400	.402	.405	.411	.412	.418	.420
June	.384	.391	.390	.389	.391	.395	.385	.392	.398	.399	.403	.408	.410	.415	.418
July	.384	.391	.390	.389	.391	.395	.385	.392	.398	.399	.403	.408	.410	.415	.418
Aug	.380	.386	.385	.385	.386	.391	.381	.387	.393	.395	.399	.404	.406	.411	.414
Sept	.375	.381	.380	.380	.381	.385	.376	.382	.388	.390	.393	.399	.400	.406	.408
Oct	.371	.378	.376	.376	.378	.382	.372	.379	.384	.386	.390	.395	.397	.402	.405
Nov	.368	.375	.374	.373	.375	.379	.369	.376	.381	.383	.387	.392	.394	.399	.402
Dec	.362	.368	.367	.367	.368	.372	.363	.369	.375	.377	.380	.385	.387	.392	.395
2005	July	Aug	Sep	Oct	Nov	Dec	Jan	Feb	Mar	Apr	May	June	July	Aug	Sep
Jan	.369	.375	.374	.374	.375	.380	.370	.376	.382	.384	.388	.393	.394	.400	.402
Feb	.364	.370	.369	.369	.370	.374	.365	.371	.377	.379	.382	.388	.389	.395	.397
Mar	.357	.364	.363	.362	.364	.368	.359	.365	.371	.372	.376	.381	.383	.388	.391
Apr	.350	.356	.355	.354	.356	.360	.351	.357	.363	.364	.368	.373	.375	.380	.383
May	.347	.353	.352	.352	.353	.357	.348	.354	.360	.361	.365	.370	.372	.377	.380
June	.345	.352	.351	.350	.352	.356	.347	.353	.358	.360	.364	.369	.370	.376	.378
July	.345	.352	.351	.350	.352	.356	.347	.353	.358	.360	.364	.369	.370	.376	.378
Aug	.343	.349	.348	.347	.349	.353	.344	.350	.356	.357	.361	.366	.368	.373	.375
Sept	.339	.345	.344	.344	.345	.350	.340	.346	.352	.354	.357	.363	.364	.369	.372
Oct	.338	.344	.343	.342	.344	.348	.339	.345	.351	.352	.356	.361	.363	.368	.370
Nov	.336	.342	.341	.340	.342	.346	.337	.343	.349	.350	.354	.359	.361	.366	.368
Dec	.332	.338	.337	.337	.338	.343	.333	.340	.345	.347	.350	.355	.357	.362	.365

MONTH OF DISPOSAL

	2016			2017											
2002	Oct	Nov	Dec	Jan	Feb	Mar	Apr	May	June	July	Aug	Sep	Oct	Nov	Dec
Jan	.528	.532	.541	.532	.549	.554	.561	.568	.571	.575	.585	.587	.589	.591	.605
Feb	.524	.528	.537	.528	.544	.549	.557	.563	.567	.570	.581	.583	.584	.587	.600
Mar	.517	.521	.531	.521	.538	.543	.551	.557	.560	.564	.574	.577	.578	.581	.594
Apr	.507	.511	.520	.511	.528	.533	.540	.546	.550	.553	.563	.566	.567	.570	.583
May	.503	.507	.516	.507	.523	.528	.536	.542	.545	.549	.559	.561	.562	.565	.578
June	.503	.507	.516	.507	.523	.528	.536	.542	.545	.549	.559	.561	.562	.565	.578
July	.505	.509	.518	.507	.526	.531	.538	.545	.548	.551	.562	.564	.565	.568	.581
Aug	.501	.505	.514	.505	.522	.527	.534	.540	.544	.547	.557	.560	.561	.563	.577
Sept	.491	.495	.504	.495	.511	.516	.524	.530	.533	.537	.547	.549	.550	.553	.566
Oct	.488	.492	.501	.492	.509	.514	.521	.527	.531	.534	.544	.546	.547	.550	.563
Nov	.486	.490	.499	.490	.506	.511	.519	.525	.528	.531	.542	.544	.545	.548	.561
Dec	.483	.487	.496	.487	.504	.509	.516	.522	.525	.529	.539	.541	.542	.545	.558
2003	Oct	Nov	Dec	Jan	Feb	Mar	Apr	May	June	July	Aug	Sep	Oct	Nov	Dec
Jan	.484	.488	.497	.488	.504	.510	.517	.523	.526	.530	.540	.542	.543	.546	.559
Feb	.477	.481	.490	.481	.497	.502	.509	.515	.519	.522	.532	.534	.535	.538	.551
Mar	.472	.476	.485	.476	.492	.497	.504	.510	.514	.517	.527	.529	.530	.533	.546
Apr	.461	.465	.474	.465	.481	.486	.493	.499	.503	.506	.516	.518	.519	.522	.535
May	.459	.463	.472	.463	.479	.484	.491	.497	.500	.504	.513	.516	.517	.520	.532
June	.461	.464	.473	.464	.480	.485	.493	.499	.502	.505	.515	.517	.518	.521	.534
July	.461	.464	.473	.464	.480	.485	.493	.499	.502	.505	.515	.517	.518	.521	.534
Aug	.458	.462	.471	.462	.478	.483	.490	.496	.499	.503	.513	.515	.516	.519	.531
Sept	.451	.455	.464	.455	.471	.476	.483	.489	.492	.495	.505	.507	.508	.511	.524
Oct	.450	.454	.463	.454	.470	.475	.482	.488	.491	.495	.504	.507	.508	.510	.523
Nov	.449	.453	.462	.453	.469	.474	.481	.487	.490	.494	.504	.506	.507	.510	.522
Dec	.443	.447	.456	.447	.463	.468	.475	.481	.484	.487	.497	.499	.500	.503	.516
2004	Oct	Nov	Dec	Jan	Feb	Mar	Apr	May	June	July	Aug	Sep	Oct	Nov	Dec
Jan	.446	.450	.459	.450	.466	.471	.478	.484	.487	.490	.500	.502	.504	.506	.519
Feb	.441	.445	.453	.445	.460	.465	.472	.478	.482	.485	.495	.497	.498	.501	.513
Mar	.434	.438	.447	.438	.454	.459	.466	.472	.475	.478	.488	.490	.491	.494	.507
Apr	.426	.430	.438	.430	.445	.450	.457	.463	.466	.470	.479	.481	.482	.485	.498
May	.420	.424	.432	.424	.439	.444	.451	.457	.460	.463	.473	.475	.476	.479	.491
June	.418	.421	.430	.421	.437	.442	.449	.454	.458	.461	.471	.473	.474	.476	.489
July	.418	.421	.430	.421	.437	.442	.449	.454	.458	.461	.471	.473	.474	.476	.489
Aug	.413	.417	.425	.417	.432	.437	.444	.450	.453	.456	.466	.468	.469	.472	.484
Sept	.408	.411	.420	.411	.427	.432	.439	.444	.448	.451	.460	.463	.464	.466	.478
Oct	.404	.408	.416	.408	.423	.428	.435	.441	.444	.447	.457	.459	.460	.462	.475
Nov	.401	.405	.413	.405	.420	.425	.432	.438	.441	.444	.453	.456	.457	.459	.471
Dec	.394	.398	.407	.398	.413	. 418	.425	.431	.434	.437	.447	.449	.450	.452	.464
2005	Oct	Nov	Dec	Jan	Feb	Mar	Apr	May	June	July	Aug	Sep	Oct	Nov	Dec
Jan	.402	.406	.414	.406	.421	.426	.433	.438	.442	.445	.454	.456	.457	.460	.472
Feb	.397	.400	.409	.400	.416	.420	.427	.433	.436	.439	.449	.451	.452	.455	.467
Mar	.390	.394	.402	.394	.409	.414	.420	.426	.429	.433	.442	.444	.445	.448	.460
Apr	.382	.386	.394	.386	.401	.406	.412	.418	.421	.424	.434	.436	.437	.439	.451
May	.379	.383	.391	.383	.398	.403	.409	.415	.418	.421	.431	.433	.434	.436	.448
June	.378	.381	.390	.381	.396	.401	.408	.414	.417	.420	.429	.431	.432	.435	.447
July	.378	.381	.390	.381	.396	.401	.408	.414	.417	.420	.429	.431	.432	.435	.447
Aug	.375	.379	.387	.379	.394	.398	.405	.411	.414	.417	.426	.428	.429	.432	.444
Sept	.371	.375	.383	.375	.390	.395	.401	.407	.410	.413	.423	.425	.426	.428	.440
Oct	.370	.374	.382	.374	.389	.393	.400	.406	.409	.412	.421	.423	.424	.427	.439
Nov	.368	.371	.380	.371	.386	.391	.398	.403	.407	.410	.419	.421	.422	.425	.436
Dec	.364	.368	.376	.368	.383	.387	.394	.400	.403	.406	.415	.417	.418	.421	.433

MONTH OF DISPOSAL

	2015						2016								
2006	July	Aug	Sep	Oct	Nov	Dec	Jan	Feb	Mar	Apr	May	June	July	Aug	Sep
Jan	.337	.343	.342	.342	.343	.347	.338	.344	.350	.352	.355	.360	.362	.367	.370
Feb	.332	.338	.337	.336	.338	.342	.333	.339	.344	.346	.350	.355	.356	.361	.364
Mar	.326	.332	.331	.331	.332	.336	.327	.333	.339	.341	.344	.349	.351	.356	.358
Apr	.316	.322	.321	.321	.322	.326	.317	.323	.329	.330	.334	.339	.340	.346	.348
May	.308	.314	.313	.313	.314	.318	.309	.315	.321	.322	.326	.331	.332	.337	.340
June	.303	.309	.308	.307	.309	.313	.304	.310	.315	.317	.320	.325	.327	.332	.335
July	.303	.309	.308	.307	.309	.313	.304	.310	.315	.317	.320	.325	.325	.327	.335
Aug	.298	.304	.303	.303	.304	.308	.299	.305	.311	.312	.316	.321	.322	.327	.330
Sept	.292	.298	.297	.297	.298	.302	.293	.299	.305	.306	.310	.315	.316	.321	.324
Oct	.290	.296	.295	.295	.296	.300	.291	.297	.303	.304	.308	.313	.314	.319	.322
Nov	.286	.292	.291	.290	.292	.296	.287	.293	.298	.300	.303	.308	.310	.315	.317
Dec	.276	.282	.281	.280	.282	.286	.277	.283	.288	.290	.293	.298	.299	.304	.307
2007	July	Aug	Sep	Oct	Nov	Dec	Jan	Feb	Mar	Apr	May	June	July	Aug	Sep
Jan	.283	.289	.288	.287	.289	.293	.284	.290	.295	.297	.300	.305	.307	.312	.314
Feb	.273	.279	.278	.278	.279	.283	.274	.280	.286	.287	.290	.295	.297	.302	.304
Mar	.265	.271	.270	.270	.271	.275	.266	.272	.277	.279	.282	.287	.289	.294	.296
Apr	.259	.265	.264	.263	.265	.269	.260	.266	.271	.273	.276	.281	.282	.287	.290
May	.254	.260	.259	.258	.260	.264	.255	.261	.266	.268	.271	.276	.277	.282	.285
June	.247	.253	.252	.252	.253	.257	.248	.254	.260	.261	.264	.269	.271	.275	.278
July	.255	.261	.260	.259	.261	.264	.256	.262	.267	.268	.272	.277	.278	.283	.285
Aug	.247	.253	.252	.252	.253	.257	.248	.254	.260	.261	.264	.269	.271	.275	.278
Sept	.243	.249	.248	.248	.249	.253	.244	.250	.255	.257	.260	.265	.266	.271	.274
Oct	.238	.244	.243	.242	.244	.247	.239	.245	.250	.251	.255	.259	.261	.266	.268
Nov	.233	.239	.238	.237	.239	.243	.234	.240	.245	.247	.250	.255	.256	.261	.263
Dec	.226	.232	.231	.230	.232	.236	.227	.233	.238	.239	.243	.248	.249	.254	.256
2008	July	Aug	Sep	Oct	Nov	Dec	Jan	Feb	Mar	Apr	May	June	July	Aug	Sep
Jan	.233	.238	.237	.237	.238	.242	.234	.239	.245	.246	.249	.254	.255	.260	.263
Feb	.223	.229	.228	.228	.229	.233	.224	.230	.235	.237	.240	.245	.246	.251	.253
Mar	.219	.225	.224	.223	.225	.229	.220	.226	.231	.232	.236	.240	.242	.247	.249
Apr	.208	.214	.213	.213	.214	.218	.209	.215	.220	.221	.225	.229	.231	.236	.238
May	.202	.208	.207	.206	.208	.212	.203	.209	.214	.215	.219	.223	.225	.229	.232
June	.193	.198	.197	.197	.198	.202	.194	.199	.204	.206	.209	.214	.215	.220	.222
July	.194	.200	.199	.199	.200	.204	.195	.201	.206	.207	.211	.215	.217	.221	.224
Aug	.191	.196	.195	.195	.196	.200	.192	.197	.202	.203	.207	.211	.213	.217	.220
Sept	.184	.190	.189	.188	.190	.193	.185	.190	.196	.197	.200	.205	.206	.211	.213
Oct	.188	.193	.192	.192	.193	.197	.189	.194	.199	.201	.204	.209	.210	.215	.217
Nov	.197	.203	.202	.201	.203	.206	.198	.204	.209	.210	.213	.218	.219	.224	.226
Dec	.215	.220	.219	.219	.220	.224	.216	.221	.226	.228	.231	.236	.237	.242	.244
2009	July	Aug	Sep	Oct	Nov	Dec	Jan	Feb	Mar	Apr	May	June	July	Aug	Sep
Jan	.231	.237	.236	.235	.237	.240	.232	.238	.243	.244	.248	.252	.254	.258	.261
Feb	.223	.229	.228	.228	.229	.233	.224	.230	.235	.237	.240	.245	.246	.251	.253
Mar	.224	.230	.229	.228	.230	.233	.225	.230	.236	.237	.240	.245	.247	.251	.252
Apr	.223	.228	.227	.227	.228	.232	.224	.229	.235	.236	.239	.244	.245	.250	.252
May	.215	.221	.220	.219	.221	.225	.216	.222	.227	.228	.232	.236	.238	.242	.245
June	.212	.217	.216	.216	.217	.221	.213	.218	.224	.225	.228	.233	.234	.239	.241
July	.212	.217	.216	.216	.217	.221	.213	.218	.224	.225	.228	.233	.234	.239	.241
Aug	.206	.212	.211	.210	.212	.215	.207	.213	.218	.219	.222	.227	.229	.233	.236
Sept	.201	.207	.206	.205	.207	.210	.202	.208	.213	.214	.217	.222	.223	.228	.230
Oct	.197	.203	.202	.201	.203	.206	.198	.204	.209	.210	.213	.218	.219	.224	.226
Nov	.194	.199	.199	.198	.199	.203	.195	.200	.205	.207	.210	.215	.216	.221	.223
Dec	.186	.192	.191	.190	.192	.195	.187	.193	.198	.199	.202	.207	.208	.213	.215

MONTH OF DISPOSAL

	2016			*2017*											
2006	Oct	Nov	Dec	Jan	Feb	Mar	Apr	May	June	July	Aug	Sep	Oct	Nov	Dec
Jan	.369	.373	.381	.373	.388	.392	.399	.405	.408	.411	.420	.422	.423	.426	.438
Feb	.364	.367	.375	.367	.382	.387	.393	.399	.402	.405	.415	.417	.418	.420	.432
Mar	.358	.362	.370	.362	.376	.381	.388	.393	.396	.399	.409	.411	.412	.414	.426
Apr	.348	.351	.359	.351	.366	.370	.377	.383	.386	.389	.398	.400	.401	.404	.415
May	.339	.343	.351	.343	.358	.362	.369	.374	.377	.380	.389	.392	.393	.395	.407
June	.334	.338	.346	.338	.352	.357	.363	.369	.372	.375	.384	.386	.387	.389	.401
July	.334	.338	.346	.338	.352	.357	.363	.369	.372	.375	.384	.386	.387	.389	.401
Aug	.329	.333	.341	.333	.347	.352	.358	.364	.367	.370	.379	.381	.382	.385	.396
Sept	.323	.327	.335	.327	.341	.346	.352	.358	.361	.364	.373	.375	.376	.378	.390
Oct	.321	.325	.333	.325	.339	.344	.350	.356	.359	.362	.371	.373	.374	.376	.388
Nov	.317	.320	.328	.320	.335	.339	.346	.351	.354	.357	.366	.368	.369	.371	.383
Dec	.306	.310	.318	.310	.324	.329	.335	.340	.343	.346	.355	.357	.358	.361	.372
2007	Oct	Nov	Dec	Jan	Feb	Mar	Apr	May	June	July	Aug	Sep	Oct	Nov	Dec
Jan	.313	.317	.325	.317	.331	.336	.342	.348	.351	.354	.363	.365	.366	.368	.379
Feb	.304	.307	.315	.307	.322	.326	.332	.338	.341	.344	.353	.355	.355	.358	.369
Mar	.295	.299	.307	.299	.313	.318	.324	.329	.332	.335	.344	.346	.347	.349	.361
Apr	.289	.293	.300	.293	.307	.311	.317	.323	.326	.329	.337	.339	.340	.343	.354
May	.284	.288	.295	.288	.302	.306	.312	.318	.321	.323	.332	.334	.335	.338	.349
June	.277	.281	.288	.281	.295	.299	.305	.311	.314	.316	.325	.327	.328	.330	.342
July	.285	.288	.296	.288	.302	.307	.313	.318	.321	.324	.333	.335	.336	.338	.349
Aug	.277	.281	.288	.281	.295	.299	.305	.311	.314	.316	.325	.327	.328	.330	.342
Sept	.273	.276	.284	.276	.290	.295	.301	.306	.309	.312	.321	.323	.324	.326	.337
Oct	.268	.271	.279	.271	.285	.289	.295	.301	.303	.306	.315	.317	.318	.320	.331
Nov	.263	.266	.274	.266	.280	.284	.290	.296	.299	.301	.310	.312	.313	.315	.326
Dec	.256	.259	.266	.259	.273	.277	.283	.288	.291	.294	.303	.304	.305	.308	.319
2008	Oct	Nov	Dec	Jan	Feb	Mar	Apr	May	June	July	Aug	Sep	Oct	Nov	Dec
Jan	.262	.265	.273	.265	.279	.284	.290	.295	.298	.301	.309	.311	.312	.315	.326
Feb	.253	.256	.263	.256	.270	.274	.280	.285	.288	.291	.299	.301	.302	.305	.316
Mar	.248	.252	.259	.252	.265	.270	.276	.281	.284	.287	.295	.297	.298	.300	.311
Apr	.237	.241	.248	.241	.254	.258	.264	.270	.272	.275	.284	.286	.286	.289	.300
May	.231	.234	.242	.234	.248	.252	.258	.263	.266	.269	.277	.279	.280	.282	.293
June	.221	.225	.232	.225	.238	.242	.248	.253	.256	.259	.267	.269	.270	.272	.283
July	.223	.226	.234	.226	.240	.244	.250	.255	.258	.261	.269	.271	.272	.274	.285
Aug	.219	.222	.230	.222	.236	.240	.246	.251	.254	.256	.265	.267	.267	.270	.280
Sept	.212	.216	.223	.216	.229	.233	.239	.244	.247	.250	.258	.260	.261	.263	.273
Oct	.216	.220	.227	.220	.233	.237	.243	.248	.251	.254	.262	.264	.265	.267	.277
Nov	.226	.229	.237	.229	.243	.247	.253	.258	.261	.263	.272	.274	.275	.277	.288
Dec	.244	.247	.255	.247	.261	.265	.271	.276	.279	.282	.290	.292	.293	.295	.306
2009	Oct	Nov	Dec	Jan	Feb	Mar	Apr	May	June	July	Aug	Sep	Oct	Nov	Dec
Jan	.260	.264	.271	.264	.277	.282	.288	.293	.296	.299	.307	.309	.310	.313	.324
Feb	.253	.256	.263	.256	.270	.274	.280	.285	.288	.291	.299	.301	.302	.305	.316
Mar	.253	.257	.264	.257	.270	.274	.281	.286	.289	.292	.300	.302	.303	.305	.316
Apr	.252	.255	.263	.255	.269	.273	.279	.285	.287	.290	.299	.301	.302	.304	.315
May	.244	.248	.255	.248	.261	.266	.272	.277	.280	.282	.291	.293	.294	.296	.307
June	.241	.244	.252	.244	.258	.262	.268	.273	.276	.279	.287	.289	.290	.292	.303
July	.241	.244	.252	.244	.258	.262	.268	.273	.276	.279	.287	.289	.290	.292	.303
Aug	.235	.238	.246	.238	.252	.256	.262	.267	.270	.273	.281	.283	.284	.286	.297
Sept	.230	.233	.241	.233	.247	.251	257	.262	.265	.268	.276	.278	.279	.281	.292
Oct	.226	.229	.237	.229	.243	.247	.253	.258	.261	.263	.272	.274	.275	.277	.288
Nov	.223	.226	.233	.226	.239	.243	.249	.254	.257	.260	.268	.270	.271	.273	.284
Dec	.215	.218	.225	.218	.231	.235	.241	.246	.249	.252	.260	.262	.263	.265	.276

MONTH OF DISPOSAL

2010	2015						2016								
	July	Aug	Sep	Oct	Nov	Dec	Jan	Feb	Mar	Apr	May	June	July	Aug	Sep
Jan	.187	.192	.191	.191	.192	.196	.188	.193	.198	.200	.203	.207	.209	.213	.216
Feb	.180	.185	.184	.184	.185	.189	.181	.186	.191	.193	.196	.200	.202	.206	.208
Mar	.172	.177	.176	.176	.177	.181	.173	.178	.183	.184	.188	.192	.193	.198	.200
Apr	.161	.166	.165	.165	.166	.170	.162	.167	.172	.173	.176	.181	.182	.187	.189
May	.157	.162	.161	.161	.162	.165	.157	.163	.168	.169	.172	.177	.178	.182	.185
June	.154	.159	.158	.158	.159	.163	.155	.160	.165	.166	.170	.174	.175	.180	.182
July	.157	.162	.161	.161	.162	.165	.157	.163	.168	.169	.172	.177	.178	.182	.185
Aug	.152	.157	.156	.156	.157	.161	.153	.158	.163	.164	.167	.172	.173	.178	.180
Sept	.148	.153	.152	.152	.153	.157	.149	.154	.159	.160	.163	.168	.169	.174	.176
Oct	.145	.151	.150	.149	.151	.154	.146	.151	.156	.158	.161	.165	.167	.171	.173
Nov	.140	.146	.145	.144	.146	.149	.141	.146	.151	.153	.156	.160	.161	.166	.168
Dec	.132	.137	.137	.136	.137	.141	.133	.138	.143	.144	.148	.152	.153	.158	.160
2011	July	Aug	Sep	Oct	Nov	Dec	Jan	Feb	Mar	Apr	May	June	July	Aug	Sep
Jan	.129	.134	.134	.133	.134	.138	.130	.135	.140	.141	.145	.149	.150	.155	.157
Feb	.118	.123	.122	.122	.123	.127	.119	.124	.129	.130	.133	.137	.139	.143	.145
Mar	.112	.117	.117	.116	.117	.121	.113	.118	.123	.124	.127	.132	.133	.137	.139
Apr	.103	.108	.108	.107	.108	.112	.104	.109	.114	.115	.118	.122	.124	.128	.130
May	.099	.105	.104	.103	.105	.108	.100	.105	.110	.111	.114	.119	.120	.124	.126
Jun	.099	.105	.104	.103	.105	.108	.100	.105	.110	.111	.114	.119	.120	.124	.126
July	.102	.107	.106	.106	.107	.110	.103	.108	.112	.114	.117	.121	.122	.127	.129
Aug	.095	.100	.100	.099	.100	.104	.096	.101	.106	.107	.110	.114	.116	.120	.122
Sept	.087	.092	.091	.091	.092	.095	.088	.093	.098	.099	.102	.106	.107	.111	.113
Oct	.087	.092	.091	.090	.092	.095	.087	.092	.097	.098	.101	.105	.107	.111	.113
Nov	.084	.089	.088	.088	.089	.093	.085	.090	.095	.096	.099	.103	.104	.109	.111
Dec	.080	.085	.084	.084	.085	.089	.081	.086	.091	.092	.095	.099	.100	.104	.107
2012	July	Aug	Sep	Oct	Nov	Dec	Jan	Feb	Mar	Apr	May	June	July	Aug	Sep
Jan	.087	.092	.091	.090	.092	.095	.087	.092	.097	.098	.101	.105	.107	.111	.113
Feb	.078	.083	.082	.082	.083	.086	.079	.084	.088	.090	.093	.097	.098	.102	.104
Mar	.074	.079	.078	.078	.079	.082	.075	.080	.084	.086	.088	.093	.094	.098	.100
Apr	.066	.071	.071	.070	.071	.075	.067	.072	.077	.078	.081	.085	.086	.090	.092
May	.067	.072	.071	.071	.072	.075	.068	.073	.077	.078	.081	.085	.087	.091	.093
June	.069	.074	.074	.073	.074	.078	.070	.075	.080	.081	.084	.088	.089	.093	.096
July	.068	.073	.072	.072	.073	.076	.069	.074	.078	.080	.083	.087	.088	.092	.094
Aug	.064	.069	.068	.068	.069	.072	.065	.070	.074	.076	.079	.083	.084	.088	.090
Sept	.059	.064	.063	.063	.064	.067	.060	.065	.069	.070	.073	.077	.079	.083	.085
Oct	.053	.058	.057	.057	.058	.061	.054	.059	.063	.064	.067	.071	.072	.077	.079
Nov	.053	.058	.057	.057	.058	.061	.054	.059	.063	.064	.067	.071	.072	.077	.079
Dec	.048	.053	.052	.051	.053	.056	.049	.053	.058	.059	.062	.066	.067	.071	.073
2013	July	Aug	Sep	Oct	Nov	Dec	Jan	Feb	Mar	Apr	May	June	July	Aug	Sep
Jan	.052	.057	.056	.056	.057	.060	.053	.058	.062	.063	.066	.070	.072	.076	.078
Feb	.044	.049	.048	.048	.049	.053	.045	.050	.055	.056	.059	.063	.064	.068	.070
Mar	.040	.045	.044	.043	.045	.048	.041	.045	.050	.051	.054	.058	.059	.063	.065
Apr	.036	.041	.040	.040	.041	.044	.037	.042	.046	.048	.051	.055	.056	.060	.062
May	.034	.039	.038	.038	.039	.042	.035	.040	.044	.046	.048	.052	.054	.058	.060
June	.036	.040	.040	.039	.040	.044	.036	.041	.046	.047	.050	.054	.055	.059	.061
July	.036	.040	.040	.039	.040	.044	.036	.041	.046	.047	.050	.054	.055	.059	.061
Aug	.030	.035	.034	.034	.035	.038	.031	.036	.040	.041	.044	.048	.049	.053	.055
Sept	.027	.031	.031	.030	.031	.035	.027	.032	.037	.038	.040	.044	.046	.050	.052
Oct	.027	.031	.031	.030	.031	.035	.027	.032	.037	.038	.040	.044	.046	.050	.052
Nov	.026	.031	.030	.029	.031	.034	.027	.031	.036	.037	.040	.044	.045	.049	.051
Dec	.024	.029	.028	.027	.029	.032	.025	.029	.034	.035	.038	.042	.043	.047	.049

MONTH OF DISPOSAL

	2016			2017											
2010	Oct	Nov	Dec	Jan	Feb	Mar	Apr	May	June	July	Aug	Sep	Oct	Nov	Dec
Jan	.215	.218	.226	.218	.232	.236	.242	.247	.250	.252	.261	.263	.263	.266	.276
Feb	.208	.211	.219	.211	.224	.229	.234	.240	.242	.245	.253	.255	.256	.258	.269
Mar	.200	.203	.210	.203	.216	.220	.226	.231	.234	.237	.245	.246	.247	.250	.260
Apr	.189	.192	.199	.192	.205	.209	.215	.219	.222	.225	.233	.235	.236	.238	.248
May	.184	.187	.195	.187	.200	.204	.210	.215	.218	.220	.229	.230	.231	.233	.244
June	.182	.185	.192	.185	.198	.202	.207	.212	.215	.218	.226	.228	.228	.231	.241
July	.184	.187	.195	.187	.200	.204	.210	.215	.218	.220	.229	.230	.231	.233	.244
Aug	.180	.183	.190	.183	.196	.200	.205	.210	.213	.216	.224	.225	.226	.229	.239
Sept	.175	.178	.186	.178	.191	.195	.201	.206	.209	.211	.219	.221	.222	.224	.234
Oct	.173	.176	.183	.176	.189	.193	.198	.203	.206	.209	.217	.218	.219	.221	.232
Nov	.168	.171	.178	.171	.183	.187	.193	.198	.201	.203	.211	.213	.214	.216	.226
Dec	.159	.162	.169	.162	.175	.179	.185	.190	.192	.195	.203	.204	.205	.208	.218
2011	Oct	Nov	Dec	Jan	Feb	Mar	Apr	May	June	July	Aug	Sep	Oct	Nov	Dec
Jan	.156	.159	.166	.159	.172	.176	.182	.186	.189	.192	.200	.201	.202	.204	.214
Feb	.145	.148	.155	.148	.160	.164	.170	.175	.177	.180	.188	.189	.190	.192	.202
Mar	.139	.142	.149	.142	.154	.158	.164	.169	.171	.174	.182	.183	.184	.186	.196
Apr	.130	.133	.140	.133	.145	.149	.154	.159	.162	.164	.172	.174	.174	.177	.186
May	.126	.129	.136	.129	.141	.145	.151	.155	.158	.160	.168	.170	.170	.173	.182
June	.126	.129	.136	.129	.141	.145	.151	.155	.158	.160	.168	.170	.170	.173	.182
July	.128	.131	.138	.131	.144	.147	.153	.158	.160	.163	.170	.172	.173	.175	.185
Aug	.122	.125	.131	.125	.137	.141	.146	.151	.153	.156	.163	.165	.166	.168	.178
Sept	.113	.116	.123	.116	.128	.132	.137	.142	.145	.147	.155	.156	.157	.159	.169
Oct	.113	.116	.122	.116	.128	.132	.137	.142	.144	.147	.154	.156	.157	.159	.168
Nov	.110	.113	.120	.113	.125	.129	.135	.139	.142	.144	.152	.153	.154	.156	.166
Dec	.106	.109	.116	.109	.121	.125	.130	.135	.137	.140	.147	.149	.150	.152	.162
2012	Oct	Nov	Dec	Jan	Feb	Mar	Apr	May	June	July	Aug	Sep	Oct	Nov	Dec
Jan	.113	.116	.122	.116	.128	.132	.137	.142	.144	.147	.154	.156	.157	.159	.168
Feb	.104	.107	.113	.107	.119	.123	.128	.133	.135	.138	.145	.147	.148	.150	.159
Mar	.100	.103	.109	.103	.115	.118	.124	.128	.131	.133	.141	.142	.143	.145	.155
Apr	.092	.095	.101	.095	.107	.111	.116	.120	.123	.125	.133	.134	.135	.137	.147
May	.092	.095	.102	.095	.107	.111	.116	.121	.123	.126	.133	.135	.136	.138	.147
June	.095	.098	.105	.098	.110	.114	.119	.124	.126	.129	.136	.138	.139	.141	.150
July	.094	.097	.103	.097	.109	.112	.118	.122	.125	.127	.135	.136	.137	.139	.149
Aug	.090	.093	.099	.093	.105	.108	.114	.118	.121	.123	.130	.132	.133	.135	.144
Sept	.084	.087	.094	.087	.099	.103	.108	.113	.115	.118	.125	.127	.127	.129	.139
Oct	.078	.081	.088	.081	.093	.096	.102	.106	.109	.111	.118	.120	.121	.123	.132
Nov	.078	.081	.088	.081	.093	.096	.102	.106	.109	.111	.118	.120	.121	.123	.132
Dec	.073	.076	.082	.076	.088	.091	.096	.101	.103	.106	.113	.115	.115	.118	.127
2013	Oct	Nov	Dec	Jan	Feb	Mar	Apr	May	June	July	Aug	Sep	Oct	Nov	Dec
Jan	.077	.080	.087	.080	.092	.096	.101	.105	.108	.110	.118	.119	.120	.122	.131
Feb	.069	.072	.079	.072	.084	.088	.093	.097	.100	.102	.109	.111	.112	.114	.123
Mar	.065	.068	.074	.068	.079	.083	.088	.092	.095	.097	.105	.106	.107	.109	.118
Apr	.061	.064	.071	.064	.076	.079	.085	.089	.091	.094	.101	.103	.103	.105	.115
May	.059	.062	.068	.062	.074	.077	.082	.087	.089	.092	.099	.100	.101	.103	.112
June	.060	.063	.070	.063	.075	.078	.084	.088	.091	.093	.100	.102	.103	.105	.114
July	.060	.063	.070	.063	.075	.078	.084	.088	.091	.093	.100	.102	.103	.105	.114
Aug	.055	.058	.064	.058	.069	.073	.078	.082	.085	.087	.094	.096	.097	.099	.108
Sept	.051	.054	.060	.054	.066	.069	.074	.079	.081	.083	.091	.092	.093	.095	.104
Oct	.051	.054	.060	.054	.066	.069	.074	.079	.081	.083	.091	.092	.093	.095	.104
Nov	.050	.053	.060	.053	.065	.068	.073	.078	.080	.083	.090	.091	.092	.094	.103
Dec	.048	.051	.057	.051	.063	.066	.071	.076	.078	.080	.087	.089	.090	.092	.101

MONTH OF DISPOSAL

	2015						2016								
2014	July	Aug	Sep	Oct	Nov	Dec	Jan	Feb	Mar	Apr	May	June	July	Aug	Sep
Jan	.024	.029	.028	.027	.029	.032	.025	.029	.034	.035	.038	.042	.043	.047	.049
Feb	.017	.022	.021	.021	.022	.025	.018	.023	.027	.028	.031	.035	.036	.040	.042
Mar	.015	.020	.019	.018	.020	.023	.016	.020	.025	.026	.029	.033	.034	.038	.040
Apr	.011	.016	.015	.015	.016	.019	.012	.017	.021	.022	.025	.029	.030	.034	.036
May	.011	.015	.014	.014	.015	.018	.011	.016	.020	.021	.024	.028	.029	.033	.035
June	.010	.014	.013	.012	.014	.017	.010	.014	.019	.020	.023	.027	.028	.032	.034
July	.010	.015	.014	.014	.015	.018	.011	.016	.020	.021	.024	.028	.029	.033	.035
Aug	.006	.011	.010	.010	.011	.014	.007	.012	.016	.017	.020	.024	.025	.029	.031
Sep	.004	.009	.008	.007	.009	.012	.005	.009	.014	.015	.017	.021	.023	.026	.028
Oct	.003	.008	.007	.007	.008	.011	.004	.009	.013	.014	.017	.021	.022	.026	.028
Nov	.006	.011	.010	.009	.011	.014	.007	.011	.016	.017	.019	.023	.025	.028	.030
Dec	.004	.009	.008	.008	.009	.012	.005	.010	.014	.015	.018	.022	.023	.027	.029
2015	July	Aug	Sep	Oct	Nov	Dec	Jan	Feb	Mar	Apr	May	June	July	Aug	Sep
Jan	.013	.017	.016	.016	.017	.020	.013	.018	.022	.023	.026	.030	.031	.035	.037
Feb	.007	.012	.011	.011	.012	.015	.008	.013	.017	.018	.021	.025	.026	.030	.032
Mar	.006	.011	.010	.009	.011	.014	.007	.011	.016	.017	.019	.023	.025	.028	.030
Apr	.002	.007	.006	.006	.007	.010	.003	.008	.012	.013	.016	.020	.021	.025	.027
May	.000	.005	.004	.004	.005	.008	.001	.006	.010	.011	.014	.018	.019	.023	.025
June	.000	.003	.003	.002	.003	.007	.000	.004	.008	.010	.012	.016	.017	.021	.023
July	—	.005	.004	.003	.005	.008	.001	.005	.010	.011	.014	.017	.019	.022	.024
Aug	—	—	.000	.000	.000	.003	.000	.001	.005	.006	.009	.013	.014	.018	.020
Sep	—	—	—	.000	.001	.004	.000	.002	.006	.007	.010	.013	.015	.018	.020
Oct	—	—	—	—	.001	.004	.000	.002	.006	.007	.010	.014	.015	.019	.021
Nov	—	—	—	—	—	.003	.000	.001	.005	.006	.009	.013	.014	.018	.020
Dec	—	—	—	—	—	—	.000	.000	.002	.003	.006	.010	.011	.015	.017
2016	July	Aug	Sep	Oct	Nov	Dec	Jan	Feb	Mar	Apr	May	June	July	Aug	Sep
Jan	—	—	—	—	—	—	—	.005	.009	.010	.013	.017	.018	.022	.024
Feb	—	—	—	—	—	—	—	—	.004	.005	.008	.012	.013	.017	.019
Mar	—	—	—	—	—	—	—	—	.001	.004	.008	.009	.013	.015	
Apr	—	—	—	—	—	—	—	—	—	.003	.007	.008	.011	.013	
May	—	—	—	—	—	—	—	—	—	—	.004	.005	.009	.011	
June	—	—	—	—	—	—	—	—	—	—	—	.001	.005	.007	
July	—	—	—	—	—	—	—	—	—	—	—	—	.004	.006	
Aug	—	—	—	—	—	—	—	—	—	—	—	—	—	.002	
Sep	—	—	—	—	—	—	—	—	—	—	—	—	—	—	—
Oct	—	—	—	—	—	—	—	—	—	—	—	—	—	—	—
Nov	—	—	—	—	—	—	—	—	—	—	—	—	—	—	—
Dec	—	—	—	—	—	—	—	—	—	—	—	—	—	—	—
2017	July	Aug	Sep	Oct	Nov	Dec	Jan	Feb	Mar	Apr	May	June	July	Aug	Sep
Jan	—	—	—	—	—	—	—	—	—	—	—	—	—	—	—
Feb	—	—	—	—	—	—	—	—	—	—	—	—	—	—	—
Mar	—	—	—	—	—	—	—	—	—	—	—	—	—	—	—
Apr	—	—	—	—	—	—	—	—	—	—	—	—	—	—	—
May	—	—	—	—	—	—	—	—	—	—	—	—	—	—	—
June	—	—	—	—	—	—	—	—	—	—	—	—	—	—	—
July	—	—	—	—	—	—	—	—	—	—	—	—	—	—	—
Aug	—	—	—	—	—	—	—	—	—	—	—	—	—	—	—
Sep	—	—	—	—	—	—	—	—	—	—	—	—	—	—	—
Oct	—	—	—	—	—	—	—	—	—	—	—	—	—	—	—
Nov	—	—	—	—	—	—	—	—	—	—	—	—	—	—	—
Dec	—	—	—	—	—	—	—	—	—	—	—	—	—	—	—

MONTH OF DISPOSAL

	2016			2017											
2014	Oct	Nov	Dec	Jan	Feb	Mar	Apr	May	June	July	Aug	Sep	Oct	Nov	Dec
Jan	.048	.051	.057	.051	.063	.066	.071	.076	.078	.080	.087	.089	.090	.092	.101
Feb	.042	.044	.051	.044	.056	.059	.065	.069	.071	.074	.081	.082	.083	.085	.094
Mar	.039	.042	.048	.042	.053	.057	.062	.066	.069	.071	.078	.080	.080	.082	.091
Apr	.036	.038	.045	.038	.050	.053	.058	.063	.065	.067	.074	.076	.077	.079	.088
May	.035	.038	.044	.038	.049	.052	.057	.062	.064	.066	.073	.075	.076	.078	.087
June	.033	.036	.042	.036	.047	.051	.056	.060	.062	.065	.072	.073	.074	.076	.085
July	.034	.037	.043	.037	.048	.052	.057	.061	.064	.066	.073	.075	.075	.077	.086
Aug	.030	.033	.039	.033	.044	.048	.053	.057	.060	.062	.069	.070	.071	.073	.082
Sep	.028	.031	.037	.031	.042	.045	.050	.055	.057	.059	.066	.068	.069	.071	.080
Oct	.028	.030	.036	.030	.042	.045	.050	.054	.057	.059	.066	.068	.068	.070	.079
Nov	.030	.033	.039	.033	.044	.047	.053	.057	.059	.061	.068	.070	.071	.073	.082
Dec	.028	.031	.037	.031	.042	.046	.051	.055	.057	.060	.067	.068	.069	.071	.080
2015	Oct	Nov	Dec	Jan	Feb	Mar	Apr	May	June	July	Aug	Sep	Oct	Nov	Dec
Jan	.037	.040	.046	.040	.051	.054	.060	.064	.066	.069	.076	.077	.078	.080	.089
Feb	.032	.034	.041	.034	.046	.049	.054	.058	.061	.063	.070	.072	.072	.074	.083
Mar	.030	.033	.039	.033	.044	.047	.053	.057	.059	.061	.068	.070	.071	.073	.082
Apr	.026	.029	.035	.029	.040	.044	.049	.053	.055	.058	.065	.066	.067	.069	.078
May	.024	.027	.033	.027	.038	.042	.047	.051	.053	.056	.063	.064	.065	.067	.076
June	.023	.025	.032	.025	.037	.040	.045	.049	.052	.054	.061	.063	.063	.065	.074
July	.024	.027	.033	.027	.038	.041	.046	.051	.053	.055	.062	.064	.065	.067	.075
Aug	.019	.022	.028	.022	.033	.037	.042	.046	.048	.050	.057	.059	.060	.062	.070
Sep	.020	.023	.029	.023	.034	.037	.042	.047	.049	.051	.058	.060	.060	.062	.071
Oct	.020	.023	.029	.023	.034	.038	.043	.047	.049	.052	.059	.060	.061	.063	.072
Nov	.019	.022	.028	.022	.033	.037	.042	.046	.048	.050	.057	.059	.060	.062	.070
Dec	.016	.019	.025	.019	.030	.033	.038	.043	.045	.047	.054	.056	.056	.058	.067
2016	Oct	Nov	Dec	Jan	Feb	Mar	Apr	May	June	July	Aug	Sep	Oct	Nov	Dec
Jan	.023	.026	.032	.026	.037	.041	.046	.050	.052	.054	.061	.063	.064	.066	.075
Feb	.018	.021	.027	.021	.032	.036	.041	.045	.047	.050	.057	.058	.059	.061	.070
Mar	.014	.017	.023	.017	.028	.031	.036	.041	.043	.045	.052	.054	.054	.056	.065
Apr	.013	.016	.022	.016	.027	.030	.035	.039	.042	.044	.051	.052	.053	.055	.064
May	.010	.013	.019	.013	.024	.027	.032	.037	.039	.041	.048	.050	.050	.052	.061
June	.006	.009	.015	.009	.020	.024	.029	.033	.035	.037	.044	.046	.046	.048	.057
July	.005	.008	.014	.008	.019	.022	.027	.032	.034	.036	.043	.044	.045	.047	.056
Aug	.002	.004	.010	.004	.015	.019	.023	.028	.030	.032	.039	.040	.041	.043	.052
Sep	.000	.002	.008	.002	.013	.017	.022	.026	.028	.030	.037	.039	.039	.041	.050
Oct	—	.003	.009	.003	.014	.017	.022	.026	.028	.031	.037	.039	.040	.042	.050
Nov	—	—	.006	.000	.011	.014	.019	.023	.026	.028	.035	.036	.037	.039	.047
Dec	—	—	—	.000	.005	.008	.013	.017	.019	.022	.028	.030	.031	.033	.041
2017	Oct	Nov	Dec	Jan	Feb	Mar	Apr	May	June	July	Aug	Sep	Oct	Nov	Dec
Jan	—	—	—	—	.011	.014	.019	.023	.026	.028	.035	.036	.037	.039	.047
Feb	—	—	—	—	—	.003	.008	.012	.015	.017	.023	.025	.026	.028	.036
Mar	—	—	—	—	—	—	.005	.009	.011	.013	.020	.022	.022	.024	.033
Apr	—	—	—	—	—	—	—	.004	.006	.008	.015	.017	.017	.019	.028
May	—	—	—	—	—	—	—	—	.002	.004	.011	.013	.013	.015	.024
June	—	—	—	—	—	—	—	—	—	.002	.009	.010	.011	.013	.021
July	—	—	—	—	—	—	—	—	—	—	.007	.008	.009	.011	.019
Aug	—	—	—	—	—	—	—	—	—	—	—	.001	.002	.004	.012
Sep	—	—	—	—	—	—	—	—	—	—	—	—	.001	.003	.011
Oct	—	—	—	—	—	—	—	—	—	—	—	—	—	.002	.010
Nov	—	—	—	—	—	—	—	—	—	—	—	—	—	—	.008
Dec	—	—	—	—	—	—	—	—	—	—	—	—	—	—	—

Retail prices index

	Jan	Feb	Mar	Apr	May	Jun
1982	78.73	78.76	79.44	81.04	81.62	81.85
1983	82.61	82.97	83.12	84.28	84.64	84.84
1984	86.84	87.20	87.48	88.64	88.97	89.20
1985	91.20	91.94	92.80	94.78	95.21	95.41
1986	96.25	96.60	96.73	97.67	97.85	97.79
1987	100.00	100.40	100.60	101.80	101.90	101.90
1988	103.30	103.70	104.10	105.80	106.20	106.60
1989	111.00	111.80	112.30	114.30	115.00	115.40
1990	119.50	120.20	121.40	125.10	126.20	126.70
1991	130.20	130.90	131.40	133.10	133.50	134.10
1992	135.60	136.30	136.70	138.80	139.30	139.30
1993	137.90	138.80	139.30	140.60	141.10	141.00
1994	141.30	142.10	142.50	144.20	144.70	144.70
1995	146.00	146.90	147.50	149.00	149.60	149.80
1996	150.20	150.90	151.50	152.60	152.90	153.00
1997	154.40	155.00	155.40	156.30	156.90	157.50
1998	159.50	160.30	160.80	162.60	163.50	163.40
1999	163.40	163.70	164.10	165.20	165.60	165.60
2000	166.60	167.50	168.40	170.10	170.70	171.10
2001	171.10	172.00	172.20	173.10	174.20	174.40
2002	173.30	173.80	174.50	175.70	176.20	176.20
2003	178.40	179.30	179.90	181.20	181.50	181.30
2004	183.10	183.80	184.60	185.70	186.50	186.80
2005	188.90	189.60	190.50	191.60	192.00	192.20
2006	193.40	194.20	195.00	196.50	197.70	198.50
2007	201.60	203.10	204.40	205.40	206.20	207.30
2008	209.80	211.40	212.10	214.00	215.10	216.80
2009	210.10	211.40	211.30	211.50	212.80	213.40
2010	217.90	219.20	220.70	222.80	223.60	224.10
2011	229.00	231.30	232.50	234.40	235.20	235.20
2012	238.00	239.90	240.80	242.50	242.40	241.80
2013	245.80	247.60	248.70	249.50	250.00	249.70
2014	252.60	254.20	254.80	255.70	255.90	256.30
2015	255.40	256.70	257.10	258.00	258.50	258.90
2016	258.80	260.00	261.10	261.40	262.10	263.10
2017	265.50	268.40	269.30	270.60	271.70	272.30

Retail prices index, cont.

	Jul	Aug	Sep	Oct	Nov	Dec
1982	81.88	81.90	81.85	82.26	82.66	82.51
1983	85.30	85.68	86.06	86.36	86.67	86.89
1984	89.10	89.94	90.11	90.67	90.95	90.87
1985	95.23	95.49	95.44	95.59	95.92	96.05
1986	97.52	97.82	98.30	98.45	99.29	99.62
1987	101.80	102.10	102.40	102.90	103.40	103.30
1988	106.70	107.90	108.40	109.50	110.00	110.30
1989	115.50	115.80	116.60	117.50	118.50	118.80
1990	126.80	128.10	129.30	130.30	130.00	129.90
1991	133.80	134.10	134.60	135.10	135.60	135.70
1992	138.80	138.90	139.40	139.90	139.70	139.20
1993	140.70	141.30	141.90	141.80	141.60	141.90
1994	144.00	144.70	145.00	145.20	145.30	146.00
1995	149.10	149.90	150.60	149.80	149.80	150.70
1996	152.40	153.10	153.80	153.80	153.90	154.40
1997	157.50	158.50	159.30	159.50	159.60	160.00
1998	163.00	163.70	164.40	164.50	164.40	164.40
1999	165.10	165.50	166.20	166.50	166.70	167.30
2000	170.50	170.50	171.70	171.60	172.10	172.20
2001	173.30	174.00	174.60	174.30	173.60	173.40
2002	175.90	176.40	177.60	177.90	178.20	178.50
2003	181.30	181.60	182.50	182.60	182.70	183.50
2004	186.80	187.40	188.10	188.60	189.00	189.90
2005	192.20	192.60	193.10	193.30	193.60	194.10
2006	198.50	199.20	200.10	200.40	201.10	202.70
2007	206.10	207.30	208.00	208.90	209.70	210.90
2008	216.50	217.20	218.40	217.70	216.00	212.90
2009	213.40	214.40	215.30	216.00	216.60	218.00
2010	223.60	224.50	225.30	225.80	226.80	228.40
2011	234.70	236.10	237.90	238.00	238.50	239.40
2012	242.10	243.00	244.20	245.60	245.60	246.80
2013	249.70	251.00	251.90	251.90	252.10	253.40
2014	256.00	257.00	257.60	257.70	257.10	257.50
2015	258.60	259.80	259.60	259.50	259.80	260.60
2016	263.40	264.40	264.90	264.80	265.50	267.10
2017	272.90	274.70	275.10	275.30	275.80	278.10

Leases

SEE TOLLEY'S TAX COMPUTATIONS 216.3.
Depreciation table (TCGA 1992 Sch 8 para 1)

Yrs	%	Yrs	%	Yrs	%	Yrs	%
50 (or more)	100	37	93.497	24	79.622	11	50.038
49	99.657	36	92.761	23	78.055	10	46.695
48	99.289	35	91.981	22	76.399	9	43.154
47	98.902	34	91.156	21	74.635	8	39.399
46	98.490	33	90.280	20	72.770	7	35.414
45	98.059	32	89.354	19	70.791	6	31.195
44	97.595	31	88.371	18	68.697	5	26.722
43	97.107	30	87.330	17	66.470	4	21.983
42	96.593	29	86.226	16	64.116	3	16.959
41	96.041	28	85.053	15	61.617	2	11.629
40	95.457	27	83.816	14	58.971	1	5.983
39	94.842	26	82.496	13	56.167	0	0
38	94.189	25	81.100	12	53.191		

Formula: Fraction of expenditure disallowed—

$$\frac{AE - D}{AE}$$

Where:

AE is the percentage for duration of lease at acquisition or expenditure; and
D is the percentage for duration of lease at disposal.

Fractions of years: Add one-twelfth of the difference between the percentage for the whole year and the next higher percentage for each additional month. Odd days under 14 are not counted; 14 odd days or more count as a month.

Short leases: premiums treated as rent (TCGA 1992 Sch 8 para 5; ITTOIA 2005 ss 277–281A; CTA 2009 s 217–221A) Part of premium for grant of a short lease which is chargeable to income tax as property income:

$$P - (2\% \times (n - 1) \times P)$$

Where:

P is the amount of premium;
n is the number of complete years which lease has to run when granted.

Length of lease (complete years)	Amount chargeable to CGT %	Income tax charge %	Length of lease (complete years)	Amount chargeable to CGT %	Income tax charge %	Length of lease (complete years)	Amount chargeable to CGT %	Income tax charge %
Over 50	100	0	34	66	34	17	32	68
50	98	2	33	64	36	16	30	70
49	96	4	32	62	38	15	28	72
48	94	6	31	60	40	14	26	74
47	92	8	30	58	42	13	24	76
46	90	10	29	56	44	12	22	78
45	88	12	28	54	46	11	20	80
44	86	14	27	52	48	10	18	82
43	84	16	26	50	50	9	16	84
42	82	18	25	48	52	8	14	86
41	80	20	24	46	54	7	12	88
40	78	22	23	44	56	6	10	90
39	76	24	22	42	58	5	8	92
38	74	26	21	40	60	4	6	94
37	72	28	20	38	62	3	4	96
36	70	30	19	36	64	2	2	98
35	68	32	18	34	66	1 or less	0	100

Corporation tax

Rates for non-ring fence profits

SEE TOLLEY'S TAX COMPUTATIONS 101.2.
(CTA 2010 ss 3, 18–34; F(No 2)A 2015 s 7)

Financial year	2015	2016	2017	2018	2019	2020
Main rate	20%	20%	19%	19%	19%	19%[1]
Tax credit: from 6 April	10%	N/A[2]	N/A[2]	N/A[2]	N/A[2]	N/A[2]

[1] For financial year 2020 the main rate was originally reduced to 17% but will now remain at 19% until at least financial year 2022.
[2] Tax credits are abolished from 6 April 2016.
[3] The power to set the rate of corporation tax in Northern Ireland has been devolved to the Northern Ireland Assembly in relation to such financial year as HM Treasury may appoint.

Bank levy see p 65. **Patent box** see p 64. **Diverted profits tax** see p 65. **Bank corporation tax surcharge** see p 65. **Tax charge on restitution interest** see p 66.

Rates for ring fence profits

(CTA 2010 ss 279A–279H)

Financial year	2015	2016	2017	2018	2019	2020
Main rate	30%	30%	30%	30%	30%	30%
Small profits rate	19%	19%	19%	19%	19%	19%
lower limit[1]	£300,000	£300,000	£300,000	£300,000	£300,000	£300,000
upper limit[1]	£1.5m	£1.5m	£1.5m	£1.5m	£1.5m	£1.5m
marginal relief fraction	11/400	11/400	11/400	11/400	11/400	11/400

[1] Reduced proportionally for accounting periods of less than 12 months. The limits are divided by the number of related 51% group companies, including the company in question.

Marginal relief

From 1 April 2015 Applies to ring fence profits only. The small ring fence profits rate applies to taxable total profits where augmented profits (see below) do not exceed the lower limit. Where a company's ring fence profits exceed the lower limit but do not exceed the upper limit, the charge to corporation tax on the company's taxable total profits is reduced by an amount calculated in accordance with a statutory formula—

$$R \times (U - A) \times \frac{N}{A}$$

where—
R is the marginal relief fraction;
U is the upper limit;
N is the amount of the taxable total profits;
A is the amount of the augmented profits—its adjusted taxable total profits plus exempt ABGH distributions (before 6 April 2016, franked investment income) (other than from UK companies in the same group or owned by a consortium of which the recipient is a member). A company's adjusted taxable total profits are its profits chargeable to corporation tax as if no part of its chargeable gains and allowable losses for the period were liable to capital gains tax instead of to corporation tax.

Corporation tax reliefs

Disincorporation relief *before 1 April 2018*

(FA 2013 ss 58–61)
With effect for disincorporations between 1 April 2013 and 31 March 2018 inclusive, joint claims may be made by a company and its shareholders to allow goodwill or interests in land not held as trading stock to be transferred at a reduced value so that no corporation tax will be payable by the company on the transfer. Relief is restricted to cases where the market value of the assets allowed for disincorporation relief does not exceed £100,000. Joint claims must be made to HMRC within two years of the date of the transfer and other eligibility criteria also apply. Shareholders to whom the assets are transferred will inherit the transfer value for the purpose of capital gains tax.

Gifts of pre-eminent objects

(FA 2012 Sch 14)

Companies which gift pre-eminent objects to the nation will receive a reduction in their UK tax liability of 20% of the value of the object they are donating. The gift must be accepted as pre-eminent by the Arts Council under the Cultural Gifts Scheme.

Patent box

(CTA 2010 Pt 8A)

The patent box allows companies to elect to apply a 10% corporation tax rate to a proportion of profits attributable to qualifying patents, whether paid separately as royalties or embedded in the sales price of products, and to certain other qualifying intellectual property rights such as regulatory data protection (also called 'data exclusivity'), supplementary protection certificates and plant variety rights from 1 April 2013. In the first year the proportion of profits qualifying for the 10% rate was 60% and this was increased annually to 100% from April 2017. Thus, for financial year 2014 the proportion was 70%, for 2015 it was 80%, and for 2016 it was 90%.

Real Estate Investment Trusts (REITs)

(CTA 2010 ss 518–609)

Qualifying rental income from and gains on disposals of investment properties by UK companies within the REIT scheme are exempt from corporation tax.

Research and development

(CTA 2009 ss 1039–1142)

Deduction scheme

SEE TOLLEY'S TAX COMPUTATIONS 117.1.

An 'SME' incurring R&D expenditure in a 12-month accounting period can obtain relief for 230% of that expenditure.

SMEs not yet in profit or which have not yet started to trade can claim relief upfront as a cash payment of 14.5% of 'surrenderable loss' (R&D tax credit). Proposed to be limited from 1 April 2021 to three times the company's total PAYE and NICs payment for the period.

An 'SME' can also claim relief where it incurs expenditure on work contracted to it by a large company or by any person otherwise than in the course of carrying on a chargeable trade; or expenditure which is subsidised; or expenditure subject to the project limit of €7.5m. The relief is 130% of the expenditure.

An 'SME' is a company with less than 500 employees and either annual turnover of €100m or less or annual balance sheet total of €86m or less.

Large companies can claim a similar relief to that for SMEs above, including tax credits, for expenditure incurred before 1 April 2017 on certain vaccines research.

Before 1 April 2016 large companies incurring R&D expenditure could obtain relief for 130% of that expenditure. From that date they must use the 'Above the line' credit scheme outlined below.

'Above the line' credit scheme for large companies

SEE TOLLEY'S TAX COMPUTATIONS 117.2.

Large companies (and certain SMEs with sub-contracted or subsidised R&D, or R&D subject to the project limit) can claim R&D relief as a taxable above the line (ATL) credit to the value of 13% (12% for expenditure before 1 April 2020, 11% for expenditure between 1 April 2015 and 1 January 2018) of their qualifying R&D expenditure (49% for ring fence trades). The credit is fully payable, net of tax, to companies with no corporation tax liability. The scheme was initially optional from 1 April 2013. Companies that did not elect to claim the ATL credit could continue claiming R&D relief under the large company deduction scheme (see above) until 31 March 2016. The ATL credit became mandatory for such companies on 1 April 2016. Universities and charities are unable to claim the credit for expenditure incurred on or after 1 August 2015.

Annual tax on enveloped dwellings

(FA 2013 ss 94–174, Schs 33–35)

A charge is imposed on certain non-natural persons (NNPs), ie companies, partnerships with at least one company member, and collective investment schemes which hold UK residential dwellings valued above a certain limit on specified valuation dates. The limit is £500,000 from 1 April 2016 (£1 million between 1 April 2015 and 1 April 2016). Returns and payment are due by 30 April each year. If the payer is not chargeable for the full year, a later repayment claim can be made. Various reliefs from the charge apply and companies may be able to submit relief declaration returns. A charge to capital gains tax at 28% also applies to disposals before 6 April 2019 of such properties, whether by UK resident or non-resident NNPs. See also p 139 regarding the 15% stamp duty land tax which can apply to acquisitions of such properties.

Annual tax charge

Property value[1]	Annual tax 2015–16	Annual tax 2016–17	Annual tax 2017–18	Annual tax 2018–19	Annual tax 2019–20	Annual tax 2020–21
More than £500,000 to £1m	N/A	£3,500	£3,500	£3,600	£3,650	£3,700
More than £1m to £2m	£7,000	£7,000	£7,050	£7,250	£7,400	£7,500
More than £2m to £5m	£23,350	£23,350	£23,550	£24,250	£24,800	£25,200
More than £5m to £10m	£54,450	£54,450	£54,950	£56,550	£57,900	£58,850
More than £10m to £20m	£109,050	£109,050	£110,100	£113,400	£116,100	£118,050
More than £20m	£218,200	£218,200	£220,350	£226,950	£232,350	£236,250

[1]   The valuation is the market value on the last previous valuation date. The first valuation date was 1 April 2012 and then every five years thereafter. Other valuation dates can apply in certain circumstances, for example when a new property is purchased. The valuation is applied on the first day of the chargeable period if the chargeable person is within the charge on that day, otherwise the first day in the chargeable period on which they are first within the charge.

Relief codes for relief declaration returns

	Code for type of relief
Property rental business	1
Dwellings open to the public	2
Property developers	3
Property traders	4
Financial institutions acquiring dwellings	5
Regulated home reversion plans	5A
Occupation by certain employees etc	6
Farmhouses	7
Providers of social housing	8

Bank corporation tax surcharge

(CTA 2010 ss 269D–269DO)
From 1 January 2016 a surcharge of 8% is levied on profits of banking companies and building societies.

Bank levy

(FA 2011 Sch 19 para 6)
A bank levy is charged based on the total chargeable equity and liabilities reported in the relevant balance sheets of affected banks, banking and building society groups at the end of the chargeable period. It is payable through the existing corporation tax self-assessment system. It is not charged on the first £20 billion of chargeable liabilities.

	1.1.16–31.12.16	1.1.17–31.12.17	1.1.18–31.12.18	1.1.19–31.12.19	1.1.20–31.12.20	1.1.21–31.12.21
Short-term chargeable liabilities	0.18%	0.17%	0.16%	0.15%	0.14%	0.1%
Long-term chargeable equity and liabilities	0.09%	0.085%	0.08%	0.075%	0.07%	0.05%

Diverted profits tax

(FA 2015 ss 77–116)
A diverted profits tax of 25% applies to counter the use of aggressive tax planning techniques by multinational enterprises to divert profits from the UK. There are two basic rules which apply. The first rule counteracts arrangements by which foreign companies exploit the permanent establishment rules, and comes into effect if a person is carrying on activity in the UK in connection with supplies of goods and services by a non-UK resident company to customers in the UK, provided that the detailed conditions are met. The second rule applies to certain arrangements which lack economic substance involving entities with an existing UK taxable presence.

Digital services tax

From April 2020 a digital services tax (DST) of 2% applies to revenues which are attributable to UK users and are from digital services activities that fall into three categories: a social media service; an internet search engine; or an online marketplace. There is an annual threshold of £500m digital services revenues and £25m UK digital services revenues below which the DST will not apply, and businesses with low margins or losses can make a safe-harbour election which allows a calculation of DST based on operating margins.

Loans to participators

SEE TOLLEY'S TAX COMPUTATIONS 104.2.

(CTA 2010 s 455)

A charge of 32.5% of the loan made or benefit conferred applies (25% for loans made and benefits conferred before 6 April 2016).

Tax charge on restitution interest

(CTA 2010 ss 357YA–357YW)

Where tax has been overpaid by a company as a result of a mistake in law or following unlawful collection of tax by HMRC a restitution award may be made. Where the award is made as a result of a judgment or an agreement between the parties which became final on or after 21 October 2015, the interest element of the award, whether arising before, on or after 21 October 2015, is chargeable to corporation tax at a special rate of 45%.

Environmental taxes and other levies

Aggregates levy

(FA 2001 ss 16–49, Schs 4–10)

Levy on commercial exploitation of aggregates including rock, gravel or sand together with any other substance incorporated or naturally occurring with it. Applies to all aggregate (not recycled) extracted in the UK or territorial waters unless exempt. Before 1 April 2014 exemptions applied to quarried or mined products such as clay, shale, slate, metal and metal ores, gemstones, semi-precious gemstones and industrial minerals. From 1 April 2014, the Government had to suspend these exemptions, exclusions and reliefs as they were the subject of a State aid investigation by the European Commission. Following conclusion of the investigation, all the exemptions except that for shale were reinstated on 1 August 2015 with retrospective effect from 1 April 2014. There is an exempt process for shale which is not used as aggregate for construction purposes which applies from 1 April 2014. This enables a person who has commercially exploited and accounted for the levy chargeable on such shale to claim a tax credit for it, when it is used in this new exempt process (HMRC Brief 6/2015).

The aggregates levy has been devolved to the Scottish Parliament. From a date to be appointed a replacement tax will apply in Scotland.

From 1 April 2009	£2.00 per tonne

Air passenger duty

(FA 1994 s 30, Sch 5A)

The rates for all *direct* long haul flights (ie in band B) departing from Northern Ireland are devolved to the Northern Ireland Assembly and set at £0.

Children under the age of 2 years on the date of the flight without their own seat are exempt from charge in all classes of travel. From 1 May 2015, children under the age of 12 years on the date of the flight are exempt from charge in standard class. From 1 March 2016 this exemption applies to children under age 16.

Air passenger duty has been devolved to the Scottish Parliament. A replacement tax (air departure tax) is planned to apply in Scotland from a date to be determined.

Reduced rate (lowest class of travel)

Band and distance of capital city of destination country from UK in miles	1.4.15–31.3.16	1.4.16–31.3.17	1.4.17–31.3.18	1.4.18–31.3.19	1.4.19–31.3.20	1.4.20–31.3.21	From 1.4.21
Band A (0–2,000)	£13	£13	£13	£13	£13	£13	£13
Band B (over 2,000)	£71	£73	£75	£78	£78	£80	£82

Standard rate (all classes other than lowest class)[1]

Band and distance of capital city of destination country from UK in miles	1.4.15–31.3.16	1.4.16–31.3.17	1.4.17–31.3.18	1.4.18–31.3.19	1.4.19–31.3.20	1.4.20–31.3.21	From 1.4.21
Band A (0–2,000)	£26	£26	£26	£26	£26	£26	£26
Band B (over 2,000)	£142	£146	£150	£156	£172	£176	£180

Higher rate (flights aboard aircraft of 20 tonnes and above with fewer than 19 seats)

Band and distance of capital city of destination country from UK in miles	1.4.15–31.3.16	1.4.16–31.3.17	1.4.17–31.3.18	1.4.18–31.3.19	1.4.19–31.3.20	1.4.20–31.3.21	From 1.4.21
Band A (0–2,000)	£78	£78	£78	£78	£78	£78	£78
Band B (over 2,000)	£426	£438	£450	£468	£515	£528	£541

[1] If a class of travel provides a seat pitch in excess of 1.016 metres (40 inches) the standard rate is the minimum rate that applies, even if it is the lowest or only class of travel.

The following specifies which countries come into band A and band B.

Band A territories — 0–2,000 miles from London		
Albania	Greenland	Morocco
Algeria	Guernsey[1]	Netherlands
Andorra	Hungary	Norway (including Svalbard)
Austria	Iceland	Poland
Azores	Republic of Ireland	Portugal (including Madeira)
Belarus	Isle of Man	Romania
Belgium	Italy (including Sicily and Sardinia)	Russian Federation (west of the Urals)
Bosnia and Herzegovina	Jersey[1]	San Marino
Bulgaria	Republic of Kosovo	Serbia
Croatia	Latvia	Slovak Republic
Cyprus	Libya	Slovenia
Czech Republic	Liechtenstein	Spain (including the Balearic Islands and the Canary Islands)
Denmark (including the Faroe Islands)	Lithuania	Sweden
Estonia	Luxembourg	Switzerland
Finland	former Yugoslav Republic of Macedonia	Tunisia
France (including Corsica)	Malta	Turkey
Germany	Moldova	Ukraine
Gibraltar	Monaco	Western Sahara
Greece	Montenegro	

[1]   HMRC guidance refers to the Channel Islands, rather than Guernsey and Jersey.

Band B — Journey ends in any other place.

Climate change levy

(FA 2000 s 30, Sch 6)

Levy on supply for industrial or commercial purposes of energy in the form of electricity, gas, petroleum and hydrocarbon gas supplied in a liquid state, coal and lignite, coke and semi-coke of coal or lignite and petroleum coke.

Taxable commodity supplied	Rate[1]						
	1.4.15– 31.3.16	1.4.16– 31.3.17	1.4.17– 31.3.18	1.4.18– 31.3.19	1.4.19– 31.3.20	**1.4.20– 31.3.21**	1.4.21– 31.3.22
Electricity	0.554p per kWh	0.559p per kWh	0.568p per kWh	0.583p per kWh	0.847p per kWh	**0.811p per kWh**	0.775p per kWh
Gas supplied by a gas utility or any gas supplied in a gaseous state that is of a kind supplied by a gas utility	0.193p per kWh	0.195p per kWh	0.198p per kWh	0.203p per kWh	0.339p per kWh	**0.406p per kWh**	0.465p per kWh
Any petroleum gas, or other gaseous hydrocarbon supplied in a liquid state	1.240p per kg	1.251p per kg	1.272p per kg	1.304p per kg	2.175p per kg	**2.175p per kg**	2.175p per kWh
Any other taxable commodity	1.512p per kg	1.526p per kg	1.551p per kg	1.591p per kg	2.653p per kg	**3.174p per kg**	3.640p per kg

[1] Rate at which payable if supply is not a reduced-rate supply. The levy is charged at a reduced rate for facilities covered by a climate change agreement, generally 19% of the full rate (22% from 1 April 2019 to 31 March 2020; 35% from 1 April 2014 to 31 March 2019) but 8% for electricity supplies (7% from 1 April 2019 to 31 March 2020; 10% from 1 April 2013 to 31 March 2019). From 1 April 2020 there is a reduced rate of 23% for liquefied petroleum (previous reduced rate was same as other taxable commodities). Supplies of taxable commodities used in metallurgical and mineralogical processes are exempt. From 1 August 2015 electricity generated from renewable sources is no longer eligible for exemption when supplied under a renewable source contract. From 1 April 2021 reduced rate for taxable commodities other than electricity and liquefied petroleum will be 17%.

Carbon price support rates for climate change levy and fuel duty

Supplies of solid fossil fuels, gas and liquefied petroleum gas used in most forms of electricity generation are liable to the CPS rates of CCL, which differs from the main CCL rates (see above) levied on consumers' use of these commodities (and electricity). Oils and bioblends are not taxable commodities for CCL purposes, and are taxed under the fuel duty regime. There are, however, CPS rates of fuel duty for oils and bioblends used in the generation of electricity. The carbon price floor does not apply to Northern Ireland. The CPS rate is reduced by the carbon capture percentage where there is a supply of fossil fuels to an electricity generator which uses carbon capture and storage (CCS) technology. Small scale Combined Heat and Power (CHP) stations are not subject to the CPS rate. From 1 April 2015 fossil fuels used in a CHP station to generate good quality electricity consumed on-site are also excluded.

Supplies of commodity	Rate	
	1.4.15–31.3.16	**1.4.16–31.3.22**
Gas supplied by a gas utility or any gas supplied in a gaseous state that is of a kind supplied by a gas utility	0.334p per kWh	**0.331p per kWh**
Any petroleum gas, or other gaseous hydrocarbon supplied in a liquid state	5.307p per kg	**5.280p per kg**
Coal and other taxable solid fossil fuels	156.86p per gross gigajoule	**154.79p per gross gigajoule**
Gas oil; rebated bioblend; kerosene[1]	4.99p per litre	**4.916p per litre**
Fuel oil; other heavy oil; rebated light oil	5.73p per litre	**5.711p per litre**

[1] The CPS rates of fuel duty apply to duty paid kerosene used in electricity generation.

Fuel duty

(HODA 1979 s 6; SI 2011/2935; SI 2015/550)

A Rural Fuel Duty relief scheme for retailers of road fuel on the Inner and Outer Hebrides, the Northern Isles, the Islands of the Clyde and the Isles of Scilly applies until 31 October 2023. Retailers of road fuel within these areas are eligible to register with HMRC to claim back 5p per litre relief on unleaded petrol and diesel for retail sale within the eligible areas. The retailers have 60 days following registration for the scheme to reduce the cost of every litre of road fuel sold by the equivalent amount of the relief claimed (HMRC Brief 40/2011). The scheme applies until 31 March 2020 to the postal town of Hawes in North Yorkshire, and the following postcode districts: EX35, LA17, NE48, IV14, IV21, IV22, IV26, IV27, IV54, KW12, PA38, PA80, PH19, PH23, PH36, PH41 (HMRC Brief 3/2015).

	Petrol/diesel	Biodiesel or bioethanol	LPG used as road fuel	Natural gas used as road fuel	Red diesel	Fuel oil	Aqua-methanol
From 14 November 2016	**57.95p per litre**	**57.95p per litre**	**31.61p per kg**	**24.70p per kg**	**11.14p per litre**	**10.70p per litre**	**7.90p per litre**
From 6pm 23 March 2011 to 13 November 2016	57.95p per litre	57.95p per litre	31.61p per kg	24.70p per kg	11.14p per litre	10.70p per litre	57.95p per litre

Insurance premium tax

(FA 1994 ss 48–74, Schs 6A, 7, 7A)

IPT is a tax on premiums received under insurance contracts other than those which are specifically exempt.

	Standard rate	Higher rate[1]
From 1.6.17	**12.0%**	**20.0%**
1.10.16–31.5.17[3]	10.0%	20.0%
1.11.15–30.9.16[2]	9.5%	20.0%
4.1.11–31.10.15	6.0%	20.0%

[1]   The higher rate applies to sales of motor cars, light vans and motorcycles, electrical or mechanical domestic appliances, and travel insurance.

[2]   9.5% rate applies from 1 March 2016 for insurers who use a special accounting scheme rather than the cash receipt method, and where the premium relates to risks covered by the terms of a contract entered into before 1 November 2015.

[3]   10% rate applies from 1 February 2017 for insurers who use a special accounting scheme rather than the cash receipt method, and where the premium relates to risks covered by the terms of a contract entered into before 1 October 2016.

Landfill tax

(FA 1996 ss 39–71, 197, Sch 5; SI 1996/1527; SI 1996/1528; Notice LFT1)

Tax on disposal of material (before 1 April 2018, waste) imposed on operators of landfill sites calculated by reference to the weight and type of material deposited. Exemption applies to mining and quarrying material, dredging material, pet cemeteries, disposals of NATO material, and inert material used to fill working and old quarries. From 1 April 2018 the scope of the tax is extended to disposals of material at sites operating without the appropriate licence or permit, and the exemptions above will not apply to these sites. The power to raise landfill tax devolved to the Scottish Parliament from 1 April 2015 (see table below) and to the Welsh Government from 1 April 2018 (see table below).

Period	Active waste per tonne	Inert waste per tonne[2]	Maximum credit[1]
From 1.4.21	£96.70	£3.10	TBA
1.4.20–31.3.21	£94.15	£3.00	5.3%
1.4.19–31.3.20	£91.35	£2.90	5.3%
1.4.18–31.3.19	£88.95	£2.80	5.3%
1.4.17–31.3.18	£86.10	£2.70	5.3%
1.4.16–31.3.17	£84.40	£2.65	4.2%
1.4.15–31.3.16	£82.60	£2.60	5.7%

[1] Tax credits are available to operators who make donations to environmental trusts of 90% of the donation to the maximum percentage above of the tax payable in a 12-month period (Landfill Communities Fund). Tax credits do not apply to disposals of material at sites operating without the appropriate licence or permit.

[2] For details of waste materials liable at the lower rate see SI 2011/1017 as amended and HMRC Briefs 15/2012 and 18/2012. The lower rate does not apply to disposals of material at sites operating without the appropriate licence or permit.

Scottish landfill tax

(Landfill Tax (Scotland) Act 2014; SSI 2019/58; SSI 2020/65)

Tax replaces landfill tax in Scotland from 1 April 2015.

Period	Active waste per tonne	Inert waste per tonne[2]	Maximum credit[1]
1.4.20–31.3.21	£94.15	£3.00	5.6%
1.4.19–31.3.20	£91.35	£2.90	5.6%
1.4.18–31.3.19	£88.95	£2.80	5.6%
1.4.17–31.3.18	£86.10	£2.70	5.6%
1.4.16–31.3.17	£84.40	£2.65	5.6%
1.4.15–31.3.16	£82.60	£2.60	5.6%

[1] Tax credits are available to operators who make donations to environmental trusts of 90% of the donation to the maximum percentage above of the tax payable in a 12-month period (Scottish Landfill Communities Fund).

[2] For details of waste materials liable at the lower rate see SSIs 2015/45 and 2016/93.

Landfill disposals tax (Wales)

(Landfill Disposals Tax (Wales) Act 2017; SI 2018/131; SI 2018/1209; SI 2020/95)

Tax replaces landfill tax in Wales from 1 April 2018.

Period	Active waste per tonne	Inert waste per tonne	Unauthorised disposals rate
1.4.20–31.3.21	£94.15	£3.00	£141.20
1.4.19–31.3.20	£91.35	£2.90	£137.00
1.4.18–31.3.19	£88.95	£2.80	£133.45

[1] The Landfill Disposals Tax Communities Scheme will be established as a grant scheme and will not be delivered by means of a tax credit.

Vehicle excise duty

(VERA 1994 Sch 1)

Vehicle tax, or 'road tax' is charged according to CO_2 emissions, as follows:

Standard rate for cars registered before 1 April 2017

Band	CO_2 (g/km)	2018–19 Standard rate	2019–20 Standard rate	2020–21 Standard rate
A	Up to 100	£0	£0	£0
B	101–110	£20	£20	£20
C	111–120	£30	£30	£30
D	121–130	£120	£125	£125[2]
E	131–140	£140	£145	£150
F	141–150	£155	£160	£165
G	151–165	£195	£200	£205
H	166–175	£230	£235	£240
I	176–185	£250	£260	£265
J	186–200	£290	£300	£305
K	201–225	£315	£325	£330
L	226–255	£540	£555	£565
M	Over 255	£555	£570	£580

[1] There is an alternative fuel discount of £10 for all cars. For cars registered on or after 1 April 2017 the first-year rate of tax applies in the year of purchase of a new vehicle. In later years, the standard rate applies. There are no first-year rates for cars registered before 1 April 2017. Cars with a list price above £40,000 when new have an additional rate of £325 per year (£320 before 1 April 2020; £310 before 1 April 2019) for the first 5 years in which the standard rate is paid. From 1 April 2018 there is a separate first-year rate for diesel cars that do not meet the Euro 6d emissions standard.

[2] This figure is in Finance Bill 2020 which differs from the figure announced in Budget 2020 of £130.

Standard and first-year rates for cars registered on or after 1 April 2017

CO_2 (g/km)	2018–19 Standard rate	2018–19 first-year rate	2018–19 first-year rate diesel vehicles	2019–20 Standard rate	2019–20 first-year rate	2019–20 first-year rate diesel vehicles	2020–21 Standard rate	2020–21 first-year rate	2020–21 first-year rate diesel vehicles
0	£0	£0	£0	£0	£0	£0	£0	£0	£0
1–50	£140	£10	£25	£145	£10	£25	£150	£10	£25
51–75	£140	£25	£105	£145	£25	£110	£150	£25	£110
76–90	£140	£105	£125	£145	£110	£130	£150	£110	£135
91–100	£140	£125	£145	£145	£130	£150	£150	£135	£155
101–110	£140	£145	£165	£145	£150	£170	£150	£155	£175
111–130	£140	£165	£205	£145	£170	£210	£150	£175	£215
131–150	£140	£205	£515	£145	£210	£530	£150	£215	£540
151–170	£140	£515	£830	£145	£530	£855	£150	£540	£870
171–190	£140	£830	£1,240	£145	£855	£1,280	£150	£870	£1,305
191–225	£140	£1,240	£1,760	£145	£1,280	£1,815	£150	£1,305	£1,850
226–255	£140	£1,760	£2,070	£145	£1,815	£2,135	£150	£1,850	£2,175
Over 255	£140	£2,070	£2,070	£145	£2,135	£2,135	£150	£2,175	£2,175

Light goods vehicle rates

Tax class	2018–19	2019–20	2020–21
Light goods vehicle[1]	£250	£260	£265
Euro 4 & 5 LGV	£140	£140	£140

[1] Registered on or after 1 March 2001.

Motorcycle rates

VED band	2018–19	2019–20	2020–21
Up to 150 cc	£19	£20	£20
151–400 cc	£42	£43	£44
401–600 cc	£64	£66	£67
Over 600 cc	£88	£91	£93

Income tax

Starting, basic, higher and additional rates

(ITA 2007 ss 6–21)

Band of taxable income	Band	Rate[1]	Tax	Cumulative tax
£	£	%	£	£
2020–21				
0–37,500	37,500	20	7,500	7,500
37,501–150,000	112,500	40	45,000	52,500
Over 150,000	–	45	–	–
2019–20				
0–37,500	37,500	20	7,500	7,500
37,501–150,000	112,500	40	45,000	52,500
Over 150,000	–	45	–	–
2018–19				
0–34,500	34,500	20	6,900	6,900
34,501–150,000	115,500	40	46,200	53,100
Over 150,000	–	45	–	–
2017–18				
0–33,500	33,500	20	6,700	6,700
33,501–150,000	116,500	40	46,600	53,300
Over 150,000	–	45	–	–
2016–17				
0–32,000	32,000	20	6,400	6,400
32,001–150,000	118,000	40	47,200	53,600
Over 150,000	–	45	–	–
2015–16				
0–31,785	31,785	20	6,357	6,357
31,786–150,000	118,215	40	47,286	53,643
Over 150,000	–	45	–	–

[1]   A Scottish rate of income tax applies from 6 April 2016 and a Welsh rate of income tax applies from 6 April 2019 — see below.

Scottish rate of income tax

SEE TOLLEY'S TAX COMPUTATIONS **1.8**.
(Scotland Act 1998 s 80C)

Band of taxable income	Band	Rate	Tax	Cumulative tax
£	£	%	£	£
2020–21				
0–2,085	2,085	19	396	396
2,086–12,658	10,573	20	2,114	2,510
12,659–30,930	18,272	21	3,837	6,347
30,931–150,000	119,070	41	48,818	55,165
Over 150,000	–	46	–	–
2019–20				
0–2,049	2,049	19	389	389
2,050–12,444	10,395	20	2,079	2,468
12,445–30,930	18,486	21	3,882	6,350
30,931–150,000	119,070	41	48,818	55,168
Over 150,000	–	46	–	–
2018–19				
0–2,000	2,000	19	380	380
2,001–12,150	10,150	20	2,030	2,410
12,151–31,580	19,430	21	4,080	6,490
31,581–150,000	118,420	41	48,552	55,042
Over 150,000	–	46	–	–
2017–18				
0–31,500	31,500	20	6,300	6,300
31,501–150,000	118,500	40	47,400	53,700
Over 150,000	–	45	–	–

Band of taxable income	Band	Rate	Tax	Cumulative tax
£	£	%	£	£
2016–17				
0–32,000	32,000	20	6,400	6,400
32,001–150,000	118,000	40	47,200	53,600
Over 150,000	–	45	–	–

From 6 April 2016 a Scottish rate of income tax applies to Scottish taxpayers' non-dividend, non-savings income. From 2017–18 the Scottish Parliament can set its own Scottish income tax rates and bands. For 2018–19 onwards the higher rate and additional rate are increased by 1% over UK rates, and the basic rate band is split into three, giving a total of five tax bands. In 2017–18 the tax rates remained the same as the rest of the UK but the basic rate band applying to non-dividend, non-savings income was £31,500 rather than £33,500. In 2016–17 the basic, higher and additional rates were calculated by reducing each of the UK basic, higher and additional rates by ten percentage points and then adding a Scottish rate of 10% resulting in the rates being the same as for the rest of the UK. The UK basic rate band still applies to Scottish taxpayers' dividend and savings income. The definition of a Scottish taxpayer is based on the location of an individual's main place of residence.

Welsh rate of income tax

(Government of Wales Act 2006; Wales Act 2014)

Band of taxable income	Band	Rate	Tax	Cumulative tax
£	£	%	£	£
2020–21				
0–37,500	37,500	20	7,500	7,500
37,501–150,000	112,500	40	45,000	52,500
Over 150,000	–	45	–	–
2019–20				
0–37,500	37,500	20	7,500	7,500
37,501–150,000	112,500	40	45,000	52,500
Over 150,000	–	45	–	–

A Welsh rate of income tax of 10% applies for Welsh taxpayers from 6 April 2019. The Welsh basic, higher and additional rates are calculated by reducing each of the UK basic, higher and additional rates by ten percentage points and then adding the Welsh rate resulting in the rates being the same as for the rest of the UK. The rate is charged on non-savings, non-dividends income.

Taxation of savings

SEE TOLLEY'S TAX COMPUTATIONS 1.2, 1.3.

(ITA 2007 ss 6–21)

A starting rate for savings band for individuals applies. For **2015–16 onwards it is £5,000**. Where an individual's taxable non-savings income is less than this limit, there is a **0% starting rate for 2015–16 onwards** for savings up to the limit. Where taxable non-savings income exceeds the limit, the starting rate for savings does not apply. Savings income includes interest from banks and building societies, interest distributions from authorised unit trusts, interest on gilts and other securities including corporate bonds, purchased life annuities and discounts.

From 6 April 2016 a personal savings allowance (PSA) is available to basic and higher rate taxpayers but not to additional rate taxpayers. The allowance is **£1,000 per year for basic rate taxpayers and £500 per year for higher rate taxpayers**. Savings income above the allowance is taxable at the basic or higher rate as appropriate, with savings income generally being treated as the second top slice of income behind dividends. The PSA is not a deduction in arriving at total income or taxable income. **A 0% rate of income tax applies** to savings income covered by the PSA. It operates in conjunction with the 0% starting rate for savings and income taxable at this rate does not fall within the PSA. Also from 6 April 2016, banks, building societies and National Savings are no longer required to deduct 20% tax at source from interest payable. From 6 April 2017 there is no requirement to deduct income tax at source from interest distributions from open-ended investment companies, authorised unit trusts and investment trust companies and from interest on peer-to-peer loans. Savings income within an ISA continues to be tax-free, and does not need to be covered by the PSA.

For tax years before 2016–17, where income did not exceed the basic rate limit, there was no further tax to pay on savings income from which 20% tax had been deducted. Any tax over-deducted was repayable. Higher rate taxpayers liable to pay tax at 40% and additional rate taxpayers liable to pay tax at 45% on that part of their savings income falling above the basic rate limit or higher rate limit (as applicable) were entitled to a credit for any tax deducted at source. Non-taxpayers and those whose total savings income is eligible for the 0% starting rate could apply to have interest paid without deduction of tax.

Taxation of dividends

SEE TOLLEY'S TAX COMPUTATIONS 1.1.

(ITA 2007 ss 6–21)

For 2018–19 onwards a **dividend allowance of £2,000** is available to all taxpayers (£5,000 for 2016–17 and 2017–18). A **0% rate of income tax applies** to dividends covered by the allowance. The rates of tax on dividend income above the allowance are 7.5% for dividend income falling within the basic rate band, 32.5% for dividend income falling within the higher rate band, and 38.1% for dividend income falling within the additional rate band. The dividend allowance is not a deduction in arriving at total income or taxable income. UK and foreign dividends (except those foreign dividends taxed under the remittance basis) form the top slice of taxable income.

For tax years before 2016–17, where income did not exceed the basic rate limit the tax rate was 10% (applied to the dividend grossed-up by a tax credit of 1/9) so that the liability was met by the tax credit. Higher rate taxpayers were liable to pay tax at 32.5% on that part of their dividend income falling above the basic rate limit and additional rate taxpayers were liable to pay tax at 37.5% on that part of their dividend income falling above the higher rate limit. Tax credits are abolished from 6 April 2016.

Taxation of trusts

SEE TOLLEY'S TAX COMPUTATIONS 27.2.

	Trust rate	Dividend trust rate
2016–17 onwards	**45%**	**38.1%**
2013–14 to 2015–16	45%	37.5%

First slice of income: The first £1,000 of income arising to a trust chargeable at the trust rate or the dividend trust rate is instead chargeable at the basic, savings or dividend rate.
Vulnerable beneficiaries: Trustees can be taxed (on election) on trust income as if it were income of the vulnerable beneficiary taking into account the beneficiary's personal allowances, starting and basic rate bands (FA 2005 ss 23–45).

Construction industry sub-contractors

(SI 2007/46)

	Rate of tax deduction at source
Registered sub-contractors	20%
Unregistered sub-contractors	30%

Child benefit income tax charge

SEE TOLLEY'S TAX COMPUTATIONS 29.1.

(ITEPA 2003 ss 681B–H; Social Security Administration Act 1992, s 13A)

Where an individual or their partner is in receipt of child benefit a high income child benefit charge can arise. The charge is applied to the higher earner. Taxpayers with adjusted net income between £50,000 and £60,000 are subject to an income tax charge of 1% of the amount of child benefit for every £100 of income that exceeds £50,000. For taxpayers with income above £60,000, the amount of the charge will equal the amount of child benefit received. Alternatively, a taxpayer with expected income over £60,000 can elect not to receive any child benefit. The election has effect for weeks beginning after it is made. It can be revoked at any time to restore payment of child benefit, and, where the election was made in the erroneous belief that the charge would arise, it may be revoked up to two years after the end of the tax year to which it relates in order for child benefit to be paid for the period.

Charities and Community Amateur Sports Clubs (CASCs)

Gift Aid and Gift Aid Small Donations schemes

SEE TOLLEY'S TAX COMPUTATIONS 5.1.

Under the **Gift Aid scheme** an individual donor can claim higher rate relief and, if applicable, additional rate relief on the grossed up amount of a monetary donation against income tax and capital gains tax. The charity or CASC claims basic rate relief on the grossed up amount of the donation. Donors must make a declaration that they are UK taxpayers to allow the charity to reclaim the repayment. One declaration can cover a series of donations to the same charity and the declaration can be made in writing, including fax, email and text, or orally, although an oral declaration is not effective until a written confirmation is sent to the donor. Template declarations are provided on Gov.uk. A declaration can be backdated for up to four years prior to the declaration. The basic rate tax deemed to have been deducted by the donor at source is clawed back if the donor's tax liability is insufficient to match it. Donors may elect in their self-assessment tax returns for donations to be treated as made in the preceding tax year for higher rate (and if applicable, additional rate) relief purposes.

Relief for payments under charitable covenants is given under the Gift Aid scheme.

The **Gift Aid Small Donations scheme** allows charities and CASCs to claim a gift aid style payment on broadly £8,000 (£5,000 before 6 April 2016) of small cash donations or, from 6 April 2017, contactless payments of up to £30 each (£20 before 6 April 2019) in circumstances where it is often difficult to obtain a gift aid declaration, such as street collections. The donations must not have been the subject of a gift aid declaration and must not be deductible in calculating the individual's income.

(ITA 2007 ss 413–430; Small Charitable Donations Act 2012; SI 2019/337)

Gifts in kind

Relief is available for gifts by traders to charities, community amateur sports clubs or educational establishments of goods produced or sold or of plant or machinery used for the purposes of the trade (CAA 2001 s 63(2)–(4); ITTOIA 2005 ss 107–109; CTA 2009 ss 105–107; CTA 2010 ss 658–671).

Gifts of land, shares and securities etc

Relief is available where a person disposes of listed shares and securities, unit trust units, AIM shares, etc or of freehold or leasehold interests in land to a charity by way of a gift or sale at an undervalue. The amount deductible from total income is the market value of the shares etc on the date of disposal plus incidental disposal costs less any consideration or value of benefits received by the donor or a connected person. This is in addition to any capital gains tax relief (ITA 2007 ss 431–446).

Payroll giving

Under the payroll giving scheme, employees authorise their employer to deduct charitable donations from their pay and receive tax relief on their donation at their top rate of tax (FA 2000 s 38; ITEPA 2003 ss 713–715; SI 1986/2211 as amended).

Inheritance tax relief see p 112. **Capital gains tax** see p 38. **Gifts of pre-eminent objects** see p 103.

Table of income tax reliefs

	2020–21	2019–20
	£	£
Basic personal allowance[6]	12,500	12,500
Total income limit[5]	100,000	100,000
Not beneficial if individual's total income exceeds	125,000	125,000
Transferable marriage allowance[7]	1,250	1,250
Age allowance		
Total income limit[1]	N/A	N/A
Personal allowance born after 5.4.1938 but before 6.4.1948[6]	N/A	N/A
Not beneficial if individual's total income exceeds	N/A	N/A
Personal allowance born before 6.4.1938	N/A	N/A
Not beneficial if individual's total income exceeds	N/A	N/A
Married couple's allowance[2]		
Either partner aged 75 and over and born before 6 April 1935		
Minimum amount	3,510	3,450
Total income limit[3]	30,200	29,600
Maximum amount	9,075	8,915
Reduced to minimum if:[3, 6]		
born after 5.4.1948 and total income over	41,330	40,530
born after 5.4.1938 but before 6.4.1948 and total income over	41,330	40,530
born before 6.4.1938 and total income over	41,330	40,530
Blind person's allowance[4]	2,500	2,450
Dividend allowance[8]	2,000	2,000
Personal savings allowance[8]		
Basic rate taxpayer	1,000	1,000
Higher rate taxpayer	500	500
Trading allowance[9]	1,000	1,000
Property allowance[9]	1,000	1,000

[1] The higher personal allowances for years before 2016–17 were available if the claimant's adjusted net income did not exceed the statutory income limit. If the limit was exceeded the maximum allowance was reduced by one-half of the excess until it was reduced to the basic personal allowance, but subject to a further reduction as outlined in note 5 if the adjusted net income exceeded £100,000.

[2] The universal married couple's allowance was withdrawn for 2000–01 onwards but continues to be available to any married couple or, from 2005–06, civil partnership where at least one spouse or partner was born before 6 April 1935. The relief is given as a reduction in income tax liability restricted to the lower of 10% of the amount of the allowance or the claimant's total income tax liability.

For marriages before 5 December 2005, married couple's allowance is given to the husband (subject to right of transfer to the wife), the amount being determined by the level of the husband's income. For marriages and civil partnerships entered into on or after that date, the allowance is given to whichever of the two partners has the higher total income for the tax year in question, the amount being determined by the level of that partner's income (subject to the right to transfer half or all of the basic allowance or excess allowances to the partner). Couples married before 5 December 2005 could make a joint election to be brought within the rules for couples marrying on or after that date.

SEE TOLLEY'S TAX COMPUTATIONS 1.7.

[3] The higher married couple's allowance is available if the claimant's adjusted net income does not exceed the statutory income limit (subject to relief given as a reduction in tax liability as in note 2 above). If the limit is exceeded the maximum allowance is reduced by one-half of the excess (less any reduction made in the personal age allowance as in note 1 above for years before 2016–17) but it cannot be reduced to less than the basic couple's allowance.

National insurance contributions – self-employed

SEE TOLLEY'S TAX COMPUTATIONS 507.1.

		2020–21	2019–20
Class 2	Flat rate per week	£3.05	£3.00
	Small profits threshold/ small earnings exception	6,475	6,365
Class 4	Band	9,500–50,000	8,632–50,000
	Rate	40,500@9%	41,368@9%
	Amount payable to upper limit	3,645.00	3,723.12
	Charge on profits above the limit	2%	2%

Table of income tax reliefs (cont.)

2018–19	2017–18	2016–17	2015–16	2014–15
£	£	£	£	£
11,850	11,500	11,000	10,600	10,000
100,000	100,000	100,000	100,000	100,000
123,700	123,000	122,000	121,200	120,000
1,190	1,150	1,100	1,060	N/A
N/A	N/A	N/A	27,700	27,000
N/A	N/A	N/A	N/A	10,500
N/A	N/A	N/A	N/A	28,000
N/A	N/A	N/A	10,660	10,660
N/A	N/A	N/A	27,820	28,320
3,360	3,260	3,220	3,220	3,140
28,900	28,000	27,700	27,700	27,000
8,695	8,445	8,355	8,355	8,165
39,570	38,370	37,970	37,970	37,050
39,570	38,370	37,970	37,970	38,050
39,570	38,370	37,970	38,090	38,370
2,390	2,320	2,290	2,290	2,230
2,000	5,000	5,000	N/A	N/A
1,000	1,000	1,000	N/A	N/A
500	500	500	N/A	N/A
1,000	1,000	N/A	N/A	N/A
1,000	1,000	N/A	N/A	N/A

4   The allowance is available for persons registered blind but not for persons registered partially-sighted.

5   The basic personal allowance for income tax is gradually reduced to nil for individuals with adjusted net incomes in excess of £100,000. The reduction is £1 for every £2 of income over the limit. SEE TOLLEY'S TAX COMPUTATIONS 1.5.

6   For 2014–15 and 2015–16 the differing levels of personal allowances applied based on specified dates of birth. For 2015–16 there was one level of basic personal allowance for individuals born after 5 April 1938, and an age allowance for those born before 6 April 1938. From 2016–17 onwards there is one personal allowance regardless of age.

7   From 2015–16 a spouse or civil partner who is not liable to income tax above the basic rate (or Scottish intermediate rate from 2018–19) is able to transfer an amount of their personal allowance to their spouse or civil partner, provided the transferee is also not liable to income tax above the basic rate (or Scottish intermediate rate from 2018–19). Married couples or civil partnerships entitled to claim the married couple's allowance will not be entitled to make a transfer. With effect from 29 November 2017, regardless of when death occurred, transfers can be made on behalf of a deceased spouse or partner or from a surviving spouse / partner to a deceased spouse / partner. SEE TOLLEY'S TAX COMPUTATIONS 1.6.

8   See p 77 for the tax rates applying where allowance is exceeded.

9   See p 102 for details.

National insurance contributions – self-employed (cont.)

2018–19	2017–18	2016–17	2015–16	2014–15
£2.95	£2.85	£2.80	£2.80	£2.75
6,205	6,025	5,965	5,965	5,885
8,424–46,350	8,164–45,000	8,060–43,000	8,060–42,385	7,956–41,865
37,926@9%	36,836@9%	34,940@9%	34,325@9%	33,909@ 9%
3,413.34	3,315.24	3144.60	3089.25	3,051.81
2%	2%	2%	2%	2%

Cars, vans and related benefits

Cars

SEE TOLLEY'S TAX COMPUTATIONS 9.3.

The income tax charge is based on a percentage of the car's price graduated according to the level of the car's carbon dioxide measured in grams per kilometre (g/km). (ITEPA 2003 ss 114–148, 169)

Car benefit – Cars first registered before 6 April 2020[9]				Car benefit – Cars first registered on or after 6 April 2020[9]			
CO_2 emissions (g/km)	Electric range (miles)	% of list price		CO_2 emissions (g/km)	Electric range (miles)	% of list price	
2020–21		Petrol	Diesel[1]	2020–21		Petrol	Diesel[1]
0	N/A	0%	0%	0	N/A	0%	0%
1–50	>130	2%	6%	1–50	>130	0%	0%
1–50	70–129	5%	9%	1–50	70–129	3%	7%
1–50	40–69	8%	12%	1–50	40–69	6%	10%
1–50	30–39	12%	16%	1–50	30–39	10%	14%
1–50	<30	14%	18%	1–50	<30	12%	16%
51–54		15%	19%	51–54		13%	17%
55–59		16%	20%	55–59		14%	18%
60–64		17%	21%	60–64		15%	19%
65–69		18%	22%	65–69		16%	20%
70–74		19%	23%	70–74		17%	21%
75–79		20%	24%	75–79		18%	22%
80–84		21%	25%	80–84		19%	23%
85–89		22%	26%	85–89		20%	24%
90–94		23%	27%	90–94		21%	25%
95–99		24%	28%	95–99		22%	26%
100–104		25%	29%	100–104		23%	27%
105–109		26%	30%	105–109		24%	28%
110–114		27%	31%	110–114		25%	29%
115–119		28%	32%	115–119		26%	30%
120–124		29%	33%	120–124		27%	31%
125–129		30%	34%	125–129		28%	32%
130–134		31%	35%	130–134		29%	33%
135–139		32%	36%	135–139		30%	34%
140–144		33%	37%	140–144		31%	35%
145–149		34%	37%	145–149		32%	36%
150–154		35%	37%	150–154		33%	37%
155–159		36%	37%	155–159		34%	37%
160 or more		37%	37%	160–164		35%	37%
				165–169		36%	37%
				170 or more		37%	37%

CO₂ emissions (g/km) 2017–18	% of list price Petrol	Diesel[1]	CO₂ emissions (g/km) 2018–19	% of list price Petrol	Diesel[1]	CO₂ emissions (g/km) 2019–20	% of list price Petrol	Diesel[1]
0–50	9%[5]	12%	0–50	13%[6]	17%	0–50	16%[7]	20%
51–75	13%	16%	51–75	16%	20%	51–75	19%	23%
76–94	17%	20%	76–94	19%	23%	76–94	22%	26%
95–99	18%	21%	95–99	20%	24%	95–99	23%	27%
100–104	19%	22%	100–104	21%	25%	100–104	24%	28%
105–109	20%	23%	105–109	22%	26%	105–109	25%	29%
110–114	21%	24%	110–114	23%	27%	110–114	26%	30%
115–119	22%	25%	115–119	24%	28%	115–119	27%	31%
120–124	23%	26%	120–124	25%	29%	120–124	28%	32%
125–129	24%	27%	125–129	26%	30%	125–129	29%	33%
130–134	25%	28%	130–134	27%	31%	130–134	30%	34%
135–139	26%	29%	135–139	28%	32%	135–139	31%	35%
140–144	27%	30%	140–144	29%	33%	140–144	32%	36%
145–149	28%	31%	145–149	30%	34%	145–149	33%	37%
150–154	29%	32%	150–154	31%	35%	150–154	34%	37%
155–159	30%	33%	155–159	32%	36%	155–159	35%	37%
160–164	31%	34%	160–164	33%	37%	160–164	36%	37%
165–169	32%	35%	165–169	34%	37%	165 or more	37%	37%
170–174	33%	36%	170–174	35%	37%			
175–179	34%	37%	175–179	36%	37%			
180–184	35%	37%	180 or more	37%	37%			
185–189	36%	37%						
190 or more	37%	37%						

CO₂ emissions (g/km) 2014–15	% of list price Petrol	Diesel[1]	CO₂ emissions (g/km) 2015–16	% of list price Petrol	Diesel[1]	CO₂ emissions (g/km) 2016–17	% of list price Petrol	Diesel[1]
1–75	5%[2]	8%	0–50	5%[3]	8%	0–50	7%[4]	10%
N/A	10%	13%	51–75	9%	12%	51–75	11%	14%
76–94	11%	14%	76–94	13%	16%	76–94	15%	18%
95–99	12%	15%	95–99	14%	17%	95–99	16%	19%
100–104	13%	16%	100–104	15%	18%	100–104	17%	20%
105–109	14%	17%	105–109	16%	19%	105–109	18%	21%
110–114	15%	18%	110–114	17%	20%	110–114	19%	22%
115–119	16%	19%	115–119	18%	21%	115–119	20%	23%
120–124	17%	20%	120–124	19%	22%	120–124	21%	24%
125–129	18%	21%	125–129	20%	23%	125–129	22%	25%
130–134	19%	22%	130–134	21%	24%	130–134	23%	26%
135–139	20%	23%	135–139	22%	25%	135–139	24%	27%
140–144	21%	24%	140–144	23%	26%	140–144	25%	28%
145–149	22%	25%	145–149	24%	27%	145–149	26%	29%
150–154	23%	26%	150–154	25%	28%	150–154	27%	30%
155–159	24%	27%	155–159	26%	29%	155–159	28%	31%
160–164	25%	28%	160–164	27%	30%	160–164	29%	32%
165–169	26%	29%	165–169	28%	31%	165–169	30%	33%
170–174	27%	30%	170–174	29%	32%	170–174	31%	34%
175–179	28%	31%	175–179	30%	33%	175–179	32%	35%
180–184	29%	32%	180–184	31%	34%	180–184	33%	36%
185–189	30%	33%	185–189	32%	35%	185–189	34%	37%
190–194	31%	34%	190–194	33%	36%	190–194	35%	37%
195–199	32%	35%	195–199	34%	37%	195–199	36%	37%
200–204	33%	35%	200–204	35%	37%	200 or more	37%	37%
205–209	34%	35%	205–209	36%	37%			
210 or more	35%	35%	210 or more	37%	37%			

[1] **Diesel cars:** A 4% (3% before 6 April 2018) supplement applies to diesel cars up to a maximum of 37%. The supplement will not apply to cars registered on or after 1 September 2017 if they meet the Euro 6d emissions standards.

[2] **For 2014–15:** No benefit applies to cars which are incapable of producing carbon dioxide when driven.

[3] **For 2015–16:** The 5% rate applies to cars which are incapable of producing carbon dioxide when driven.

[4] **For 2016–17:** The 7% rate applies to cars which are incapable of producing carbon dioxide when driven.

[5] **For 2017–18:** The 9% rate applies to cars which are incapable of producing carbon dioxide when driven.

[6] **For 2018–19:** The 13% rate applies to cars which are incapable of producing carbon dioxide when driven.

[7] **For 2019–20:** The 16% rate applies to cars which are incapable of producing carbon dioxide when driven.

[8] **For 2020–21 onwards:** For all cars first registered from 6 April 2020 a new regime for calculating a car's CO₂ emissions, known as the Worldwide harmonised Light vehicles Test Procedure (WLTP) applies.

This replaces emissions testing under the New European Driving Cycle (NEDC). NEDC emissions values still apply to cars first registered between 1 October 1999 and 5 April 2020 inclusive.

[9] **For 2021–22 – For cars first registered before 6 April 2020:** A 1% rate will apply for zero-emission cars. The other percentages will remain the same. **For cars first registered on or after 6 April 2020:** A 1% rate will apply for zero-emission cars. The appropriate percentage for cars emitting 1–50g/km will range from 1% to 13%, depending on the number of zero-emission miles the car can travel. For cars emitting 51–54g/km 14% will apply, and the percentage will then increase by 1% for every 5g/km of emissions until the maximum 37% will apply for emissions of 170g/km and above (petrol cars).

Cars registered after 28 February 2001

For cars registered on or after 1.3.01, the definitive CO_2 emissions figure is recorded on the vehicle registration document. For cars first registered between 1.1.98 and 28.2.01, the Vehicle Certification Agency supply relevant information on their website at carfueldata.direct.gov.uk and in their free, twice-yearly edition of the 'New Car Fuel Consumption & Emission Figures' booklet.

Cars registered on or after 1 January 1998 with no CO_2 emission figures

Cylinder capacity of car[2]	Appropriate percentage[1]					
	2015–16	2016–17	2017–18	2018–19	2019–20	2020–21
1,400cc or less	15%	16%	18%	20%	23%	24%
Over 1,400cc up to 2,000cc	25%	27%	29%	31%	34%	35%
Over 2,000cc:	37%	37%	37%	37%	37%	37%
Cars incapable of producing CO_2 when driven	5%	7%	9%	13%	16%	0%[3]

[1] **Diesel cars:** A 4% (3% before 6 April 2018) supplement applies to diesel cars up to a maximum of 37%. The supplement will not apply to cars registered on or after 1 September 2017 if they meet the Euro 6d emissions standards.

[2] **No cylinder capacity:** For a car with no cylinder capacity 37% applies.

[3] **2021–22:** The percentage will be 1%. Other percentages will remain the same.

Cars registered before 1.1.98: For 2015–16 tax is charged on 15% of the list price for engines to 1,400cc, 22% for engines of 1,401 to 2,000cc and 32% for engines above 2,000cc. For 2016–17 tax is charged on 16% of the list price for engines to 1,400cc, 27% for engines of 1,401 to 2,000cc and 37% for engines above 2,000cc. For 2017–18 the percentages are 18%, 29%, and 37% respectively. For 2018–19 the percentages are 20%, 31% and 37% respectively. For 2019–20 the percentages are 23%, 34% and 37% respectively. **For 2020–21 onwards** the percentages are 24%, 35%, and 37% respectively. Cars without a cylinder capacity are taxed on 37% (32% before 2016–17) of the list price.

Automatic cars for disabled drivers: CO_2 figure reduced to equivalent for manual car (ITEPA 2003 s 138).

Car unavailable for part of year: Value of the benefit is reduced proportionately (ITEPA 2003 s 143).

National Insurance: Also used to calculate the national insurance contributions payable by employers on the benefit of cars they provide for the private use of their employees, see p 122.

The cash equivalent is reduced proportionately where the car is not available for the whole tax year. The amount (as so reduced) is reduced by any payments made by the employee for private use.

List price of car:

(1) Includes qualifying accessories, excluding accessories provided after car made available if its list price was less than £100. Accessories designed for use only by disabled people also excluded. From 6 April 2011 accessories do not include certain security enhancements provided to meet the threat to an employee's personal physical security arising from the nature of the employment. Where a car is manufactured so as to be capable of running on road fuel gas, its price is proportionately reduced by so much of that price as is reasonably attributable to it being manufactured in that way. Where a new car is converted to run on road fuel gas, the equipment is not regarded as an accessory. With effect from 6 April 2009 disabled drivers of automatic cars who hold a disabled person's badge can use the list price of an equivalent manual car.

(2) Reduced by capital contributions made by employee up to £5,000.

(3) Classic cars (aged 15 years or more and with a market value of £15,000 or more at end of tax year): substitute market value at end of tax year if higher than adjusted list price. Reduction for capital contributions applies.

(ITEPA 2003 ss 120–132)

Vans and fuel for vans

SEE TOLLEY'S TAX COMPUTATIONS 9.3.

(ITEPA 2003 ss 114–119, 154–164, 168, 169A, 170; SI 2020/199)

Van benefit[1]	Vans which emit CO_2 when driven	Vans which do not emit CO_2 when driven[2]
2020–21	£3,490	£2,792
2019–20	£3,430	£2,058
2018–19	£3,350	£1,340
2017–18	£3,230	£646
2016–17	£3,170	£634
2015–16	£3,150	£630

[1] Vehicle weight up to 3,500kg.

[2] For 2015–16, 2016–17 and 2017–18, 20% of the van benefit charge for vans which emit CO_2 applies. 40% of the charge applies in 2018–19, 60% of the charge applies in 2019–20, and 80% in 2020–21. Current legislation provides that 90% of the full charge applies in 2021–22, with the rates equalised in 2022–23, but the Government proposes to reduce the charge to zero from 2021–22.

[3] No charge applies to employees who have to take their van home and private use is restricted other than for ordinary commuting (insignificant use is disregarded).

Van fuel benefit	
2020–21	£666
2019–20	£655
2018–19	£633
2017–18	£610
2016–17	£598
2015–16	£594

The fuel charge applies where the van benefit charge applies (though not where the reduced charge for zero-emission vans applies) and fuel is provided for private use.

Related benefits

Parking facilities: No taxable benefit for work place provision of car or van parking spaces, or parking for bicycles or motorcycles (ITEPA 2003 s 237).

Vehicle-battery charging: No taxable benefit for work place provision from 6 April 2018 of charging facilities for electric or plug-in hybrid cars or vans used by the employee (ITEPA 2003 s 237A).

Cycles and cyclist's safety equipment: No taxable benefit in respect of the provision to employees of bicycles or cycling safety equipment for travel to and from work (ITEPA 2003 s 244) nor for subsequent transfer to the employee at market value (ITEPA 2003 s 206).

On-call emergency vehicles: No tax or NIC charge where emergency service workers have private use of their emergency vehicle (when on call for tax years before 2017–18) (ITEPA 2003 s 248A).

Bus services: No taxable benefit in respect of the provision of works buses with a seating capacity of 9 or more provided to employees (or their children) to travel to and from work (ITEPA 2003 s 242).

Car and motorcycle hire: restricted allowances

SEE TOLLEY'S TAX COMPUTATIONS 116.1.

(ITTOIA 2005 ss 48–50B; CTA 2009 ss 56–58B; SI 2016/984)

Hire period from April 2009 (subject to transitional provisions), the disallowance is a flat rate of 15%. This applies only to cars with CO_2 emissions exceeding 110g/km from 1 April 2018 (130g/km before 1 April 2018, 160g/km before 1 April 2013 (corporation tax) or 6 April 2013 (income tax)). **From April 2021 the threshold will be reduced to 50g/km.**

Capital allowances see p 29.

Car fuel: company cars

SEE TOLLEY'S TAX COMPUTATIONS 9.3.

(ITEPA 2003 ss 149–153)

The same percentage figures on p 82 used to calculate the car benefit charge for the company car, which are directly linked to the car's CO_2 emissions, are used to calculate the benefit charge for fuel provided for private motoring. The relevant percentage figure is multiplied by £21,700 for 2014–15, by £22,100 for 2015–16, by £22,200 for 2016–17, by £22,600 for 2017–18, by £23,400 for 2018–19, by £24,100 for 2019–20 and by **£24,500 for 2020–21**.

Benefit is reduced to nil if employee is required to, and does, make good all fuel provided for private use. No taxable benefit where employer only provides fuel for business travel. Charge is proportionately reduced where employee stops receiving free fuel part way through tax year, but where free fuel is subsequently provided in same tax year, full year's charge is payable. Benefit is proportionately reduced where a car is not available or is incapable of being used for part of a year (being at least 30 days).

Car benefit – Cars first registered before 6 April 2020			
CO_2 emissions (g/km)	Electric range (miles)	Petrol	Diesel
2020–21		£	£
0	N/A	0	0
1–50	>130	490	1,470
1–50	70–129	1,225	2,205
1–50	40–69	1,960	2,940
1–50	30–39	2,940	3,920
1–50	<30	3,430	4,410
51–54		3,675	4,655
55–59		3,920	4,900
60–64		4,165	5,145
65–69		4,410	5,390
70–74		4,655	5,635
75–79		4,900	5,880
80–84		5,145	6,125
85–89		5,390	6,370
90–94		5,635	6,615
95–99		5,880	6,860
100–104		6,125	7,105
105–109		6,370	7,350
110–114		6,615	7,595
115–119		6,860	7,840
120–124		7,105	8,085
125–129		7,350	8,330
130–134		7,595	8,575
135–139		7,840	8,820
140–144		8,085	9,065
145–149		8,330	9,065
150–154		8,575	9,065
155–159		8,820	9,065
160 or more		9,065	9,065

Car benefit – Cars first registered on or after 6 April 2020			
CO_2 emissions (g/km)	Electric range (miles)	Petrol	Diesel
2020–21		£	£
0	N/A	0	0
1–50	>130	0	0
1–50	70–129	735	1,715
1–50	40–69	1,470	2,450
1–50	30–39	2,450	3,430
1–50	<30	2,940	3,920
51–54		3,185	4,165
55–59		3,430	4,410
60–64		3,675	4,655
65–69		3,920	4,900
70–74		4,165	5,145
75–79		4,410	5,390
80–84		4,655	5,635
85–89		4,900	5,880
90–94		5,145	6,125
95–99		5,390	6,370
100–104		5,635	6,615
105–109		5,880	6,860
110–114		6,125	7,105
115–119		6,370	7,350
120–124		6,615	7,595
125–129		6,860	7,840
130–134		7,105	8,085
135–139		7,350	8,330
140–144		7,595	8,575
145–149		7,840	8,820
150–154		8,085	9,065
155–159		8,330	9,065
160–164		8,575	9,065
165–169		8,820	9,065
170 or more		9,065	9,065

CO$_2$ emissions (g/km)	Petrol	Diesel	CO$_2$ emissions (g/km)	Petrol	Diesel	CO$_2$ emissions (g/km)	Petrol	Diesel
2017–18	£	£	**2018–19**	£	£	**2019–20**	£	£
0–50	2,034	2,712	0–50	3,042	3,978	0–50	3,856	4,820
51–75	2,938	3,616	51–75	3,744	4,680	51–75	4,579	5,543
76–94	3,842	4,520	76–94	4,446	5,382	76–94	5,302	6,266
95–99	4,068	4,746	95–99	4,680	5,616	95–99	5,543	6,507
100–104	4,294	4,972	100–104	4,914	5,850	100–104	5,784	6,748
105–109	4,520	5,198	105–109	5,148	6,084	105–109	6,025	6,989
110–114	4,746	5,424	110–114	5,382	6,318	110–114	6,266	7,230
115–119	4,972	5,650	115–119	5,616	6,552	115–119	6,507	7,471
120–124	5,198	5,876	120–124	5,850	6,786	120–124	6,748	7,712
125–129	5,424	6,102	125–129	6,084	7,020	125–129	6,989	7,953
130–134	5,650	6,328	130–134	6,318	7,254	130–134	7,230	8,194
135–139	5,876	6,554	135–139	6,552	7,488	135–139	7,471	8,435
140–144	6,102	6,780	140–144	6,786	7,722	140–144	7,712	8,676
145–149	6,328	7,006	145–149	7,020	7,956	145–149	7,953	8,917
150–154	6,554	7,232	150–154	7,254	8,190	150–154	8,194	8,917
155–159	6,780	7,458	155–159	7,488	8,424	155–159	8,435	8,917
160–164	7,006	7,684	160–164	7,722	8,658	160–164	8,676	8,917
165–169	7,232	7,910	165–169	7,956	8,658	165 or more	8,917	8,917
170–174	7,458	8,136	170–174	8,190	8,658			
175–179	7,684	8,362	175–179	8,424	8,658			
180–184	7,910	8,362	180 or more	8,658	8,658			
185–189	8,136	8,362						
190 or more	8,362	8,362						

CO$_2$ emissions (g/km)	Petrol	Diesel	CO$_2$ emissions (g/km)	Petrol	Diesel	CO$_2$ emissions (g/km)	Petrol	Diesel
2014–15	£	£	**2015–16**	£	£	**2016–17**	£	£
–	–	–	0–50	1,105	1,768	0–50	1,554	2,220
1–75	1,085	1,736	51–75	1,989	2,652	51–75	2,442	3,108
76–94	2,387	3,038	76–94	2,873	3,536	76–94	3,330	3,996
95–99	2,604	3,255	95–99	3,094	3,757	95–99	3,552	4,218
100–104	2,821	3,472	100–104	3,315	3,978	100–104	3,774	4,440
105–109	3,038	3,689	105–109	3,536	4,199	105–109	3,996	4,662
110–114	3,255	3,906	110–114	3,757	4,420	110–114	4,218	4,884
115–119	3,472	4,123	115–119	3,978	4,641	115–119	4,440	5,106
120–124	3,689	4,340	120–124	4,199	4,862	120–124	4,662	5,328
125–129	3,906	4,557	125–129	4,420	5,083	125–129	4,884	5,550
130–134	4,123	4,774	130–134	4,641	5,304	130–134	5,106	5,772
135–139	4,340	4,991	135–139	4,862	5,525	135–139	5,328	5,994
140–144	4,557	5,208	140–144	5,083	5,746	140–144	5,550	6,216
145–149	4,774	5,425	145–149	5,304	5,967	145–149	5,772	6,438
150–154	4,991	5,642	150–154	5,525	6,188	150–154	5,994	6,660
155–159	5,208	5,859	155–159	5,746	6,409	155–159	6,216	6,882
160–164	5,425	6,076	160–164	5,967	6,630	160–164	6,438	7,104
165–169	5,642	6,293	165–169	6,188	6,851	165–169	6,660	7,326
170–174	5,859	6,510	170–174	6,409	7,072	170–174	6,882	7,548
175–179	6,076	6,727	175–179	6,630	7,293	175–179	7,104	7,770
180–184	6,293	6,944	180–184	6,851	7,514	180–184	7,326	7,992
185–189	6,510	7,161	185–189	7,072	7,735	185–189	7,548	8,214
190–194	6,727	7,378	190–194	7,293	7,956	190–194	7,770	8,214
195–199	6,944	7,595	195–199	7,514	8,177	195–199	7,992	8,214
200–204	7,161	7,595	200–204	7,735	8,177	200 or more	8,214	8,214
205–209	7,378	7,595	205–209	7,956	8,177			
210 or more	7,595	7,595	210 or more	8,177	8,177			

Mileage allowances

Advisory fuel rates for company cars

Engine size	Cost per mile		
	Petrol	Diesel	LPG
From 1 March 2020			
1,400cc or less	**12p**	**–**	**8p**
1,600cc or less	**–**	**9p**	**–**
1,401–2,000cc	**14p**	**–**	**10p**
1,601–2,000cc	**–**	**11p**	**–**
Over 2,000cc	**20p**	**13p**	**14p**
1 December 2019–29 February 2020			
1,400cc or less	12p	–	8p
1,600cc or less	–	9p	–
1,401–2,000cc	14p	–	9p
1,601–2,000cc	–	11p	–
Over 2,000cc	21p	14p	14p
1 September 2019–30 November 2019			
1,400cc or less	12p	—	8p
1,600cc or less	—	10p	—
1,401–2,000cc	14p	—	10p
1,601–2,000cc	—	11p	—
Over 2,000cc	21p	14p	14p
1 June 2019–31 August 2019			
1,400cc or less	12p	—	8p
1,600cc or less	—	10p	—
1,401–2,000cc	15p	—	9p
1,601–2,000cc	—	12p	—
Over 2,000cc	22p	14p	14p
1 March 2019–31 May 2019			
1,400cc or less	11p	—	7p
1,600cc or less	—	10p	—
1,401–2,000cc	14p	—	8p
1,601–2,000cc	—	11p	—
Over 2,000cc	21p	13p	13p
1 December 2018–28 February 2019			
1,400cc or less	12p	–	8p
1,600cc or less	–	10p	–
1,401–2,000cc	15p	–	10p
1,601–2,000cc	–	12p	–
Over 2,000cc	22p	14p	15p
1 September 2018–30 November 2018			
1,400cc or less	12p	–	7p
1,600cc or less	–	10p	–
1,401–2,000cc	15p	–	9p
1,601–2,000cc	–	12p	–
Over 2,000cc	22p	13p	13p
1 June 2018–31 August 2018			
1,400cc or less	11p	–	7p
1,600cc or less	–	10p	–
1,401–2,000cc	14p	–	9p
1,601–2,000cc	–	11p	–
Over 2,000cc	22p	13p	14p
1 March 2018–31 May 2018			
1,400cc or less	11p	–	7p
1,600cc or less	–	9p	–
1,401–2,000cc	14p	–	8p
1,601–2,000cc	–	11p	–
Over 2,000cc	22p	13p	13p

Engine size	Cost per mile		
	Petrol	Diesel	LPG
1 December 2017–28 February 2018			
1,400cc or less	11p	–	7p
1,600cc or less	–	9p	–
1,401–2,000cc	14p	–	9p
1,601–2,000cc	–	11p	–
Over 2,000cc	21p	13p	14p
1 September 2017–30 November 2017			
1,400cc or less	11p	–	7p
1,600cc or less	–	9p	–
1,401–2,000cc	13p	–	8p
1,601–2,000cc	–	11p	–
Over 2,000cc	21p	12p	13p
1 June 2017–31 August 2017			
1,400cc or less	11p	–	7p
1,600cc or less	–	9p	–
1,401–2,000cc	14p	–	9p
1,601–2,000cc	–	11p	–
Over 2,000cc	21p	13p	14p
1 March 2017–31 May 2017			
1,400cc or less	11p	–	7p
1,600cc or less	–	9p	–
1,401–2,000cc	14p	–	9p
1,601–2,000cc	–	11p	–
Over 2,000cc	22p	13p	14p
1 December 2016–28 February 2017			
1,400cc or less	11p	–	7p
1,600cc or less	–	9p	–
1,401–2,000cc	14p	–	9p
1,601–2,000cc	–	11p	–
Over 2,000cc	21p	13p	13p
1 September 2016–30 November 2016			
1,400cc or less	11p	–	7p
1,600cc or less	–	9p	–
1,401–2,000cc	13p	–	9p
1,601–2,000cc	–	11p	–
Over 2,000cc	20p	13p	13p
1 June 2016–31 August 2016			
1,400cc or less	10p	–	7p
1,600cc or less	–	9p	–
1,401–2,000cc	13p	–	9p
1,601–2,000cc	–	10p	–
Over 2,000cc	20p	12p	13p
1 March 2016–31 May 2016			
1,400cc or less	10p	–	7p
1,600cc or less	–	8p	–
1,401–2,000cc	12p	–	8p
1,601–2,000cc	–	10p	–
Over 2,000cc	19p	11p	13p
1 December 2015–29 February 2016			
1,400cc or less	11p	–	7p
1,600cc or less	–	9p	–
1,401–2,000cc	13p	–	9p
1,601–2,000cc	–	11p	–
Over 2,000cc	20p	13p	13p

[1] Payments at or below these rates are tax and NIC free. The table figures will be accepted for VAT purposes.
[2] Other rates may be used if the employer can demonstrate that they are justified.
[3] Rates are currently reviewed by HMRC quarterly.
[4] Hybrid cars are treated as petrol or diesel cars accordingly.

Advisory electricity rate for company cars

Cost per mile
4p

[1] In August 2018 HMRC started publishing an advisory electricity rate, although electricity is not treated as a fuel for car fuel benefit purposes.

Authorised mileage rates

SEE TOLLEY'S TAX COMPUTATIONS 9.2.

	Rate per business mile	
Cars or vans	First 10,000 miles	Over 10,000 miles
2011–12 onwards[1]	45p	25p

[1] Where the employer pays less than the authorised rate the employee can claim tax relief for the difference (ITEPA 2003 ss 229–232, 235, 236).

	Rate per business mile
Car passengers Allowance for each fellow passenger carried	
2002–03 onwards	5p
Cycles	
2002–03 onwards[1]	20p
Motorcycles	
2002–03 onwards[1]	24p

[1] Where the employer pays less than the authorised rate the employee can claim tax relief for the difference (ITEPA 2003 ss 229–232, 235, 236).

Travel expenses of members of local authorities

(ITEPA 2003 s 235A)

From April 2016 there is an exemption for qualifying payments made by a local authority in respect of travel expenses incurred by a member on a journey between home and permanent workplace provided the member's home is in the area of the authority or within 20 miles of the boundary of the area. The exemption for mileage payments will be limited to the authorised mileage rates above.

Employment benefits and expenses payments

Pages 91 to 95 cover some common benefits and expenses payments not detailed separately elsewhere. From 6 April 2016 employees (other than lower-paid ministers of religion) earning at a rate of less than £8,500 per year will pay income tax on their benefits in kind in the same way as other employees earning at a rate of £8,500 or more. Previously all 'lower-paid' employees (ie those whose annual remuneration plus benefits was less than £8,500) were exempted from certain benefits.

Accommodation, supplies, etc used in employment duties

SEE TOLLEY'S TAX COMPUTATIONS 9.4.

(ITEPA 2003 s 316)

The provision of accommodation, supplies or services used by employees in performance of employment duties is not taxable provided:

  (a)   if the benefit is provided on premises occupied by the employer, any private use by the employee (or the employee's family or household) is not significant; or

  (b)   in any other case, the sole purpose of providing the benefit is to enable the employee to perform those duties, any private use is not significant and the benefit is not an excluded benefit (eg the provision of a motor vehicle, boat or aircraft).

Amounts which would otherwise be deductible

SEE TOLLEY'S TAX COMPUTATIONS 9.3.

(ITEPA 2003 ss 289A–289E)

From 6 April 2016 an exemption applies to expenses and benefits paid or reimbursed by the employer where the employee would be due a deduction. The exemption does not apply if the payment or reimbursement is offered in conjunction with a relevant salary sacrifice arrangement.

Assets given to employees

SEE TOLLEY'S TAX COMPUTATIONS 9.3.

(ITEPA 2003 ss 203, 204)

If new, tax chargeable on cost to employer (market value in the case of a 'lower-paid' minister of religion, and before 2016–17 in the case of all 'lower-paid' employees). If used, tax chargeable on greater of:

  (a)   market value at the time of transfer; and

  (b)   where the asset is first applied for the provision of a benefit after 5 April 1980 and a person has been chargeable to tax on its use, market value when first so applied less amounts charged to tax for use up to and including the year of transfer.

Buses to shops

(SI 2002/205)

The provision of buses for journeys of ten miles or less from the workplace to shops etc on a working day is not taxable.

Cheap loans

SEE TOLLEY'S TAX COMPUTATIONS 9.3.

(ITEPA 2003 ss 174–190)

A taxable benefit arises on employer-related loans to all employees other than 'lower-paid' ministers of religion (previously to directors or employees earning £8,500 or more a year), on the difference between the interest paid and interest payable at the 'official rate' below. There is no tax charge where:

  (a)   all the employer-related loans (or all loans not qualifying for tax relief) do not exceed £10,000;

  (b)   all the interest payable is or would be eligible for tax relief; and

  (c)   the loans are ordinary commercial loans.

The provisions can apply to alternative finance arrangements entered into after 21 March 2006.

The 'official rate' is:

From 6 April 2020	2.25%
6 April 2017 to 5 April 2020	2.50%
6 April 2015 to 5 April 2017	3.00%

The average rate for the tax year is:

2019–20	2.50%
2018–19	2.50%
2017–18	2.50%
2016–17	3.00%
2015–16	3.00%

The official rate is set in advance for the whole of the following tax year, subject to review if the typical mortgage rates were to fall sharply during a tax year. The average for a tax year is provided after the end of the year.

Childcare provision

(ITEPA 2003 ss 318–318D; CPA 2014; SI 2015/537; SI 2018/462)

No liability arises:

(a) where the premises (which are not wholly or mainly used as a private dwelling) are made available by the employer; or

(b) where the scheme is provided under arrangements with other persons, by one or more of those persons; or

(c) where (a) or (b) does not apply, on the first £55 per week of registered or approved childcare, or where the employee joins the scheme after 5 April 2011, the first £55 (basic rate taxpayers), £28 per week (higher rate taxpayers), £25 per week (additional rate taxpayers) of registered or approved childcare.

From April 2017 a 'tax-free childcare' scheme was introduced under which the Government will make a top-up payment of 25% of payments into a childcare account up to a maximum of £8,000 per year (£16,000 for a disabled child). Government support is therefore capped at a maximum of £2,000 each year per qualifying child (£4,000 for a disabled child). A child is a qualifying child until the last day of the week containing 1 September after the child's 11th birthday (16th in the case of a disabled child). There is no liability to income tax or NIC under the scheme. The scheme has now been rolled out to all eligible parents and replaces those under (b) and (c) above for new entrants from 4 October 2018, though existing recipients will continue to receive tax and NIC relief for as long as they remain eligible, provided that their employer continues to operate the scheme.

Christmas parties and annual functions

(ITEPA 2003 s 264)

Not taxable if cost does not exceed £150 per head per tax year and open to staff generally. Otherwise, fully taxable. Expenditure may be split between more than one function. (Not taxable on 'lower-paid' ministers of religion, and before 2016–17 on all 'lower-paid' employees.)

Credit tokens

(ITEPA 2003 ss 90–96A, 363)

Where money goods or services are provided to employees through credit tokens, the cost to the employer, less any employee contribution, is taxable on the employee, except if they were used to buy certain non-taxable benefits.

Disabled employees

(ITEPA 2003 ss 246, 247; SI 2002/1596)

The provision of, or payment for, transport for disabled employees for ordinary commuting is tax free. This also applies to the provision of equipment, services or facilities to disabled employees to help them carry out their duties of employment.

Employees' liability insurance

(ITEPA 2003 s 346)

This is non-taxable.

Eye tests and corrective appliances

(ITEPA 2003 s 320A)

No liability arises where the provision of tests or special corrective appliances are required under health and safety legislation and are available as required to employees generally.

Homeworkers

(ITEPA 2003 s 316A)

Employer contributions to additional household costs not taxable where employee works at home. Supporting evidence required if contributions exceed £6 per week from 6 April 2020 (previously £4) or £26 per month for monthly paid employees (previously £18).

Incidental overnight expenses

SEE TOLLEY'S TAX COMPUTATIONS 9.6.

(ITEPA 2003 ss 240, 241)

Not taxable where employee stays away from home on business and payment from employer does not exceed:

(a) £5 per night in the UK; or

(b) £10 per night overseas.

Living accommodation

SEE TOLLEY'S TAX COMPUTATIONS 9.4.

(ITEPA 2003 ss 97–113)

A taxable benefit (the 'basic charge') arises on the annual rental value (or actual rent if greater) less any sums made good by the employee. There is an additional charge (if the basic charge is not calculated on the full open market rental value) where the cost of accommodation (including costs of any capital improvements less amounts made good by the employee) exceeds £75,000. The additional charge is the excess cost over £75,000 multiplied by the official rate for cheap loans (see above) in force at the start of the tax year less any rent paid by the employee in excess of the basic charge.

For leases of ten years or less entered into on or after 22 April 2009, a lease premium paid is to be treated as if it were rent and spread over the period of the lease accordingly.

The charges are apportioned in the case of multiple occupation or if the property is provided for only part of the year or part is used exclusively for business purposes.

Exemption: No taxable benefit arises where living accommodation is provided:
  (a)   for the proper performance of duties;
  (b)   by reason that it is customary to do so; or
  (c)   by reason of special threat to the employee's security.

The above exemptions apply to a full-time working director whose interest in the company does not exceed 5%, otherwise only exemption (c) applies to directors.

Living expenses

SEE TOLLEY'S TAX COMPUTATIONS 9.4.

(ITEPA 2003 ss 313–315)

A taxable charge arises on the cost to the employer of the employee's living expenses. For the provision of assets such as furniture, see 'Use of employer's assets' below.

Where the exemption for living accommodation above applies, the tax charge relating to living expenses (including the provision of furniture and items normal for domestic occupation) is restricted to 10% of the employee's net earnings from the related employment less any sums made good by the employee.

Expenditure on alteration and structural repairs which are normally the landlord's responsibility do not give rise to a taxable benefit.

Long service awards

(ITEPA 2003 s 323)

Not taxable provided the employee has at least 20 years' service and cost to the employer does not exceed £50 for each year of service. No similar award may be made within ten years of such an award.

Meals

(ITEPA 2003 s 317)

Subsidised or free meals provided for staff generally at the workplace are not taxable. This relief does not apply if the provision of meals is made under salary sacrifice or flexible remuneration arrangements.

Medical check-ups, insurance and treatment

SEE TOLLEY'S TAX COMPUTATIONS 9.6.

(ITEPA 2003 ss 320B, 325; HMRC Employment Income Manual EIM21765)

Check-ups:

From 2009–10 onwards one screening and one check-up each year not taxable.

Insurance: Premiums paid on behalf of employees (other than 'lower-paid' ministers of religion, and before 2016–17 all 'lower-paid' employees) are taxable unless for treatment outside the UK whilst the employee is performing duties abroad.

Recommended medical treatment: From 1 January 2015 any benefit in kind or payment of earnings, up to an annual cap of £500 per employee, is not taxable where an employer meets the cost of certain recommended medical treatment in connection with an employee's return to work after a period of absence due to ill-health or injury.

Pensions advice

(SI 2002/205; ITEPA 2003 ss 308B, 308C)

Payments provided to employees in respect of advice on pensions (including on general financial and tax issues relating to pensions) are not taxable if the cost is no more than £500 (£150 before 6 April 2017 and restricted to advice on pensions).

From 6 April 2015 payments by employers in respect of independent advice provided to employees in relation to conversions and transfers of pension scheme benefits are exempt.

Personal expenses

SEE TOLLEY'S TAX COMPUTATIONS 9.2.

(ITEPA 2003 ss 70–72, 336–341)

Unless covered by specific exemptions, payments to an employee by reason of his employment in respect of expenses or allowances are taxable. Deduction is allowed for expenses the employee is obliged to incur which are:
  (a)   qualifying travelling expenses (broadly those necessarily incurred other than for ordinary commuting or private travel); or
  (b)   other amounts incurred wholly, exclusively and necessarily in the performance of employment duties.

Relocation expenses

SEE TOLLEY'S TAX COMPUTATIONS 9.5.

(ITEPA 2003 ss 271–289)

Qualifying removal expenses and benefits up to £8,000 per move in connection with job-related residential moves are not taxable. Included are expenses of disposal, acquisition, abortive acquisition, transport of belongings, travelling and subsistence, bridging loans and duplicate expenses (replacement domestic items).

Salary sacrifice and flexible benefit arrangements

(ITEPA 2003 ss 69A, 69B)

From 2017–18 the range of benefits that attract income tax and NIC advantages when provided as part of optional remuneration arrangements is limited but savings can still be made on employer pension contributions and advice, employer-provided childcare, cycle to work schemes, and ultra-low emission company cars. Arrangements in place before 6 April 2017 could continue unaffected until 5 April 2018 (with a further extension until 5 April 2021 for existing longer term agreements covering cars, living accommodation and school fees).

Scholarships

(ITEPA 2003 ss 211–215)

An employee is taxable on the cost of any scholarship from a trust fund which does not satisfy a 25% distribution test or which is paid because of the employee's employment.

Subscriptions and fees

(ITEPA 2003 ss 343–345)

Not taxable where paid to professional bodies and the employee has a contractual or professional requirement to be a member of the body.

Third party gifts

(ITEPA 2003 ss 270, 324)

Gifts during the tax year of goods and non-cash vouchers up to £250 not taxable where provided by a party unconnected with the employer and not for services provided in connection with employment.

Trivial benefits

(ITEPA 2003 ss 323A–323C)

From 6 April 2016 there is an exemption for qualifying trivial benefits in kind costing less than £50, extending to qualifying benefits provided to former employees. An annual cap of £300 applies to office holders of close companies, and employees who are family members of those office holders.

Use of employer's assets

SEE TOLLEY'S TAX COMPUTATIONS 9.3.

(ITEPA 2003 ss 203–206, 242, 244, 319, 320; HMRC Brief 02/2012)

Tax is chargeable on all employees other than 'lower-paid' ministers of religion (previously all 'lower-paid' employees) on the annual rental value of land and, for other assets, at 20% of the market value when they are first lent or the rental charge to the employer if higher. No taxable benefit arises on:

    (a)   the loan of a mobile phone or smartphone for private use. From 6 April 2006 this is restricted to one phone per employee and no longer extends to the employee's family or household but phones first loaned before 6 April 2006 are not affected by the change;

    (b)   the use of works buses (see p 85);

    (c)   cycles and cycle safety equipment (see p 85);

    (d)   to 5 April 2006, the loan of computer equipment for private use, provided use is not restricted to directors or senior staff and value of benefit does not exceed £2,500 (computers made available for private use before 6 April 2006 are not affected by the change).

No benefit arises on the subsequent purchase by an employee at market value of computer or cycling equipment previously on loan.

From 2017–18 the benefit is reduced by periods during which the asset is unavailable for private use by the employee or his family/household, or where the asset is shared by two or more employees.

Vouchers

SEE TOLLEY'S TAX COMPUTATIONS 9.6.

(ITEPA 2003 ss 73–89, 95, 96, 268–270, 362)

Vouchers are taxable as follows.

(a)	Cash vouchers	On amount for which voucher can be exchanged.
(b)	Non-cash vouchers	On cost to employer less any contribution from employee (except where used to obtain certain non-taxable benefits).
(c)	Transport vouchers	On cost to employer less any contribution from employee.

Employment exemption

Employee-ownership trusts

(ITEPA 2003 ss 312A–312I)

From 1 October 2014 an exemption from income tax applies to qualifying bonus payments of up to £3,600 per tax year made to employees, and qualifying former employees, by a company which is owned directly or indirectly by an employee-ownership trust which meets certain qualifying conditions.

For CGT relief relating to such companies see p 38.

Employment income

PAYE and national insurance thresholds

	2015–16	2016–17	2017–18	2018–19	2019–20	2020–21
	£	£	£	£	£	£
Weekly NI	155/156	155/156	157	162	166	**183/169**
Weekly PAYE	204	212	221	228	240	**240**
Monthly NI	672/676	672/676	680	702	719	**792/732**
Monthly PAYE	883	917	958	988	1,042	**1,042**

[1] For full list of national insurance rates see p 115.

PAYE settlement agreements

SEE TOLLEY'S TAX COMPUTATIONS 506.1.

(SI 2003/2682 Part 6)

These are voluntary agreements between the employer and HMRC under which the employer agrees to meet the tax payable on certain expenses and benefits in kind that are given to his employees. Once an agreement has been signed for a tax year, there is no need to:

- enter the items covered on form P11D (and before 2016–17, form P9D);
- operate PAYE on them, or
- calculate a liability for included items which are liable for Class 1 or Class 1A NICs.

The employer pays Class 1B NICs on the items included in PAYE settlement agreements and on the total amount of tax payable. To be effective for a tax year, an agreement must be signed before 6 July following the end of the year and tax must be paid by 19 October following (or 22 October where paid electronically). They are most suited for payments and benefits provided on an irregular basis, or where benefits are for a group of employees and apportionment is difficult.

From 2018–19, the requirement for employers to agree annually with HMRC which employee expenses and benefits may be included is removed. Employers are now able to create an enduring agreement with HMRC which will remain in place for subsequent tax years unless varied or cancelled by the employer or HMRC.

Personal service companies

SEE TOLLEY'S TAX COMPUTATIONS 20.1.

(ITEPA 2003 ss 48–61)

These provisions are commonly known under the name 'IR35' and apply where personal services are provided to a client through an intermediary – normally the worker's personal service company. The effect of the legislation is to treat the worker as an employee of the client for working out the 'deemed employment payment'. The computation involves taking into account all payments and benefits, including those paid direct to the worker for a tax year other than by the intermediary for his services. Certain, restricted, allowable expenses, are deducted from 'earnings'. Finally, any payments or benefits received by the worker from the intermediary are deducted. Tax (under PAYE) and NIC is calculated and the amounts due are payable by the worker and his company. From 2013–14 the provisions are extended to office holders.

For public sector engagements from April 2017 the liability to pay the correct employment taxes moves from the worker's own company to the public sector body or agency/third party paying the company, and the amount will be deducted from the amount paid to the company. The normal 5% flat rate deduction from payments for the worker's services cannot be made in computing the deemed employment payment.

Managed service companies

(ITEPA 2003 ss 61A–61J)

Where an individual provides his services through a managed service company (as defined) all payments made to him by the company are deemed to be employment income and PAYE and NIC have to be applied.

Termination payments

SEE TOLLEY'S TAX COMPUTATIONS 6.1.

(ITEPA 2003 ss 401–416)

The following lump sum payments are exempt from tax:

(a)   Payments in connection with the cessation of employment on the death, injury or disability of the employee.

(b)   Payments under tax-exempt pension schemes by way of compensation for loss of employment (o of earnings due to ill-health) or which can properly be regarded as a benefit earned by past service

(c)   Certain payments of terminal grants to members of the armed forces.

(d)   Certain benefits under superannuation schemes for civil servants in Commonwealth oversea territories.

(e)   Payments in respect of foreign service broadly before 14 September 2017 (but see note below where the period of foreign service comprises:

(i)   75% of the whole period of service; or

(ii)   the whole of the last 10 years of service; or

(iii)   where the period of service exceeded 20 years, one-half of that period, including any 10 c the last 20 years.

Otherwise, a proportion of the payment is exempt, as follows:

$$\frac{\text{length of foreign service}}{\text{length of total service}} \times \text{amount otherwise chargeable}$$

(f)   The first £30,000 of genuine ex gratia payments (where there is no 'arrangement' by the employer t make the payment).

(g)   Statutory redundancy payments (included in computing £30,000 limit in (f) above).

Foreign service relief is abolished for termination payments and benefits to employees who are UK resident i the tax year in which the employment is terminated. This applies where the date of the termination is on or afte 6 April 2018 and the termination payment, or other benefit, is received after 13 September 2017. Foreign servic relief continues in termination cases where the employee is non-UK resident in the year of termination, and fo UK residents where the payment or benefit is in connection with a change of duties or earnings rather than wit termination of the employment. Reductions for foreign service are also retained for seafarers and extended t employees of the Royal Fleet Auxiliary.

Termination payments

SEE TOLLEY'S TAX COMPUTATIONS 6.1.

(ITEPA 2003 ss 401–416)

The following lump sum payments are exempt from tax:

(a) Payments in connection with the cessation of employment on the death, injury or disability of the employee.

(b) Payments under tax-exempt pension schemes by way of compensation for loss of employment (or of earnings due to ill-health) or which can properly be regarded as a benefit earned by past service.

(c) Certain payments of terminal grants to members of the armed forces.

(d) Certain benefits under superannuation schemes for civil servants in Commonwealth overseas territories.

(e) Payments in respect of foreign service broadly before 14 September 2017 (but see note below) where the period of foreign service comprises:

(i) 75% of the whole period of service; or

(ii) the whole of the last 10 years of service; or

(iii) where the period of service exceeded 20 years, one-half of that period, including any 10 of the last 20 years.

Otherwise, a proportion of the payment is exempt, as follows:

$$\frac{\text{length of foreign service}}{\text{length of total service}} \times \text{amount otherwise chargeable}$$

(f) The first £30,000 of genuine ex gratia payments (where there is no 'arrangement' by the employer to make the payment).

(g) Statutory redundancy payments (included in computing £30,000 limit in (f) above).

Foreign service relief is abolished for termination payments and benefits to employees who are UK resident in the tax year in which the employment is terminated. This applies where the date of the termination is on or after 6 April 2018 and the termination payment, or other benefit, is received after 13 September 2017. Foreign service relief continues in termination cases where the employee is non-UK resident in the year of termination, and for UK residents where the payment or benefit is in connection with a change of duties or earnings rather than with termination of the employment. Reductions for foreign service are also retained for seafarers and extended to employees of the Royal Fleet Auxiliary.

Fixed rate expenses

For most classes of industry fixed rate allowances for the upkeep of tools and special clothing have been agreed between HMRC and the trade unions concerned. Alternatively, the individual employee may claim as a deduction his or her actual expenses (ITEPA 2003 s 367). (HMRC Employment Income Manual EIM32712.)

Industry	Occupation		Deduction
Agriculture	All workers[1]		100
Airlines	See note 5 below		
Aluminium	(a)	Continual casting operators, process operators, de-dimplers, driers, drill punchers, dross unloaders, firemen[2], furnace operators and their helpers, leaders, mould-men, pourers, remelt department labourers, roll flatteners	140
	(b)	Cable hands, case makers, labourers, mates, truck drivers and measurers, storekeepers	80
	(c)	Apprentices	60
	(d)	All other workers[1]	120
Banks and building societies	Uniformed doormen and messengers		60
Brass and copper	Braziers, coppersmiths, finishers, fitters, moulders, turners and all other workers		120
Building	(a)	Joiners and carpenters	140
	(b)	Cement works, roofing felt and asphalt labourers	80
	(c)	Labourers and navvies	60
	(d)	All other workers	120
Building materials	(a)	Stone masons	120
	(b)	Tilemakers and labourers	60
	(c)	All other workers	80
Clothing	(a)	Lacemakers, hosiery bleachers, dyers, scourers and knitters, knitwear bleachers and dyers	60
	(b)	All other workers	60
Constructional engineering[3]	(a)	Blacksmiths and their strikers, burners, caulkers, chippers, drillers, erectors, fitters, holders up, markers off, platers, riggers, riveters, rivet heaters, scaffolders, sheeters, template workers, turners, welders	140
	(b)	Banksmen, labourers, shop-helpers, slewers, straighteners	80
	(c)	Apprentices and storekeepers	60
	(d)	All other workers	100
Electrical and electricity supply	(a)	Those workers incurring laundry costs only	60
	(b)	All other workers	120
Engineering (trades ancillary to)	(a)	Pattern makers	140
	(b)	Labourers, supervisory and unskilled workers	80
	(c)	Apprentices and storekeepers	60
	(d)	Motor mechanics in garage repair shops	120
	(e)	All other workers	120
Fire service	Uniformed firefighters and fire officers		80
Food	All workers		60
Forces personnel	See note 7 below		
Forestry	All workers		100
Glass	All workers		80
Healthcare staff in the NHS, private hospitals and nursing homes	(a)	Ambulance staff on active service	185
	(b)	Nurses and midwives, chiropodists, dental nurses, occupational, speech, physiotherapists and other therapists, healthcare assistants, phlebotomists and radiographers. See note 8 below for shoes and stockings/tights/socks allowances	125
	(c)	Plaster room orderlies, hospital porters, ward clerks, sterile supply workers, hospital domestics, hospital catering staff	125
	(d)	Laboratory staff, pharmacists, pharmacy assistants	80
	(e)	Uniformed ancillary staff: maintenance workers, grounds staff, drivers, parking attendants and security guards, receptionists and other uniformed staff	80
Heating	(a)	Pipe fitters and plumbers	120
	(b)	Coverers, laggers, domestic glaziers, heating engineers and their mates	120
	(c)	All gas workers, all other workers	100
Iron mining	(a)	Fillers, miners and underground workers	120
	(b)	All other workers	100
Iron and steel	(a)	Day labourers, general labourers, stockmen, time keepers, warehouse staff and weighmen	80
	(b)	Apprentices	60
	(c)	All other workers	140
Leather	(a)	Curriers (wet workers), fellmongering workers, tanning operatives (wet)	80
	(b)	All other workers	60

Industry	Occupation			Deduction
Particular engineering[4]	(a)	Pattern makers		140
	(b)	Chainmakers, cleaners, galvanisers, tinners and wire drawers in the wire drawing industry, tool-makers in the lock making industry		120
	(c)	Apprentices and storekeepers		60
	(d)	All other workers		80
Police force	Uniformed police officers (ranks up to and including Chief Inspector) Community Support officers and other police service employees — see note 6 below			140
Precious metals	All workers			100
Printing	(a)	Letterpress section — electrical engineers (rotary presses), electro-typers, ink and roller makers, machine minders (rotary), maintenance engineers (rotary presses) and stereotypers		140
	(b)	Bench hands (periodical and bookbinding section), compositors (letterpress section), readers (letterpress section), telecommunications and electronic section wire room operators, warehousemen (paper box making section)		60
	(c)	All other workers		100
Prisons	Uniformed prison officers			80
Public service	(i)	Dock and inland waterways		
		(a)	Dockers, dredger drivers, hopper steerers	80
		(b)	All other workers	60
	(ii)	Public transport		
		(a)	Garage hands (including cleaners)	80
		(b)	Conductors and drivers	60
Quarrying	All workers			100
Railways	(See the appropriate category for craftsmen, eg engineers, vehicles etc.) All other workers			100
Seamen	Carpenters			
	(a)	Passenger liners		165
	(b)	Cargo vessels, tankers, coasters and ferries		140
Shipyards	(a)	Blacksmiths and their strikers, boilermakers, burners, carpenters, caulkers, drillers, furnacemen (platers), holders up, fitters, platers, plumbers, riveters, sheet iron workers, shipwrights, tubers, welders		140
	(b)	Labourers		80
	(c)	Apprentices and storekeepers		60
	(d)	All other workers		100
Textiles and textile printing	(a)	Carders, carding engineers, overlookers and technicians in spinning mills		120
	(b)	All other workers		80
Vehicles	(a)	Builders, railway vehicle repairers, and railway wagon lifters		140
	(b)	Railway vehicle painters and letterers, and builders' and repairers' assistants		80
	(c)	All other workers		60
Wood & furniture	(a)	Carpenters, cabinet makers, joiners, wood carvers and woodcutting machinists		140
	(b)	Artificial limb makers (other than in wood), organ builders and packaging case makers		120
	(c)	Coopers not providing own tools, labourers, polishers and upholsterers		60
	(d)	All other workers		100

[1] 'All workers' and 'all other workers' refer only to manual workers who have to bear the cost of upkeep of tools and special clothing. They do not extend to other employees such as office staff.

[2] 'Firemen' means persons engaged to light and maintain furnaces.

[3] 'Constructional engineering' means engineering undertaken on a construction site, including buildings, shipyards, bridges, roads and other similar operations.

[4] 'Particular engineering' means engineering undertaken on a commercial basis in a factory or workshop for the purposes of producing components such as wire, springs, nails and locks.

[5] A basic flat rate expenses allowance of £1,022 applies to all uniformed commercial pilots, co-pilots and other flight deck crew working in the UK (but not stewards/stewardesses). A further £110 allowance is allowed for the cost of travel to certain regular specified activities. Stewards/stewardesses may claim basic flat rate expenses of £720.

[6] The allowance for police officers applies to community support officers. Other police service employees who must clean their own uniform can claim a deduction of £60.

[7] A flat-rate expenses allowance applies in relation to the laundering of uniforms for naval ratings and other ranks. The annual amount is £80 for the Royal Navy and £100 for the Army, RAF and Royal Marines.

[8] A flat-rate expenses allowance applies of £12 per year for the renewal or repair of shoes, and £6 per year for stockings/tights/socks where the wearing of a prescribed style or colour (style only for shoes) is obligatory for nurses, midwives, auxiliaries, students, dental nurses, nursing assistants and healthcare assistants or workers.

[9] Correct as at 20 March 2020.

Apprenticeship levy

(FA 2016 ss 98–121)

From April 2017 an apprenticeship levy applies to UK employers in both the private and public sectors. It is set at a rate of 0.5% of an employer's pay bill and paid through PAYE. Each employer receives an allowance of £15,000 to offset against their levy payment. This means that the levy will only be paid on any pay bill in excess of £3 million. The pay bill is the total of employee earnings subject to Class 1 secondary National Insurance Contributions, as if disregarding the secondary and upper secondary thresholds.

Investment reliefs

Community investment tax relief

(ITA 2007 ss 333–382; CTA 2010 ss 218–269)

Investments made by an individual or company in an accredited community development finance institution (CDFI) are eligible for tax relief up to 25%. The investment may be a loan or a subscription for shares or securities. Tax relief may be claimed for the tax year or accounting period in which the investment is made and each of the four subsequent years. Relief for each year is broadly 5% of the invested amount, but from April 2013 any unused balance of the 5% annual relief can be carried forward, although not beyond the 5-year investment period, and only as long as some part of the investment remains within the CDFI. In addition, to comply with European State aid rules, from 1 April 2013 there is a limit on the amounts of relief a company can obtain in any 3-year period — the amount of CITR relief and any de minimis aid from other sources must not exceed €200,000.

Enterprise investment scheme

(ITA 2007 ss 156–257; SI 2018/931)

The EIS applies to investments in qualifying unquoted companies trading in the UK. Eligible shares must be held for at least three years from the issue date or commencement of trade if later. The following reliefs apply subject to this and other conditions.

Relief on investment

SEE TOLLEY'S TAX COMPUTATIONS 10.1 ONWARDS.

Maximum investment: if amount over £1,000,000 invested in Knowledge Intensive Companies	**From 2018–19**	**£2,000,000**
Maximum investment: otherwise	**From 2012–13**	**£1,000,000**
Maximum carry-back to preceding year	**From 2009–10**	**No restriction (subject to annual maximum)**
Rate of relief	**From 2011–12**	**30%**[1]

[1]   Given as a deduction against income tax liability.

Other reliefs (TCGA 1992 ss 150A–150C, Sch 5B)
SEE TOLLEY'S TAX COMPUTATIONS 210.1, 210.2, 210.3.
  (a)   A gain on a disposal of shares on which EIS relief has been given and not withdrawn is exempt from capital gains tax (see p 39).
  (b)   Deferral relief is available for gains on assets where the disposal proceeds are reinvested in eligible shares in a qualifying company within one year before and three years after the disposal.
  (c)   A loss on a disposal of shares on which EIS relief has been given may be relieved against income tax or capital gains tax.

Seed enterprise investment scheme

(ITA 2007 ss 257A–257HG)

SEIS applies to investments in companies with fewer than 25 employees and assets up to £200,000 carrying on or preparing to carry on new business. Eligible shares must be held for at least three years from the issue date. The following reliefs apply subject to this and other conditions.

Relief on investment

SEE TOLLEY'S TAX COMPUTATIONS 25.1, 25.2.

Maximum investment:	**From 2012–13**	**£100,000**
Maximum carry-back to preceding year	**From 2013–14**	**No restriction (subject to annual maximum)**
Rate of relief	**From 2012–13**	**50%**[1]

[1]   Given as a deduction against income tax liability.

Other reliefs (TCGA 1992 ss 150E, 150G, Sch 5BB)

SEE TOLLEY'S TAX COMPUTATIONS 227.1, 227.2, 227.3.

   (a)   A gain on a disposal of shares on which SEIS relief has been given and not withdrawn is exempt from capital gains tax.

   (b)   Reinvestment relief is available for certain gains on assets where the disposal proceeds are reinvested in SEIS and SEIS relief is claimed (see p 40).

Social investment tax relief

(ITA 2007 ss 257J–257TE)

Between 6 April 2014 and 5 April 2021 income tax relief is available to both resident and non-UK resident individuals who subscribe for qualifying shares or make qualifying debt investments in a social enterprise which meets the requirements, and who have a UK tax liability against which to set the relief. The investment must be held for a period of three years. The following reliefs apply subject to conditions.

Relief on investment

Maximum investment:	**From 2014–15**	**£1,000,000**
Maximum carry-back to preceding year	**From 2015–16**	**No restriction (subject to annual maximum)**
Rate of relief	**From 2014–15**	**30%**[1]

[1]   Given as a deduction against income tax liability.

Other reliefs

SEE TOLLEY'S TAX COMPUTATIONS 231.1, 231.2, 231.3.

   (a)   A gain on a disposal of shares on which SITR income tax relief has been given and not withdrawn is exempt from capital gains tax where shares held for at least 3 years.

   (b)   Deferral relief is available for gains arising on assets in the period 6 April 2014 to 5 April 2021 where the disposal proceeds are reinvested in shares or debt investments which also qualify for the SITR income tax relief (see p 40).

Venture capital trusts

SEE TOLLEY'S TAX COMPUTATIONS 32.1, 32.2, 32.3.

(ITA 2007 ss 258–332)

An individual who subscribes for ordinary shares in a VCT obtains income tax reliefs at the rates in the table below subject to conditions. The shares must be held for at least five years.

Relief on investment

Maximum annual investment:	**From 2004–05**	**£200,000**
Rate of relief:	**From 2006–07**	**30%**

Other reliefs

   (a)   Dividends on shares within investment limit exempt from income tax (unless the investor's main purpose is tax avoidance) (ITTOIA 2005 s 709).

   (b)   Capital gains reliefs (see p 40).

Urban Regeneration Companies

Relief is available for expenditure incurred by businesses in making contributions to designated Urban Regeneration Companies (ITTOIA 2005 ss 82, 86; CTA 2009 ss 82, 86).

Individual savings accounts ('ISAs')

(ITTOIA 2005 ss 694–701; SI 1998/1870)

Savers can subscribe to an ISA up to the following limits per tax year.

	2015–16	2016–17	2017–18	2018–19	2019–20	**2020–21**
Overall annual subscription limit	£15,240	£15,240	£20,000	£20,000	£20,000	**£20,000**
Cash limit	£15,240	£15,240	£20,000	£20,000	£20,000	**£20,000**

[1]   From 1 July 2014 ISAs were reformed into a simpler product, the 'New ISA'. All existing ISAs became New ISAs and ISA savers are able to subscribe the full subscription amount to a cash account.

[2]   The subscription limit applies to each spouse or civil partner. From 2015–16 an additional ISA allowance is available for spouses or civil partners following the death of an ISA saver on or after 3 December 2014, equal to the value of that deceased saver's ISAs.

[3]   From 6 April 2016 there is the facility to offer a flexible account, whereby withdrawals during the year may be replaced without the replacement counting towards the subscription limit.

[4]   Shares acquired under a tax-favoured share incentive plan or SAYE option scheme may be transferred to an ISA within 90 days without tax consequences.

[5] From 6 April 2018 and subject to certain time limits, investments retained in an ISA during the administration of a deceased saver's estate will retain their tax-advantaged status.

Reliefs

(a) Investments under the scheme are free from income tax and capital gains tax. When an investment is transferred to an investor he is deemed to have made a disposal and reacquisition at market value and any notional gain is exempt from capital gains tax.

(b) Withdrawals may be made at any time without loss of tax relief.

Lifetime ISA

From 6 April 2017 individuals aged between 18 and 40 are able to save up to £4,000 per year into one Lifetime ISA and receive a 25% bonus from the Government at the end of the year. Contributions can continue to be made with the bonus paid up to the age of 50. Funds, including the Government bonus, can be used to buy a first home up to the value of £450,000 at any time from 12 months after opening the account, and can be withdrawn tax-free from age 60 for use in retirement. Withdrawals prior to that, other than by the terminally ill, will forfeit the Government bonus (plus added interest) and also attract a charge. If an individual has a Help to Buy: ISA he could transfer those savings into the Lifetime ISA in 2017–18, or continue saving into both, or open a Help to Buy: ISA after opening a Lifetime ISA, but he will only be able to use the bonus from one of the ISAs to buy a house.

Help to Buy: ISAs

Help to Buy: ISAs could be opened from 1 December 2015 to 30 November 2019 for first-time house buyers. Once opened contributions can continue until 30 November 2029. The maximum monthly savings amount is £200, and provided the balance reaches at least £1,600, the Government will provide a bonus of 25% of savings, up to a maximum bonus of £3,000 on £12,000 of savings. It is possible to deposit an additional £1,000 when the account is first opened. The interest on the account and the bonus will be tax-free. The bonus must be claimed by 1 December 2030 at the latest, and will be paid at the time of completion of the purchase of the property provided the property is worth a maximum of £450,000 in London and £250,000 elsewhere in the UK. Accounts are limited to one per person rather than one per property. See above regarding Lifetime ISAs held at the same time as Help to Buy: ISAs.

Junior individual savings accounts (Junior ISAs)

(ITTOIA 2005 s 695A; SI 1998/1870)

The Junior ISA scheme is available to all UK resident children under 18 who do not have a Child Trust Fund account or, from 6 April 2015, to those who wish to transfer a Child Trust Fund account to a Junior ISA. Children are able to have one cash and one stocks and shares Junior ISA at any time.

	2015–16	2016–17	2017–18	2018–19	2019–20	2020–21
Overall annual subscription limit	£4,080	£4,080	£4,128	£4,260	£4,368	£9,000

Miscellaneous income tax reliefs

Trading allowance and property allowance

(ITTOIA 2005 ss 783A–783AR, 783B–783BQ)

From 6 April 2017 a trading allowance and a property allowance of £1,000 each per year are available to certain individuals. They are not available on income of partners or close company participators, or where rent-a-room relief could be claimed. Where total receipts are no more than £1,000, the allowance is given automatically, no tax is payable and the income need not be declared. An election can be made for relief not to apply at all, or for partial relief to apply where receipts exceed £1,000 so that the allowance rather than expenses is deducted from gross receipts.

Employee shareholder shares

(ITEPA 2003 ss 226A–226D; SI 2013/1755)

From 1 September 2013 the first £2,000 of the value of shares acquired through the adoption of the 'employee shareholder' employment status is not subject to income tax or national insurance, provided the Employee Shareholder Agreement was entered into before 1 December 2016 (or 2 December 2016 where professional advice was given in relation to the share offer on 23 November 2016 before 1.30pm). For the capital gains tax rules see p 38.

Foster carers and shared lives carers (Qualifying care)

See Tolley's Tax Computations 30.9.

(ITTOIA 2005 ss 803–828; SI 2011/712)

Generally, local authority payments to foster carers are not taxable to the extent they do no more than meet the actual costs of caring. In other cases, and for shared lives carers:

- where gross receipts do not exceed the 'individual limit' and shared lives care is not being provided to more than three people, the carer is treated as having a nil profit and nil loss for the tax year concerned;

- where gross receipts exceed the 'individual limit' and shared lives care is not being provided to more than three people, the carer can choose to either be taxed on the excess or compute profit or loss using the normal business rules.

In addition from 2017–18 the relief is extended to include shared lives schemes that are self-funded by the person receiving care.

The 'individual limit' is made up of a fixed amount of £10,000 per residence for a full tax year plus an amount per adult or child for each week or part week that the individual provides qualifying care. The weekly amounts are £200 for a child under 11 years and £250 for a child of 11 or over and an adult.

Gift of pre-eminent objects

(FA 2012 Sch 14)

Individuals who gift pre-eminent objects to the nation will receive a reduction in their UK tax liability of 30% of the value of the object they are donating. The tax reduction can be against income or capital gains tax and can be spread forward across a period of up to five years starting with the tax year in which the object is offered. The gift must be accepted as pre-eminent by the Arts Council under the Cultural Gifts Scheme.

Life assurance premium relief

(TA 1988 s 266, Sch 14 para 7; FA 2012 Sch 39)

For premiums due and payable **before 6 April 2015**, or payable before that date and actually paid before 6 July 2015, relief for premiums paid on qualifying life assurance policies for contracts made before 14 March 1984 is available by deduction of 12.5% from admissible premiums.

Maintenance payments

SEE TOLLEY'S TAX COMPUTATIONS 16.2.

(ITTOIA 2005 ss 727, 729; ITA 2007 ss 453–456)

Where either party to the marriage or civil partnership was born before 6 April 1935 tax relief may be claimed by the payer in respect of the lower of:
- the amount of the payments in the year concerned and
- the minimum amount of the married couple's allowance for the year concerned (see p 80).

The relief is restricted to 10% of the relevant amount. The payment must be made to the former/separated spouse or civil partner. It is made gross and is not taxable in the hands of the recipient.

Rent-a-room relief

SEE TOLLEY'S TAX COMPUTATIONS 22.3.

(ITTOIA 2005 ss 784–802)

Gross annual receipts from letting furnished accommodation in the only or main home are exempt from tax up to a maximum of £7,500 (£4,250 before 6 April 2016) (provided no other taxable income is derived from a trade, letting or arrangement from which the rent-a-room receipts are derived).

If the gross receipts exceed £7,500 (£4,250 before 6 April 2016), the taxpayer can pay tax on the net receipts after deduction of expenses. Alternatively, the taxpayer can elect to pay tax on the amount by which the gross receipts exceed £7,500, without relief for the actual expenses.

An individual's maximum is halved to £3,750 (£2,125 before 6 April 2016) if during the 'relevant period' for the year (normally the tax year) some other person received income from letting accommodation in that property.

An election can be made to disapply the relief for a particular tax year (for example, if the individual would otherwise make an allowable loss).

Simplified fixed rate deductions

SEE TOLLEY'S TAX COMPUTATIONS 31.1.

(ITTOIA 2005 ss 94B–94I)

From 2013–14 individuals carrying on a trade, profession or vocation as self-employed sole traders or in partnership with other individuals can choose certain simplified expenses when calculating their profits for income tax purposes. From 2017–18 deductions for vehicle expenditure are available to those carrying on a property business. Conditions apply.

Vehicle expenditure

Kind of vehicle	Rate per business mile
Car or goods vehicle	45p for the first 10,000 miles
	25p after that
Motor cycle	24p

Use of home for business purposes

Hours worked per month	Amount per month
25 or more	£10
51 or more	£18
101 or more	£26

Premises used both as a home and for business

Note: Amount below is the non-business use amount to be deducted from the total expenses claimed. The flat rate includes all household goods and services, food and non-alcoholic drinks and utilities. It does not include mortgage interest, rent of the premises, council tax or rates. A reasonable apportionment of these expenses should be made based on the extent of the private occupation of the premises — HMRC Brief 14/2013.

Number of occupants	Disallowance amount per month
1	£350
2	£500
3 or more	£650

Capped income tax reliefs

(ITA 2007 s 24A)

The following income tax reliefs are capped. The limit is set at the greater of £50,000 or 25% of the individual's adjusted total income for the tax year. The specified reliefs which, taken together, will be limited to the extent that they can be relieved by individuals against general income are:

Trade loss relief against general income (ITA 2007 s 64)
Early trade losses relief (ITA 2007 s 72)
Post-cessation trade relief (ITA 2007 s 96)
Property loss relief against general income (ITA 2007 s 120)
Post-cessation property relief (ITA 2007 s 125)
Employment loss relief against general income (ITA 2007 s 128)
Former employees deduction for liabilities (ITEPA 2003 s 555)
Share loss relief on non-Enterprise Investment Scheme / Seed Enterprise Investment Scheme shares (ITA 2007 Pt 4 Ch 6)
Losses on deeply discounted securities (ITTOIA 2005 ss 446, 454)
Qualifying loan interest (ITA 2007 Pt 8 Ch 1)

Pension provision

(FA 2004 ss 149–284, Schs 28–36)

Tax relief on contributions

SEE TOLLEY'S TAX COMPUTATIONS 19.1.

Individual contributions: An individual may make unlimited contributions and tax relief is available on contributions up to the higher of:

• the full amount of relevant earnings; or
• £3,600 provided the scheme operates tax relief at source,

and subject to the annual allowance.

Employer contributions: Employer contributions to registered schemes are deductible for tax purposes, with statutory provision for spreading abnormally large contributions over a period of up to four years. The contributions are not treated as taxable income of the employee, although from 6 April 2013 this relief does not extend to payments for the benefit of family members.

Annual allowance

SEE TOLLEY'S TAX COMPUTATIONS 19.3.

Each individual has an annual allowance as set out in the table below. If the annual increase in an individual's rights under all registered schemes exceeds the annual allowance, the excess is chargeable at the individual's marginal rate. The individual is liable for the tax, unless he makes an election for the scheme to pay the charge if it exceeds £2,000. In such cases a consequential adjustment is made to the individual's entitlement to benefits.

Annual allowance	2014–15 to 2015–16	2016–17 to 2019–20	2020–21
Maximum	£40,000[1, 2]	£40,000[1, 2]	£40,000[1, 2]
Minimum[3]	N/A	£10,000[3]	£4,000[3]

[1]   Unused allowance can be carried forward three years.

[2]   Where members make use of flexible access to their money purchase funds from 6 April 2015 the annual allowance is effectively divided between money purchase inputs and defined benefit inputs, resulting in a 'money purchase annual allowance' of £4,000 (£10,000 before 6 April 2017) and an 'alternative annual allowance' that applies to any defined benefit inputs of £36,000 (£30,000 before 6 April 2017). The money purchase annual allowance cannot be increased by amounts brought forward.

[3]   A tapered reduction in the annual allowance applies for those with an 'adjusted income' (i.e. including pension contributions) over £240,000 (£150,000 from 6 April 2016 to 5 April 2020). The reduction is £1 for every £2 of income over the limit and the minimum allowance is £4,000 (£10,000 before 6 April 2020).

Taxable benefits

SEE TOLLEY'S TAX COMPUTATIONS 19.2, 19.3.

'Tax-free' lump sum: The maximum 'tax-free' lump sum that can be paid to a member under a registered scheme is broadly the lower of:
- 25% of the value of the pension rights; and
- 25% of the member's lifetime allowance.

Lifetime allowance: Each individual has a lifetime allowance for contributions as set out in the table below. The excess over the lifetime allowance of the benefits crystallising (usually when a pension begins to be paid) is taxable at the following rates:
- 55% if taken as a lump sum;
- 25% in other cases.

Any tax due may be deducted from the individual's benefits.

Lifetime allowance	2014–15 to 2015–16	2016–17 to 2017–18	2018–19	2019–20	2020–21
	£1,250,000	£1,000,000	£1,030,000	£1,055,000	£1,073,100

Transitional. There are transitional provisions for the protection of lump sum and other pension rights accrued before 6 April 2006. Various protections apply to protect pension rights when the lifetime allowance is decreased.

Age restrictions

Minimum pension age: The minimum pension age is 55. A pension cannot be paid before the minimum age except on grounds of ill health. Protection applies to those with existing contractual rights to draw a pension earlier and for members of pre-6 April 2006 approved schemes with early retirement ages. A reduced lifetime allowance will apply in the case of early retirement before minimum pension age except in the case of certain professions such as the police and the armed forces (SI 2005/3451).

Share schemes

Share incentive plans ('SIPs')

SEE TOLLEY'S TAX COMPUTATIONS 28.4.

(TCGA 1992 ss 236A, 238A, Schs 7C, 7D Pt 1; ITEPA 2003 ss 488–515, Sch 2)

Free share plan

2014–15 onwards	annual maximum	£3,600

Partnership share plan

2014–15 onwards	annual maximum	£1,800 or 10% of annual salary if lower

Matching shares

2000–01 onwards	Maximum number of shares given by employer to employee for each partnership share bought	2

Shares are free of tax and NICs if held in the plan for five years. Dividends are tax-free if reinvested in shares. Shares withdrawn from the plan at any time are exempt from capital gains tax and treated as acquired by the employee at their market value at that time.

If shares are withdrawn within between three and five years (with exceptions such as on death, injury, disability, retirement, redundancy, or certain cash takeovers), liability to income tax and NICs arises on the lower of their value on entering and on leaving the plan. If shares are withdrawn within three years (with similar exceptions), liability is on their value on leaving the plan.

Enterprise management incentives

SEE TOLLEY'S TAX COMPUTATIONS 28.5.

(TCGA 1992 s 238A, Sch 7D Pt 4; ITEPA 2003 ss 527–541, Sch 5)

Certain independent trading companies with gross assets not exceeding £30 million may grant share options then worth up to £250,000 (£120,000 for options granted before 16 June 2012, £100,000 for options granted before 6 April 2008) to an eligible employee. The total value of shares in respect of which unexercised qualifying options exist must not exceed £3 million. Limited to companies with fewer than 250 full-time equivalent employees for options granted on or after 21 July 2008.

Where the conditions of the scheme are complied with:
- (a) There is no charge to tax or NICs when the option is granted provided the option to acquire the shares is not at less than their market values at that date, and there is no charge on exercise providing the option is exercised within ten years.
- (b) Capital gains tax will be payable when the shares are sold, though for disposals on or after 6 April 2013, shares acquired through exercising EMI options on or after 6 April 2012 are eligible for capital gains tax entrepreneurs' relief if certain conditions are met.

Save as you earn (SAYE) share option schemes

(TCGA 1992 s 238A, Sch 7D Pt 2; ITEPA 2003 ss 516–519, Sch 3)

The scheme is linked to a savings arrangement, on which bonuses are exempt from tax, to provide funds for the acquisition of shares when the option is exercised at the end of a three or five-year contract. A five-year contract may offer the option of repayment on the seventh anniversary, although the 7-year savings period is now withdrawn. Employees who were already saving under existing SAYE contracts before 23 July 2013 were not affected by this change.

From 1 September 2018 all employees are able to take a pause of up to 12 months from saving into their SAYE scheme.

Monthly contributions to SAYE scheme

	From 6 April 2014
Minimum	£5–£10[1]
Maximum	£500

[1] The company may choose a minimum savings contribution between £5 and £10.

See HMRC website (www.gov.uk/government/publications/change-in-bonus-rates-for-save-as-you-earn-saye-share-option-schemes) for the latest bonus rates.

Where the conditions of the scheme are complied with, no income tax charge arises on the employee in respect of:
- (a) the grant of an option to acquire shares at a discount of up to 20% of the share price at time of the grant;
- (b) the exercise of the option (options must not be exercised before the bonus date subject to exceptions such as on injury, disability, redundancy, retirement, death or certain cash takeovers); or

(c)   any increase in the value of the shares.

Capital gains tax is chargeable on disposal of the shares: the CGT base cost is the consideration given by the employee for both the shares and the option.

Company share option plans ('CSOPs')

(TCGA 1992 s 238A, Sch 7D Pt 3; ITEPA 2003 ss 521–526, Sch 4)

Limit on value of shares under option held by employee at any one time

From 29 April 1996	£30,000

Scheme shares must be fully paid up, not redeemable and, for options granted before 17 July 2013, not subject to special restrictions. Only full-time directors or qualifying employees may participate in the scheme.

Where the conditions of the scheme are complied with, no tax charge arises on the employee in respect of:
(a)   the grant of an option to acquire shares[1];
(b)   the exercise of the option[2]; or
(c)   any increase in the value of the shares.

Capital gains tax is chargeable on disposal of the shares: the CGT base cost is the consideration given by the employee for both the shares and the option.

[1]   At the time the option is granted the price at which shares can be acquired must not be less than the market value of shares of the same class at that time.
[2]   The option must be exercised between three and ten years after the grant (or may be exercised less than three years after the grant where the individual ceases to be an employee due to injury, disability, redundancy or retirement, or where there are certain cash takeovers of constituent companies).

Tax credits

(TCA 2002)

Tax credits are administered and paid by HMRC, and are non-taxable. Claims must be made after the commencement of the tax year and can be backdated for a maximum of one month. Universal credit will replace tax credits. New claimants and those reporting changed circumstances are being directed to universal credit. It is intended that existing claimants will be automatically transferred by 2024 (see p 136).

Child tax credit and working tax credit

	2019–20	2020–21
	Annual amount	Annual amount
Child tax credit	£	£
Family element[1]	545	545
Child element (for each child or young person)[2]	2,780	2,830
Addition for disabled child or young person	3,355	3,415
Enhancement for severe disabled child or young person	1,360	1,385
Working tax credit	£	£
Basic element	1,960	3,040
Lone parent and couple element	2,010	2,045
30-hour element	810	825
Disability element	3,165	3,220
Severe disability element	1,365	1,390
Childcare element – up to 70% of eligible costs	Weekly	Weekly
– maximum eligible cost for one child	175	175
– maximum eligible cost for two or more children	300	300

[1]   Only one family element per family. It is not payable to those starting a family after 5 April 2017.
[2]   No child element is payable for third and subsequent children born after 5 April 2017. Does not apply to disabled child element or severely disabled child element and multiple births are protected.

Income thresholds and withdrawal rates	2019–20	2020–21
Income threshold for those entitled to CTC and WTC	£6,420	£6,530
Withdrawal rate	41%	41%
Income threshold for those entitled to CTC only	£16,105	£16,385
Income rise disregard	£2,500	£2,500
Income fall disregard	£2,500	£2,500

Calculation of award. Tax credits are awarded on an annual basis. They are initially based on the income of the claimant or joint claimants for the preceding tax year and adjusted based on actual income in the tax year in which the credit is claimed. Income broadly includes all taxable income excluding the first £300 of income from pensions, savings, property or foreign assets. If current year's income is greater than the previous year's income by less than £2,500, the award is not adjusted. If current year's income is greater than the previous year's income by £2,500 or more, the award is adjusted to reflect current year's income less £2,500. An income fall disregard of £2,500 applies so where previous year's income exceeds the current year's income by not more than £2,500, the previous year's income will be used, but where the previous year's income exceeds the current year's income by more than £2,500, the current year's income plus £2,500 will be used. In any other case current year's income is used. Where circumstances change during a tax year and different rates apply, the award is recalculated on a proportional, daily basis. Such changes must be notified to HMRC within one month if tax credit entitlement will be reduced as a result.

Eligibility. CTC is payable to UK resident single parents and couples responsible for a child or young person. WTC is payable to UK residents who are at least 16 years old and, in the case of single persons, who work at least 16 hours a week. In the case of a couple they must jointly work at least 24 hours a week and one must work at least 16 hours a week, or where only one of the couple works that person must work for at least 24 hours a week. Additionally, the claimant (or one of them if a couple) must either:

- be at least 25 years old and work at least 30 hours a week; or
- have a dependent child or children; or
- have a mental or physical disability which puts them at a disadvantage in getting a job and have previously been in receipt of some form of disability benefit; or
- be over 60 and work at least 16 hours a week, regardless of whether they have dependent children.

Renewal claim. Claims for tax credit must be renewed by 31 July.

Inheritance tax

Rates of inheritance tax

(IHTA 1984 s 7, Schs 1, 1A; HMRC Inheritance Tax Manual IHTM14593)

From 15 March 1988 onwards

SEE TOLLEY'S TAX COMPUTATIONS 305.1, 305.2.

	Rate
Cumulative gross transfer rate:	
for gross transfers on death over the cumulative chargeable transfer limit	**40%**
reduced rate on death	**36%**[1]
for gross lifetime transfers over the cumulative chargeable transfer limit	**20%**
Grossing-up net transfer rate for each £1 over the chargeable transfer limit:	
for net transfers on death not bearing own tax	**2/3**
for net lifetime transfers	**1/4**

[1] For deaths occurring on or after 6 April 2012 a reduced rate of 36% applies where at least 10% of the net estate is left to charity or registered community amateur sports clubs.

Nil rate bands[3]

SEE TOLLEY'S TAX COMPUTATIONS 310.3, 310.5.
(IHTA 1984 ss 8–8D)

Period	Limit	Period	Limit
	£		£
2009–10 to 2020–21[2]	325,000[1]	1998–99	223,000
2008–09	312,000[1]	1997–98	215,000
2007–08	300,000[1]	1996–97	200,000
2006–07	285,000	1995–96	154,000
2005–06	275,000	10.3.92–5.4.95	150,000
2004–05	263,000	6.4.91–9.3.92	140,000
2003–04	255,000	1990–91	128,000
2002–03	250,000	1989–90	118,000
2001–02	242,000	15.3.88–5.4.89	110,000
2000–01	234,000	17.3.87–14.3.88	90,000
1999–2000	231,000	18.3.86–16.3.87	71,000

[1] Any nil-rate band which is unused on a person's death can be transferred to their surviving spouse or civil partner for the purposes of the charge to tax on the death of the survivor on or after 9 October 2007.
[2] The nil rate band is frozen at £325,000 until 5 April 2021.
[3] An additional **residence nil-rate band** applies when a home is passed on death to direct descendants of the deceased on or after 6 April 2017. For **2020–21 it is £175,000** (£150,000 for 2019–20, £125,000 for 2018–19, £100,000 for 2017–18). Any unused band is transferable to a spouse or civil partner. There is a tapered withdrawal of the band for estates valued at more than £2 million. It also applies where an individual downsizes from a higher value residence to a lower value one or ceases to own a home on or after 8 July 2015 and assets of equivalent value are passed on death to direct descendants.

Capital transfer tax nil rate bands

Period	Limit	Period	Limit
	£		£
6.4.85–17.3.86	67,000	26.3.80–8.3.82	50,000
13.3.84–5.4.85	64,000	27.10.77–25.3.80	25,000
15.3.83–12.3.84	60,000	13.3.75–26.10.77	15,000
9.3.82–14.3.83	55,000		

Estate duty nil rate bands (England, Scotland and Wales)

Period	Limit	Period	Limit
	£		£
22.3.72–12.3.75	15,000	9.4.62–3.4.63	4,000
31.3.71–21.3.72	12,500	30.7.54–8.4.62	3,000
16.4.69–30.3.71	10,000	10.4.46–29.7.54	2,000
4.4.63–15.4.69	5,000	16.8.14–9.4.46	100

Delivery of accounts: due dates

(IHTA 1984 s 216)

Type of transfer	Due date
Chargeable lifetime transfers	Later of: (a) 12 months after the end of the month in which the transfer took place; and (b) three months after the date on which the person delivering the account became liable
Relevant property settlements periodic and exit charges	6 months after end of the month in which the chargeable event occurred. (For chargeable events before 6 April 2014, as for chargeable lifetime transfers, see above)[1]
PETs which become chargeable	12 months after the end of the month in which the transferor died
Gifts with reservation chargeable on death	12 months after the end of the month in which the death occurred
Transfers on death	Later of: (a) 12 months after the end of the month in which the death occurred; and (b) three months after the date on which the personal representatives first act or the person liable first has reason to believe that he is liable to deliver an account
National heritage property	6 months after the end of the month in which the chargeable event occurred

[1] Where higher IHT is payable as a result of IHTA 1984 Sch A1 or the F(No 2)A 2017 domicile changes, the delivery date is the last day of December 2017 if later than normal due date.

Delivery of accounts: excepted transfers and estates

(SI 2004/2543; SI 2008/606)

Date of transfer or death	6 April 2000–5 April 2002	6 April 2002–5 April 2003	6 April 2003–31 Aug 2006	From 1 Sept 2006
Excepted transfers:	*Value below*	*Value below*	*Value below*	*Value below*
Total chargeable transfers since 6 April	£10,000	£10,000	£10,000	£10,000
Total chargeable transfers during last ten years	£40,000	£40,000	£40,000	£40,000
Excepted estates:				
Total gross value[1]	£210,000	£220,000	(see (a) below)	(see (a) below)
Total gross value of property outside UK	£50,000	£75,000	£75,000	£100,000
Aggregate value of 'specified transfers'[2]	£75,000	£100,000	£100,000	£150,000
Settled property passing on death	–	£100,000	£100,000	£150,000

For chargeable transfers after 5 April 2007, no account need be delivered where:
(i) the transfer is of cash or quoted shares or securities and the value of the transfer and other chargeable transfers made in the preceding seven years does not exceed the IHT threshold; or
(ii) the value of the transfer and other chargeable transfers made in the preceding seven years does not exceed 80% of the IHT threshold and the value of the transfer does not exceed the net amount of the threshold available to the transferor at the time of the transfer.

For footnotes see the list below.

Excepted estates

For deaths occurring after 5 April 2004, no account need be delivered where the deceased died domiciled in the UK provided either conditions (a) or (b) below are met, and both conditions (c) and (d) below are met.

(a)   the aggregate of the gross value of the estate, and of any 'specified transfers'[2] or 'specified exempt transfers'[3] does not exceed the appropriate IHT threshold[4];

(b)   the aggregate of the gross value of the estate, and of any 'specified transfers'[2] or 'specified exempt transfers'[3] does not exceed £1,000,000; for deaths after 28 February 2011 at least part of the estate passes to the person's spouse, civil partner or to a charity; and after deducting from that aggregate figure any exempt spouse, civil partner and charity transfers and total estate liabilities[6], it does not exceed the appropriate IHT threshold[4];

(c)   the gross value of settled property or foreign assets do not exceed the limits in the above table; and

(d)   there were no chargeable lifetime transfers in the seven years before death other than specified transfers not exceeding the limits in the above table[5].

Where the deceased was never domiciled in the UK, no account need be delivered provided that the value of the estate in the UK is wholly attributable to cash and quoted shares and securities not exceeding £150,000.

[1]   See table above — This limit applies to the aggregate gross value of the estate and of 'specified transfers' and 'specified exempt transfers'. For deaths after 28 February 2011 transfers treated as normal expenditure out of income made within 7 years before death and totalling more than £3,000 in any tax year will be treated as chargeable transfers for these purposes.

[2]   'Specified transfers' are chargeable transfers of cash, quoted shares and securities and, after 6 April 2002, interests in or over land and, after 5 April 2004, personal chattels or corporeal moveable property. For deaths after 28 February 2011 transfers treated as normal expenditure out of income made within 7 years before death and totalling more than £3,000 in any tax year will be treated as chargeable transfers for these purposes.

[3]   'Specified exempt transfers' are transfers in the seven years before death between spouses or civil partners, gifts to charity, political parties or housing associations, transfers to maintenance funds for historical buildings, etc or to employee trusts.

[4]   For deaths after 5 April 2010 the IHT threshold for these purposes is increased by 100% where—

(a)   the deceased is a surviving spouse or civil partner;

(b)   a claim has been made for the transfer of the unused nil-rate band of their deceased spouse or civil partner;

(c)   all of the first deceased spouse's or civil partner's nil-rate band was unused; and

(d)   the first deceased met certain other criteria similar to those listed above for excepted estates.

[5]   For deaths after 28 February 2011 transfers treated as normal expenditure out of income made within 7 years before death and totalling more than £3,000 in any tax year will be treated as chargeable transfers for these purposes.

[6]   For deaths on or after 1 April 2014 total estate liabilities do not include those which are not discharged on or after death out of the estate in money or money's worth, or those which are prevented by any other provision in IHTA 1984 from being taken into account, or those attributable to financing the acquisition of, or maintenance or enhancement of the value of, excluded property.

Excepted settlements

No account need be delivered of property comprised in an excepted settlement (i.e. one with no qualifying interest in possession) where a chargeable event occurs after 5 April 2007 and cash not exceeding £1,000 is the only property comprised in the settlement. Other conditions to be fulfilled are that, the settlor has not provided further property, the trustees are UK resident throughout the settlement's existence and there are no related settlements.

Inheritance tax reliefs

The following is a summary of the main reliefs and exemptions under the Inheritance Tax Act 1984 (Parts II and V). The legislation should be referred to for conditions and exceptions.

Agricultural property
SEE TOLLEY'S TAX COMPUTATIONS 302.1, 302.2.

Transfer with vacant possession (or right to obtain it within 12 months); transfer on or after 1 September 1995, of land let (or treated as let) on or after that date.   100% of agricultural value

Any other case.   50% of agricultural value

Note: The 100% relief is extended in limited circumstances by Concession F17.

Annual gifts   £3,000
SEE TOLLEY'S TAX COMPUTATIONS 310.1.

Business property
SEE TOLLEY'S TAX COMPUTATIONS 304.1.

Unincorporated business.	100%	Controlling holding in fully quoted companies.	50%
Unquoted shares (including shares in AIM or USM companies) (held for 2 years or more).[1]	100%	Land, buildings, machinery or plant used in business of company or partnership.	50%
Unquoted securities which alone, or together with other such securities and unquoted shares, give the transferor control of the company (held for 2 years or more).[1]	100%		
Settled property used in life tenant's business.	100%		

[1]   Tax charges arising and transfers occurring after 5 April 1996. 10 March 1992–5 April 1996 minority holding of shares or securities of up to 25% in unquoted or USM company qualified for 50% relief; larger holdings qualified for 100% relief.

Charities, gifts to   Exempt

From 1 April 2002, Community Amateur Sports Clubs are treated as charities.

Marriage/civil partnership gifts
SEE TOLLEY'S TAX COMPUTATIONS 320.1.

Made by:		
	parent	£5,000
	remoter ancestor	£2,500
	party to marriage/civil partnership	£2,500
	other person	£1,000

National purposes
SEE TOLLEY'S TAX COMPUTATIONS 316.1 ONWARDS.

Property given or bequeathed to bodies listed in IHTA 1984 Sch 3.   Exempt

Political parties, gifts to   Exempt

Potentially exempt transfers
SEE TOLLEY'S TAX COMPUTATIONS 305.1.

Exempt if made 7 or more years before the date of death. Except for gifts with reservation etc, they include:
  (a)   transfers by individuals to other individuals or certain trusts for the disabled;
  (b)   transfers after 21 March 2006 by individuals to a bereaved minor's trust on the coming to an end of an immediate post-death interest;
  (c)   transfers before 22 March 2006 by individuals to accumulation and maintenance trusts;
  (d)   transfers by individuals into interest in possession trusts in which, for transfers after 21 March 2006, the beneficiary has a disabled person's interest; and
  (e)   certain transfers on the termination or disposal of an individual's beneficial interest in possession in settled property (in restricted circumstances following FA 2006).

Quick succession relief
SEE TOLLEY'S TAX COMPUTATIONS **319.1.**
Estate increased by chargeable transfer followed by death within 5 years.
Death within 1st year. 100%
Each additional year: decreased by 20%
Small gifts to same person £250
Spouses/civil partners with separate domicile (one not being in the UK)
SEE TOLLEY'S TAX COMPUTATIONS **310.4.**
Total exemption. £325,000[1]

[1] For transfers of value before 6 April 2013 the total exemption was £55,000. From 6 April 2013 the limit is increased to the level of the prevailing IHT nil-rate band (see p 109). For transfers of value made on or after 6 April 2013 individuals can elect to be treated as domiciled in the UK if, at any time on or after 6 April 2013 and during the period of 7 years ending with the date on which the election is made, they have a UK-domiciled spouse or civil partner. The election may be made in some cases where the UK-domiciled individual had died. Personal representatives may make an election on behalf of a deceased person in certain circumstances. Other conditions apply.

Tapering relief
The value of the estate on death is taxed as the top slice of cumulative transfers in the 7 years before death. Transfers on or within 7 years of death are taxed on their value at the date of the gift on the death rate scale, but using the scale in force at the date of death, subject to the following taper:

Years between gift and death	Percentage of full charge at death rates
0–3	100
3–4	80
4–5	60
5–6	40
6–7	20

Penalties see p 17.

National insurance contributions

(SI 2001/1004)

From 6 April 2020

SEE TOLLEY'S TAX COMPUTATIONS 504.1, 506.1, 505.1 ONWARDS.

Class 1 contributions[1]			
Earnings limits and threshold	Weekly £	Monthly £	Yearly £
Lower earnings limit	120	520	6,240
Primary threshold	183	792	9,500
Secondary threshold	169	732	8,788
Upper secondary threshold[3, 4]	962	4,167	50,000
Upper earnings limit	962	4,167	50,000
Rates			
Employees' contributions			
Weekly earnings:	£183.01–£962	12%	
	Over £962	2%	
Employers' contributions[3, 4]			
Weekly earnings:	Over £169[3, 4]	13.8%	
Women at reduced rate			
Employees' contributions			
Weekly earnings:	£183.01–£962	5.85%	
	Over £962	2%	
Employers' contributions			
Weekly earnings:	Over £169	13.8%	
Employment allowance[2]		**£4,000**	
Class 1A and Class 1B contributions		13.8%	

[1]   Employees' rates are nil for children under 16 and those over state pensionable age but employers' contributions are still payable. Employees' NICs are not payable on earnings up to the primary threshold, employers' NICs are not payable on earnings up to the secondary threshold.

[2]   An employment allowance of £4,000 per year (£3,000 from 6 April 2016 to 5 April 2020, £2,000 from 6 April 2014 to 5 April 2016) applies for businesses, charities and CASCs to be offset against their employer Class 1 secondary NICs. The allowance is claimed as part of the normal payroll process through RTI. Only one company in a group may claim. There are some excluded employers such as certain employers of domestic staff, public authorities and those which carry out functions wholly or mainly of a public nature. From 6 April 2015 the allowance was extended to employers of care and support workers where the duties of employment relate to the employer's personal, family or household affairs. From 6 April 2016 the allowance is no longer available to companies whose only employee is the director. From 6 April 2020 the allowance is only available to employers with a secondary Class 1 NICs liability below £100,000 in the preceding tax year. This £100,000 threshold will apply cumulatively in the case of connected employers.

[3]   From 6 April 2015 employers with employees under the age of 21 are no longer required to pay Class 1 secondary NICs on earnings up to the upper secondary threshold for those employees.

[4]   From 6 April 2016 employers with apprentices under the age of 25 are no longer required to pay Class 1 secondary NICs on earnings up to the upper secondary threshold for those employees.

6 April 2019–5 April 2020

SEE TOLLEY'S TAX COMPUTATIONS 504.1, 506.1, 505.1 ONWARDS.

Class 1 contributions[1]			
Earnings limits and threshold	Weekly £	Monthly £	Yearly £
Lower earnings limit	118	512	6,136
Primary threshold	166	719	8,632
Secondary threshold	166	719	8,632
Upper secondary threshold[3, 4]	962	4,167	50,000
Upper earnings limit	962	4,167	50,000
Rates			
Employees' contributions			
Weekly earnings:	£166.01–£962	12%	
	Over £962	2%	
Employers' contributions[3, 4]			
Weekly earnings:	Over £166[3, 4]	13.8%	
Women at reduced rate			
Employees' contributions			
Weekly earnings:	£166.01–£962	5.85%	
	Over £962	2%	
Employers' contributions			
Weekly earnings:	Over £166	13.8%	
Employment allowance[2]		£3,000	
Class 1A and Class 1B contributions		13.8%	

[1] Employees' rates are nil for children under 16 and those over state pensionable age but employers' contributions are still payable. Employees' NICs are not payable on earnings up to the primary threshold, employers' NICs are not payable on earnings up to the secondary threshold.

[2] An employment allowance of £3,000 per year (£2,000 from 6 April 2014 to 5 April 2016) applies for businesses, charities and CASCs to be offset against their employer Class 1 secondary NICs. The allowance is claimed as part of the normal payroll process through RTI. Only one company in a group may claim. There are some excluded employers such as certain employers of domestic staff, public authorities and those which carry out functions wholly or mainly of a public nature. From 6 April 2015 the allowance was extended to employers of care and support workers where the duties of employment relate to the employer's personal, family or household affairs. From 6 April 2016 the allowance is no longer available to companies whose only employee is the director.

[3] From 6 April 2015 employers with employees under the age of 21 are no longer required to pay Class 1 secondary NICs on earnings up to the upper secondary threshold for those employees.

[4] From 6 April 2016 employers with apprentices under the age of 25 are no longer required to pay Class 1 secondary NICs on earnings up to the upper secondary threshold for those employees.

6 April 2018–5 April 2019

Class 1 contributions[1]			
Earnings limits and threshold	Weekly £	Monthly £	Yearly £
Lower earnings limit	116	503	6,032
Primary threshold	162	702	8,424
Secondary threshold	162	702	8,424
Upper secondary threshold[3, 4]	892	3,863	46,350
Upper earnings limit	892	3,863	46,350
Rates			
Employees' contributions			
Weekly earnings:	£162.01–£892	12%	
	Over £892	2%	
Employers' contributions[3, 4]			
Weekly earnings:	Over £162[3, 4]	13.8%	
Women at reduced rate			
Employees' contributions			
Weekly earnings:	£162.01–£892	5.85%	
	Over £892	2%	
Employers' contributions			
Weekly earnings:	Over £162	13.8%	
Employment allowance[2]		**£3,000**	
Class 1A and Class 1B contributions		13.8%	

[1] Employees' rates are nil for children under 16 and those over state pensionable age but employers' contributions are still payable. Employees' NICs are not payable on earnings up to the primary threshold, employers' NICs are not payable on earnings up to the secondary threshold.

[2] An employment allowance of £3,000 per year (£2,000 from 6 April 2014 to 5 April 2016) applies for businesses, charities and CASCs to be offset against their employer Class 1 secondary NICs. The allowance is claimed as part of the normal payroll process through RTI. Only one company in a group may claim. There are some excluded employers such as certain employers of domestic staff, public authorities and those which carry out functions wholly or mainly of a public nature. From 6 April 2015 the allowance was extended to employers of care and support workers where the duties of employment relate to the employer's personal, family or household affairs. From 6 April 2016 the allowance is no longer available to companies whose only employee is the director.

[3] From 6 April 2015 employers with employees under the age of 21 are no longer required to pay Class 1 secondary NICs on earnings up to the upper secondary threshold for those employees.

[4] From 6 April 2016 employers with apprentices under the age of 25 are no longer required to pay Class 1 secondary NICs on earnings up to the upper secondary threshold for those employees.

6 April 2017–5 April 2018

Class 1 contributions[1]			
Earnings limits and threshold	Weekly £	Monthly £	Yearly £
Lower earnings limit	113	490	5,876
Primary threshold	157	680	8,164
Secondary threshold	157	680	8,164
Upper secondary threshold[3, 4]	866	3,750	45,000
Upper earnings limit	866	3,750	45,000
Rates			
Employees' contributions			
Weekly earnings:	£157.01–£866	12%	
	Over £866	2%	
Employers' contributions[3, 4]			
Weekly earnings:	Over £157[3, 4]	13.8%	
Women at reduced rate			
Employees' contributions			
Weekly earnings:	£157.01–£866	5.85%	
	Over £866	2%	
Employers' contributions			
Weekly earnings:	Over £157	13.8%	
Employment allowance[2]		**£3,000**	
Class 1A and Class 1B contributions		13.8%	

[1] Employees' rates are nil for children under 16 and those over state pensionable age but employers' contributions are still payable. Employees' NICs are not payable on earnings up to the primary threshold, employers' NICs are not payable on earnings up to the secondary threshold.

[2] An employment allowance of £3,000 per year (£2,000 from 6 April 2014 to 5 April 2016) applies for businesses, charities and CASCs to be offset against their employer Class 1 secondary NICs. The allowance is claimed as part of the normal payroll process through RTI. Only one company in a group may claim. There are some excluded employers such as certain employers of domestic staff, public authorities and those which carry out functions wholly or mainly of a public nature. From 6 April 2015 the allowance was extended to employers of care and support workers where the duties of employment relate to the employer's personal, family or household affairs. From 6 April 2016 the allowance is no longer available to companies whose only employee is the director.

[3] From 6 April 2015 employers with employees under the age of 21 are no longer required to pay Class 1 secondary NICs on earnings up to the upper secondary threshold for those employees.

[4] From 6 April 2016 employers with apprentices under the age of 25 are no longer required to pay Class 1 secondary NICs on earnings up to the upper secondary threshold for those employees.

6 April 2016–5 April 2017

Class 1 contributions[1]			
Earnings limits and threshold	Weekly £	Monthly £	Yearly £
Lower earnings limit	112	486	5,824
Primary threshold	155	672	8,060
Secondary threshold	156	676	8,112
Upper secondary threshold[3, 4]	827	3,583	43,000
Upper earnings limit	827	3,583	43,000
Rates[5]			
Employees' contributions			
Weekly earnings:	£155.01–£827	12%	
	Over £827	2%	
Employers' contributions[3, 4]			
Weekly earnings:	Over £156[3, 4]	13.8%	
Women at reduced rate			
Employees' contributions			
Weekly earnings:	£155.01–£827	5.85%	
	Over £827	2%	
Employers' contributions			
Weekly earnings:	Over £156	13.8%	
Employment allowance[2]		**£3,000**	
Class 1A and Class 1B contributions		13.8%	

[1] Employees' rates are nil for children under 16 and those over state pensionable age but employers' contributions are still payable. Employees' NICs are not payable on earnings up to the primary threshold, employers' NICs are not payable on earnings up to the secondary threshold.

[2] An employment allowance of £3,000 per year (£2,000 from 6 April 2014 to 5 April 2016) applies for businesses, charities and CASCs to be offset against their employer Class 1 secondary NICs. The allowance is claimed as part of the normal payroll process through RTI. Only one company in a group may claim. There are some excluded employers such as certain employers of domestic staff, public authorities and those which carry out functions wholly or mainly of a public nature. From 6 April 2015 the allowance was extended to employers of care and support workers where the duties of employment relate to the employer's personal, family or household affairs. From 6 April 2016 the allowance is no longer available to companies whose only employee is the director.

[3] From 6 April 2015 employers with employees under the age of 21 are no longer required to pay Class 1 secondary NICs on earnings up to the upper secondary threshold for those employees.

[4] From 6 April 2016 employers with apprentices under the age of 25 are no longer required to pay Class 1 secondary NICs on earnings up to the upper secondary threshold for those employees.

[5] Contracting out is no longer possible from 6 April 2016 as the single-tier state pension was introduced.

Class 1 contributions[1]				
Earnings limits and threshold		Weekly £	Monthly £	Yearly £
Lower earnings limit		112	486	5,824
Primary threshold		155	672	8,060
Secondary threshold		156	676	8,112
Upper secondary threshold[5]		815	3,532	42,385
Upper earnings limit		815	3,532	42,385
Upper accruals point		770	3,337	40,040
		Not contracted out	Contracted out Salary-related schemes[3]	
Employees' contributions				
Weekly earnings:	£155.01–770	12%	10.6%	
	£770.01–£815	12%	12%	
	Over £815	2%	2%	
	– rebate £112–£155		1.4%[2, 3]	
Employers' contributions[4, 5]				
Weekly earnings:	£156.01–£770[5]	13.8%	10.4%	
	Over £770[5]	13.8%	13.8%	
	– rebate £112–£156		3.4%[2, 3]	
Women at reduced rate				
Employees' contributions				
Weekly earnings:	£155.01–£815	5.85%		
	Over £815	2%		
Employers' contributions	Normal employers' contributions apply as above			
Employment allowance[4]		**£2,000**		
Class 1A and Class 1B contributions		13.8%		

[1] Employees' rates are nil for children under 16 and those over state pensionable age but employers' contributions are still payable. Employees' NICs are not payable on earnings up to the primary threshold, employers' NICs are not payable on earnings up to the secondary threshold.

[2] The rebate is given on earnings between the lower earnings limit and the primary threshold for employees, and between the lower earnings limit and the secondary threshold for employers. The rebate for employees is given to employers to the extent that insufficient contributions have been paid by the employee for offset.

[3] From 2012 the rebates for defined benefit schemes (salary-related schemes) are 3.4% for employers and 1.4% for employees. Contracting out on a defined contribution basis (money purchase schemes) is abolished from 6 April 2012. Contracting out via a personal pension plan is also not possible from 6 April 2012.

[4] From 6 April 2014 an employment allowance of £2,000 per year applies for businesses, charities and CASCs to be offset against their employer Class 1 secondary NICs. The allowance is claimed as part of the normal payroll process through RTI. Only one company in a group may claim. There are some excluded employers such as certain employers of domestic staff, public authorities and those which carry out functions wholly or mainly of a public nature. From 6 April 2015 the allowance is extended to employers of care and support workers where the duties of employment relate to the employer's personal, family or household affairs.

[5] From 6 April 2015 employers with employees under the age of 21 are no longer required to pay Class 1 secondary NICs on earnings up to the upper secondary threshold for those employees.

Class 2, 3 and 4 contributions

SEE TOLLEY'S TAX COMPUTATIONS 507.1, 513.1, 503.1 ONWARDS.

	2020–21	2019–20	2018–19
Class 2 (self-employed)[1]			
Flat rate—per week	**£3.05**	£3.00	£2.95
Share fishermen—per week	**£3.70**	£3.65	£3.60
Volunteer development workers—per week	**£6.00**	£5.90	£5.80
Small profits threshold—per year	**£6,475**	£6,365	£6,205
Class 3 (voluntary contributions)			
Flat rate—per week	**£15.30**	£15.00	£14.65
Class 4 (self-employed)[1]			
Lower annual profits limit	**£9,500**	£8,632	£8,424
Upper annual profits limit	**£50,000**	£50,000	£46,350
Rate between lower and upper limits	**9%**	9%	9%
Rate on profits above upper limit	**2%**	2%	2%
Maximum contributions			
Class 1 or Class 1/Class 2[2]	**£4,954.44**	£5,062.56	£4,642.80
– plus rate on earnings above upper limit	**2%**	2%	2%
Class 4 limiting amount[3]	**£3,806.65**	£3,882.12	£3,569.69
– plus rate on profits above upper limit	**2%**	2%	2%

[1] Not payable if pensionable age is reached by the beginning of the tax year.
[2] Where an earner has more than one employment (including self-employment), liability for Class 1 or Class 1 and Class 2 contributions cannot exceed a maximum amount equal to 53 employees' Class 1 contributions at the maximum standard rate, plus 2% on earnings over the individual's upper earnings limit (which varies depending on individual circumstances).
[3] Where Class 4 contributions are payable in addition to Class 1 and/or Class 2 contributions, liability for Class 4 contributions cannot exceed such an amount as, when added to the Class 1/Class 2 contributions payable (after applying the maximum if appropriate), equals the limiting amount. The limiting amount is the maximum Class 4 contributions payable (including 2% on earnings over the upper profit limit) plus 53 Class 2 contributions.

	2017–18	2016–17	2015–16
Class 2 (self-employed)[1]			
Flat rate—per week	£2.85	£2.80	£2.80
Share fishermen—per week	£3.50	£3.45	£3.45
Volunteer development workers—per week	£5.65	£5.60	£5.60
Small earnings exception—per year	£6,025	£5,965	£5,965
Class 3 (voluntary contributions)			
Flat rate—per week	£14.25	£14.10	£14.10
Class 4 (self-employed)[1]			
Lower annual profits limit	£8,164	£8,060	£8,060
Upper annual profits limit	£45,000	£43,000	£42,385
Rate between lower and upper limits	9%	9%	9%
Rate on profits above upper limit	2%	2%	2%
Maximum contributions			
Class 1 or Class 1/Class 2[2]	£4,509.24	£4,273.92	£4,197.60
– plus rate on earnings above upper limit	2%	2%	2%
Class 4 limiting amount[3]	£3,466.29	£3,293.00	£3,237.65
– plus rate on profits above upper limit	2%	2%	2%

[1] Not payable if pensionable age is reached by the beginning of the tax year.
[2] Where an earner has more than one employment (including self-employment), liability for Class 1 or Class 1 and Class 2 contributions cannot exceed a maximum amount equal to 53 employees' Class 1 contributions at the maximum standard rate, plus 2% on earnings over the individual's upper earnings limit (which varies depending on individual circumstances).
[3] Where Class 4 contributions are payable in addition to Class 1 and/or Class 2 contributions, liability for Class 4 contributions cannot exceed such an amount as, when added to the Class 1/Class 2 contributions payable (after applying the maximum if appropriate), equals the limiting amount. The limiting amount is the maximum Class 4 contributions payable (including 2% on earnings over the upper profit limit) plus 53 Class 2 contributions.

Employers' contributions: benefits in kind

Class 1A NICs are payable by employers on most taxable benefits in kind, excluding benefits:
  (1)   included in a PAYE settlement agreement (see p 95);
  (2)   provided to 'lower-paid' ministers of religion, and before 6 April 2016 all 'lower-paid' employees (including benefits in kind and expenses payments);
  (3)   otherwise not required to be included on a P11D;
  (4)   on which Class 1 NICs were due;
  (5)   which were covered by a dispensation before 6 April 2016 (see below).

From 6 April 2016 the dispensations regime is abolished and replaced with a new exemption for paid or reimbursed amounts that would otherwise be deductible. Also from 6 April 2016 employees (other than lower-paid ministers of religion) earning at a rate of less than £8,500 per year pay income tax on their benefits in kind in the same way as other employees earning at a rate of £8,500 or more.

Class 1 and Class 1A Benefits provided under optional remuneration arrangements are not covered by existing exemptions except in limited circumstances. Where this is the case Class 1 or Class 1A NICs are due as appropriate.

Class 1B contributions are payable by employers by reference to the value of any items included in a PAYE settlement agreement (PSA) which would otherwise be earnings for Class 1 or Class 1A, including the amount of tax paid. Income tax and Class 1B contributions on a PSA are payable by 19 October after the end of the tax year to which the PSA relates (or 22 October if paid electronically).

Common benefits subject to Class 1 and Class 1A NICs (CWG5 2020)

Benefit	NICs Class	PAYE or P11D
Assets transferred to employees but not readily convertible assets	1A	P11D
Assets placed at employee's disposal for mixed business and private use	1A	P11D
Car fuel supplied for private motoring in company car	1A	P11D
Car/van fuel supplied for private motoring in privately owned car/van – supplied using company credit card, garage account, agency card or employer's own fuel pump	1A	P11D
– any other circumstances	1	P11D
Cars available for private use	1A	P11D
Car parking facilities other than at or near place of work or as part of business travel	1A	P11D
Car parking fees paid for or reimbursed to employee other than at or near place of work or as part of business travel	1	P11D
Childcare where employer contracts with provider and either the value exceeds the permitted maximum or the qualifying conditions are not met	1A	P11D
Childcare where employee reimbursed or additional salary provided to meet cost	1	PAYE
Christmas boxes – cash	1	PAYE
– goods	1A	P11D
Clothing and uniforms		
– cash payment to employee for clothing that can be worn at any time	1	PAYE or P11D[1]
– clothing provided by employer that can be worn at any time	1A	P11D
Council tax, unless employee provided with living accommodation which is not a benefit	1	P11D
Credit and charge cards – personal expenses on employer's card	1	P11D
Entertaining staff — expenses/ allowances – employer contract with provider	1A	P11D
– employee contract with provider	1	PAYE or P11D[1]
Expenses not covered by an exemption— any profit element in payment	1	P11D[4]
Food, groceries, farm produce – employer contract with provider	1A	P11D
– employee contract with provider	1	PAYE or P11D[1]
Goods transferred to employee – employer contract with provider	1A	P11D
– employee contract with provider	1	PAYE or P11D[1]
Holidays – employer contract with provider	1A	P11D
– employee contract with provider, or holiday vouchers	1	PAYE or P11D[1]
Income tax paid but not deducted from employee, or paid on notional payments not borne by employee within 90 days of receipt of each notional payment	1	P11D
Insurance premiums for pensions etc on employee's death or retirement, employee contract with provider	1	PAYE or P11D[1]
Living accommodation (beneficial)	1A	P11D

Benefit		NICs Class	PAYE or P11D
Loans	– non-qualifying	1A	P11D
	– written off	1	P11D
Meals vouchers (all values)		1	P11D
Meals provided other than at canteen or at business premises open to all staff on a reasonable scale where all employees may obtain free or subsidised meals not provided in connection with salary sacrifice or flexible remuneration arrangements		1A	P11D
Medical, dental insurance or treatment provided in the UK by employer	– employer contract with provider	1A	P11D
	– employee contract with provider	1	PAYE or P11D[1]
Mobile phone[5] — cost of private calls, employee contract with provider		1	PAYE or P11D[1]
Personal bills		1	PAYE or P11D[1]
Readily convertible assets[2]		1	PAYE
Relocation payments	– qualifying over £8,000	1A	P11D
	– non-qualifying benefits or qualifying expenses paid after relevant day	1A	P11D
	– non-qualifying expenses	1	P11D
Round sum allowances (not identified as business expense)		1	P11D
Scholarships awarded to students because of parent's employment or payment of school fees	– employer contract with provider	1A	P11D
	– employee contract with provider	1	PAYE or P11D[1]
Social functions unless ITEPA 2003 s 264 satisfied		1A	P11D
Sporting or recreational facilities unless ITEPA 2003 s 261 satisfied		1A	P11D
Subscriptions, professional and fees not allowable as tax deduction	– employer contract with provider	1A	P11D
	– employee contract with provider	1	PAYE or P11D[1]
Staff suggestions unless ITEPA 2003 s 321 satisfied	– cash payment or a non-cash voucher	1	PAYE or P11D
	– benefit in kind	1A	P11D
Telephones	– employer contract with provider, unless private use is insignificant or employee reimburses cost of all private calls	1A	P11D
	– employee contract with provider, unless used exclusively for business. If mixed use, not applicable to business calls if supported by evidence	1	PAYE or P11D[1]
Third party benefits or payments	– cash payment	1	PAYE or P11D[1]
	– non-cash voucher	1A	P11D
Training payments	– employer contract with provider, unless work-related or encouraged or required by employer	1A	P11D
	– employee contract with provider, unless work-related or encouraged or required by employer	1	PAYE or P11D[1]
Vans available for commuting and other private use		1A[3]	P11D
Van fuel provided for use in van available for commuting & other private use		1A[3]	P11D
Vouchers (other than exceptions for childcare, meals, etc)		1	P11D

[1] Payments by employer to provider should be entered on P11D. Reimbursements to the employee are subject to PAYE.

[2] See detailed information in HMRC booklet CWG2(2020) para 5.13.1.

[3] No Class 1A due if van is available mainly for employee's business travel and commuting and other private use is insignificant.

[4] Specific and distinct business expenses within the payments should be recorded in appropriate section of P11D.

[5] No limit to number of mobile phones which employer can contract to provide NIC free solely for business with insignificant private use. Only one mobile per employee NIC free for private use where employer contracts. No mobile phone may be provided NICs free to a member of an employee's family or household.

Overseas

Average rates of exchange

Note: The rates of exchange on pp 125–128 are reproduced from information provided by HMRC and are Crown copyright.

The rates for 31.3.20 were updated by HMRC on 1 April 2020 and are correct at 13 April 2020.

Average for year ending	31.03.18	31.12.18	31.03.19	31.12.19	31.03.20
Abu Dhabi (Dirham)	4.847200	4.934967	4.848117	4.686892	4.6984
Afghanistan (Afghani)	Not quoted	Not quoted	Not quoted	Not quoted	Not quoted
Albania (Lek)	151.855608	145.201667	142.6475	139.573333	140.6141667
Algeria (Dinar)	147.292983	156.345000	155.033333	152.099167	152.9641667
Angola (Readj Kwanza)	228.398717	325.015833	358.4575	447.933333	504.7191667
Antigua (EC$)	3.562625	3.627567	3.5637	3.445167	3.454033333
Argentina (Peso)	22.835108	35.519167	41.434542	58.739542	65.96833333
Armenia (Dram)	635.050192	647.473333	637.659167	613.691667	612.795
Aruba (Florin)	2.362217	2.404958	2.362617	2.284033	2.2899
Australia (A$)	1.701108	1.784817	1.795092	1.821708	1.850933333
Austria (Euro)	1.137292	1.133458	1.132983	1.134225	1.147166667
Azerbaijan (New Manat)	2.236083	2.279708	2.24215	2.164708	2.170275
Bahamas ($ pegged to US$)	1.319675	1.343550	1.319892	1.275983	1.279266667
Bahrain (Dinar)	0.497683	0.506725	0.4978	0.481017	0.482275
Bangladesh (Taka)	108.245867	112.336667	110.600833	107.621667	108.225
Barbados (BD$)	2.639350	2.687092	2.639783	2.551983	2.55855
Belarus (Rouble)	2.635217	2.710508	2.721175	2.664100	2.670708333
Belgium (Euro)	1.137292	1.133458	1.132983	1.134225	1.147166667
Belize (Dollar)	2.638883	2.685417	2.638142	2.551450	2.558416667
Benin (CFA Franc)	746.023517	743.493333	743.184167	746.490833	754.9858333
Bermuda ($ pegged to US$)	1.319675	1.343550	1.319892	1.275983	1.279266667
Bhutan (Ngultrum)	85.167267	91.165833	91.846667	89.925833	90.24666667
Bolivia (Boliviano)	9.118975	9.283917	9.120467	8.817100	8.839783333
Bosnia-Herzegovina (Marka)	2.224400	2.216842	2.215933	2.218333	2.23615
Botswana (Pula)	13.344942	13.584425	13.646925	13.675000	13.785
Brazil (Real)	4.223092	4.843425	4.944692	4.997225	5.143041667
Brunei ($)	1.794625	1.808050	1.789833	1.741092	1.746025
Bulgaria (Lev)	2.224542	2.216892	2.215967	2.218375	2.243708333
Burkina Faso (CFA Franc)	746.023517	743.493333	743.184167	746.490833	754.9858333
Burundi (Franc)	2,294.578075	2,389.508333	2,367.751667	2,346.036667	2,372.325
Cambodia (Riel)	5,336.462042	5,433.167500	5,336.055833	5,161.497500	5,191.7775
Cameroon Republic (CFA Franc)	746.023517	743.493333	743.184167	746.490833	754.9858333
Canada (Can$)	1.692158	1.735442	1.728133	1.694733	1.693958333
Cape Verde Islands (Escudo)	125.851942	125.360000	125.289167	125.342500	126.7458333
Cayman Islands (CI$)	1.082142	1.101700	1.082308	1.046317	1.049
Central African (CFA Franc)	746.023517	743.493333	743.184167	746.490833	754.9858333
Chad (CFA Franc)	746.023517	743.493333	743.184167	746.490833	754.9858333
Chile (Peso)	839.937825	856.401667	863.108333	887.849167	923.7366667
China (Renminbi Yuan)	8.793500	8.842617	8.808783	8.794575	8.87015
Colombia (Peso)	3,868.970633	3,935.857500	3,958.056667	4,146.051667	4,219.970833
Comoros (Franc)	559.516808	557.619167	557.3875	557.992500	564.3633333
Congo Brazzaville (CFA Franc)	746.023517	743.493333	743.184167	746.490833	754.9858333
Congo Dem Rep (Congolese Franc)	2,010.992158	2,167.139167	2,138.955833	7,931.699167	7,956.9025
Costa Rica (Colon)	752.461292	769.060833	766.96	750.643333	740.8725
Cote d'Ivoire (CFA Franc)	746.023517	743.493333	743.184167	746.490833	754.9858333
Croatia (Kuna)	8.478242	8.421225	8.403867	8.412700	8.515383333
Cuba (Peso)	1.319675	1.343550	1.319892	1.275983	1.279266667
Cyprus (Euro)	1.137292	1.133458	1.132983	1.134225	1.147166667
Czech Republic (Koruna)	29.617358	29.055000	29.111667	29.131667	29.315
Denmark (Krone)	8.463283	8.447250	8.449217	8.468158	8.5666

Average for year ending	31.03.18	31.12.18	31.03.19	31.12.19	31.03.20
Djibouti (Franc)	234.526925	238.769167	234.565833	226.764167	227.3475
Dominica (EC$)	3.562625	3.627567	3.5637	3.445167	3.454033333
Dominican Republic (Peso)	63.080642	66.312500	65.701667	65.210000	66.345
Dubai (Dirham)	4.847200	4.934967	4.848117	4.686892	4.6984
Ecuador (US$)	1.319675	1.343550	1.319892	1.275983	1.279266667
Egypt (£)	23.559292	23.943333	23.5325	21.734167	21.15166667
El Salvador (Colon)	11.544442	11.752500	11.545833	11.160833	11.18833333
Equatorial Guinea (CFA Franc)	746.023517	743.493333	743.184167	746.490833	754.9858333
Eritrea (Nakfa)	19.790558	20.147500	19.793333	19.135000	19.18416667
Estonia (Euro)	1.137292	1.133458	1.132983	1.134225	1.147166667
Ethiopia (Birr)	32.895250	36.927500	36.584167	36.790833	38.07
Eurozone (Euro)	1.137292	1.133458	1.132983	1.134225	1.147166667
Fiji Islands (F$)	2.695158	2.779633	2.765633	2.741392	2.765566667
Finland (Euro)	1.137292	1.133458	1.132983	1.134225	1.147166667
France (Euro)	1.137292	1.133458	1.132983	1.134225	1.147166667
French Polynesia (CFP franc)	135.713783	135.252500	135.195833	135.334167	136.88
Gabon (CFA franc)	746.023517	743.493333	743.184167	746.490833	754.9858333
Gambia (Dalasi)	61.422583	64.870000	64.351667	63.955833	64.65
Georgia (Lari)	3.262392	3.390500	3.380358	3.560042	3.6389
Germany (Euro)	1.137292	1.133458	1.132983	1.134225	1.147166667
Ghana (Cedi)	5.933550	6.255850	6.324283	6.725642	6.912391667
Greece (Euro)	1.137292	1.133458	1.132983	1.134225	1.147166667
Grenada/Wind. Isles (EC$)	3.562625	3.627567	3.5637	3.445167	3.454033333
Guatemala (Quetzal)	9.671450	10.059158	10.07415	9.897775	9.837058333
Guinea Bissau (CFA Franc)	746.023517	743.493333	743.184167	746.490833	754.9858333
Guinea Republic (Franc)	11,950.680308	12,140.861667	11,955.29083	11,730.221667	11,896.815
Guyana (G$)	273.924767	279.440833	275.079167	266.640000	267.1966667
Haiti (Gourde)	85.080417	90.108567	93.466067	110.145000	114.7375
Honduras (Lempira)	30.987350	32.034167	31.7275	31.225000	31.405
Hong Kong (HK$)	10.295567	10.527500	10.349583	9.995125	10.00035833
Hungary (Forint)	351.979692	360.226667	362.254167	367.214167	375.9525
Iceland (Krona)	138.964717	144.255000	147.640833	156.032500	157.9741667
India (Rupee)	85.167267	91.165833	91.846667	89.925833	90.24666667
Indonesia (Rupiah)	17,681.332450	18,993.146667	18,905.83083	18,081.008333	17,981.0175
Iran (Rial)	Not quoted	Not quoted	Not quoted	Not quoted	Not quoted
Iraq (Dinar)	1,561.088458	1,526.995000	1,501.203333	1,519.003333	1,522.913333
Ireland (Euro)	1.137292	1.133458	1.132983	1.134225	1.147166667
Israel (Shekel)	4.676292	4.796125	4.783058	4.590842	4.532491667
Italy (Euro)	1.137292	1.133458	1.132983	1.134225	1.147166667
Jamaica (J$)	168.302375	172.675000	171.441667	168.676667	171.3341667
Japan (Yen)	146.289275	148.226667	145.915	140.052500	140.1766667
Jordan (Dinar)	0.935658	0.953292	0.936617	0.904850	0.907083333
Kazakhstan (Tenge)	429.597750	457.677500	466.338333	486.048333	488.3433333
Kenya (Shilling)	136.063275	136.114167	133.354167	130.166667	130.45
Korea North (Won)	Not quoted	Not quoted	Not quoted	Not quoted	Not quoted
Korea South (Won)	1,468.298333	1,475.541667	1,465.995	1,472.813333	1,492.601667
Kuwait (Dinar)	0.399008	0.405575	0.399475	0.387808	0.389016667
Kyrgyz Republic (Som)	90.690142	92.521667	91.198333	89.015000	89.25
Laos (New Kip)	10,924.060200	11,289.119167	11,175.88417	11,057.975000	11,192.2025
Latvia (Euro)	1.137292	1.133458	1.132983	1.134225	1.147166667
Lebanon (£)	1,993.559733	2,032.495000	1,995.086667	1,924.861667	1,931.2
Lesotho (Loti)	17.009892	17.507500	17.850833	18.305000	18.52566667
Liberia ($ pegged to US$)	1.319675	1.343550	1.319892	1.275983	1.279266667
Libya (Dinar)	1.815833	1.827208	1.8114	1.784458	1.793108333
Lithuania (Euro)	1.137292	1.133458	1.132983	1.134225	1.147166667
Luxembourg (Euro)	1.137292	1.133458	1.132983	1.134225	1.147166667
Macao (Pataca)	10.603683	10.843333	10.659167	10.293358	10.297525
Macedonia (Denar)	70.028658	69.770000	69.740833	69.791667	70.59
Madagascar (Malagasy Ariary)	4,119.578125	4,454.696667	4,488.0575	4,618.100000	4,680.174167
Malawi (Kwacha)	957.419008	975.765833	960.068333	942.931667	947.33
Malaysia (Ringgit)	5.533767	5.409158	5.368717	5.291067	5.302833333

Average for year ending	31.03.18	31.12.18	31.03.19	31.12.19	31.03.20
Maldive Islands (Rufiyaa)	20.366883	20.729167	20.386667	19.715833	19.75166667
Mali Republic (CFA Franc)	746.023517	743.493333	743.184167	746.490833	754.9858333
Malta (Euro)	1.137292	1.133458	1.132983	1.134225	1.147166667
Mauritania (Ouguiya)	470.815583	478.062500	470.811667	455.907500	352.52
Mauritius (Rupee)	44.805200	45.548333	45.18	45.067500	46.05416667
Mexico (Peso)	24.355933	25.654167	25.420833	24.652500	24.49083333
Moldova (Leu)	23.550275	22.589167	22.28	22.281667	22.465
Mongolia (Tugrik)	3,200.468108	3,296.170833	3,311.475833	3,389.214167	3,433.8275
Montserrat (EC$)	3.562625	3.627567	3.5637	3.445167	3.454033333
Morocco (Dirham)	12.579650	12.585833	12.4575	12.225833	12.29583333
Mozambique (Metical)	81.167542	80.731667	80.041667	79.435000	80.17666667
Myanmar (Kyat)	1,793.330225	1,915.314167	1,949.66	1,959.816667	1,940.684167
Nepal (Rupee)	136.268792	145.868333	146.9575	143.885000	144.3975
Netherlands (Euro)	1.137292	1.133458	1.132983	1.134225	1.147166667
New Caledonia (CFP Franc)	135.713783	135.252500	135.195833	135.334167	136.88
New Zealand (NZ$)	1.841325	1.931267	1.925333	1.921167	1.949025
Nicaragua (Gold Cordoba)	40.021408	42.225000	41.9925	42.040833	42.62666667
Niger Republic (CFA Franc)	746.023517	743.493333	743.184167	746.490833	754.9858333
Nigeria (Naira)	449.370933	484.997500	477.175	461.618333	463.2416667
Norway (Krone)	10.743592	10.879167	10.894167	11.161667	11.34583333
Oman (Rial Omani)	0.507983	0.517233	0.508133	0.491283	0.492541667
Pakistan (Rupee)	140.586725	160.697500	167.225833	188.920000	194.5241667
Panama (Balboa)	1.319675	1.343550	1.319892	1.275983	1.279266667
Papua New Guinea (Kina)	4.220958	4.406750	4.374908	4.317808	4.341941667
Paraguay (Guarani)	7,398.514883	7,674.501667	7,676.394167	7,872.609167	8,049.758333
Peru (New Sol)	4.287767	4.402258	4.354525	4.253775	4.268375
Philippines (Peso)	66.973833	70.557500	69.8275	66.444167	65.9925
Poland (Zloty)	4.803675	4.819975	4.855567	4.871825	4.915541667
Portugal (Euro)	1.137292	1.133458	1.132983	1.134225	1.147166667
Qatar (Riyal)	4.809233	4.891900	4.805792	4.645950	4.657791667
Romania (Leu)	5.230075	5.275600	5.2947	5.370883	5.447533333
Russia (Rouble)	76.261667	83.146667	84.786667	82.883333	81.9125
Rwanda (R Franc)	1,114.911850	1,169.408333	1,162.525	1,159.481667	1,176.019167
Saotome & Principe (Dobra)	27,909.510992	27,773.471667	27,778.32167	27,830.600000	28,188.20833
Saudi Arabia (Riyal)	4.948550	5.039008	4.950583	4.785925	4.798216667
Senegal (CFA Franc)	746.023517	743.493333	743.184167	746.490833	754.9858333
Serbia (Dinar)	137.004950	134.122500	133.96	133.750000	135.0566667
Seychelles (Rupee)	18.005750	18.529167	18.2525	17.756667	17.81083333
Sierra Leone (Leone)	10,019.493117	10,709.942500	10,797.69667	11,477.059167	11,925.09167
Singapore (S$)	1.793925	1.808050	1.788167	1.739425	1.746025
Slovakia (Euro)	1.137292	1.133458	1.132983	1.134225	1.147166667
Slovenia (Euro)	1.137292	1.133458	1.132983	1.134225	1.147166667
Solomon Islands (SI$)	10.244017	10.510833	10.396667	10.222483	10.33748333
Somali Republic (Schilling)	774.117917	780.475833	764.484167	741.514167	743.9033333
South Africa (Rand)	17.009892	17.507500	17.850833	18.305000	18.52666667
Spain (Euro)	1.137292	1.133458	1.132983	1.134225	1.147166667
Sri Lanka (Rupee)	202.270817	215.935833	220.923333	228.442500	229.2983333
St Christopher & Nevis (EC$)	3.562625	3.627567	3.5637	3.445167	3.454033333
St Lucia (EC$)	3.562625	3.627567	3.5637	3.445167	3.454033333
St Vincent (EC$)	3.562625	3.627567	3.5637	3.445167	3.454033333
Sudan Republic (£)	10.180292	27.970775	39.674167	59.182500	59.365
Surinam (Dollar)	9.870767	10.025850	9.847992	9.516350	9.540825
Swaziland (Lilangeni)	17.009892	17.507500	17.850833	18.305000	18.52666667
Sweden (Krona)	11.036758	11.581667	11.714167	11.943333	12.11666667
Switzerland (Franc)	1.280883	1.311442	1.302	1.268692	1.26615
Syria (Pound)	Not quoted	Not quoted	Not quoted	Not quoted	Not quoted
Taiwan (New T$)	39.664508	40.379167	40.125833	39.425833	39.2825
Tajikistan (Somoni)	Not quoted	Not quoted	Not quoted	Not quoted	Not quoted
Tanzania (Schilling)	2,959.310350	3,055.229167	3,023.423333	2,946.275833	2,950.009167
Thailand (Baht)	43.854408	43.361667	42.57	39.945833	39.64416667
Togo Republic (CFA Franc)	746.023517	743.493333	743.184167	746.490833	754.9858333
Tonga Islands (Pa'Anga)	1.701108	1.784817	1.88715	1.876275	1.813441667

Average for year ending	31.03.18	31.12.18	31.03.19	31.12.19	31.03.20
Trinidad and Tobago (TT$)	8.918300	9.067208	8.906358	8.615733	8.637966667
Tunisia (Dinar)	3.194825	3.478283	3.612325	3.751750	3.706508333
Turkey (Lira)	4.821650	6.343417	6.743333	7.095000	7.334416667
Turkmenistan (New Manat)	4.624408	4.707442	4.625608	4.474533	4.484966667
Uganda (New Schilling)	4,771.053325	4,996.244167	4,927.553333	4,715.306667	4,722.220833
Ukraine (Hryvnia)	35.263750	36.569167	35.79	33.555000	32.53
United Arab Emirates (Dirham)	4.847200	4.934967	4.848117	4.686892	4.6984
Uruguay (Peso Uruguayo)	37.831708	40.993333	41.600833	44.200000	46.00083333
USA (US$)	1.319675	1.343550	1.319892	1.275983	1.279266667
Uzbekistan (Sum)	7,987.388717	10,827.040000	10,703.90167	11,137.847500	11,547.23667
Vanuatu (Vatu)	143.826692	148.480000	147.9225	147.373333	148.8058333
Venezuela (Bolivar Fuerte)	2,921.778875	148,482.375833	225,552.1842	315,942.907500	317,237.2425
Vietnam (Dong)	29,988.879617	30,853.250833	30,484.0975	29,637.330000	29,699.93667
Wallis & Futuna Islands (CFP Franc)	135.713783	135.252500	135.195833	135.334167	136.88
Western Samoa (Tala)	3.300658	3.419792	3.393825	3.346683	3.3766
Yemen (Republic of) (Rial)	330.259050	336.214167	330.29	319.185833	319.9191667
Zambia (Kwacha)	12.531300	13.795833	14.2625	16.060833	16.96333333
Zimbabwe (Dollar)	477.586458	486.223333	477.663333	461.775833	462.9641667

Rates of exchange on year-end dates

	31.03.18	31.12.18	31.03.19	31.12.19	31.03.20
Australia (A$)	1.8288	1.8091	1.8458	1.8743	2.0167
Canada (Can$)	1.8086	1.7395	1.7535	1.7122	1.7582
Denmark (Krone)	8.5022	8.314	8.7452	8.7442	8.4041
Eurozone (Euro)	1.1406	1.1141	1.1715	1.1705	1.1254
Hong Kong (HK$)	11.00	9.9714	10.3185	10.2117	9.6246
Japan (Yen)	149.18	139.7323	146.1715	142.91	134.16
Norway (Krone)	11.01	11.0282	11.2768	11.5128	13.1533
South Africa (Rand)	16.62	18.3206	18.6034	18.4622	22.30
Sweden (Krona)	11.74	11.2915	12.1817	12.2205	12.47
Switzerland (Franc)	1.3433	1.2555	1.3112	1.2709	1.1914
USA (US$)	1.4028	1.2736	1.3145	1.3114	1.2412

Double taxation agreements (including protocols and regulations)

Agreements in force covering taxes on income and capital gains

Country	SI/SR & O	Country	SI/SR & O
Albania	**2013/3145**		2010/2972
Algeria	**2015/1888**	Germany	1967/25
Antigua & Barbuda	**1947/2865**		1971/874
	1968/1096		**2010/2975**[1]
Argentina	**1997/1777**		2014/1874
Armenia	**2011/2722**	Ghana	**1993/1800**
Australia	**2003/3199**	Gibraltar	**2020/275**
Austria	**2019/255**	Greece	**1954/142**
Azerbaijan	**1995/762**	Grenada	**1949/361**
Bahrain	**2012/3075**		1968/1867
Bangladesh	**1980/708**	Guernsey	**2018/1345**
Barbados	**2012/3076**	Guyana	**1992/3207**
Belarus	**2018/778**	Hong Kong	**2010/2974**
Belgium	**1987/2053**	Hungary	**2011/2726**
	2010/2979	Iceland	**2014/1879**
Belize	**1947/2866**	India	**1993/1801**
	1968/573		2013/3147
	1973/2097	Indonesia	**1994/769**
Bolivia	**1995/2707**	Irish Republic	**1976/2151**
Bosnia Herzegovina[2]	**1981/1815**		1976/2152
Botswana	**2006/1925**		1995/764
British Virgin Islands	**2009/3013**		1998/3151
Brunei	**1950/1977**	Isle of Man	**2018/1347**
	1968/306	Israel	**1963/616**
	1973/2098		1971/391
	2013/3146		2019/1111
Bulgaria	**2015/1890**	Italy	**1990/2590**
Canada	**1980/709**	Ivory Coast	**1987/169**
	1980/1528	Jamaica	**1973/1329**
	1985/1996	Japan	**2006/1924**
	2003/2619		2014/1881
	2014/3274	Jersey	**2018/1348**
	2015/2011	Jordan	**2001/3924**
Cayman Islands	**2010/2973**	Kazakhstan	**1994/3211**
Chile	**2003/3200**		1998/2567
China[4]	**2011/2724**	Kenya	**1977/1299**
	2013/3142	Kiribati (and Tuvalu)	**1950/750**
Croatia[2]	**2015/1889**		1968/309
Cyprus	**2018/839**		1974/1271
	2019/1113	Korea (South)	**1996/3168**
Czech Republic[3]	**1991/2876**	Kosovo[2]	**2015/2007**
Denmark	**1980/1960**	Kuwait	**1999/2036**
	1991/2877	Latvia	**1996/3167**
	1996/3165	Lesotho[5]	**1997/2986**
Egypt	**1980/1091**		**2018/376**
Estonia	**1994/3207**	Liechtenstein	**2012/3077**
Ethiopia	**2011/2725**	Libya	**2010/243**
Falkland Islands	**1997/2985**	Lithuania	**2001/3925**
Faroes	**2007/3469**		2002/2847
Fiji	**1976/1342**	Luxembourg	**1968/1100**
Finland	**1970/153**		1980/567
	1973/1327		1984/364
	1980/710		2010/237
	1985/1997	Macedonia[2]	**2007/2127**
	1991/2878	Malawi	**1956/619**
	1996/3166		1964/1401
France	**2009/226**		1968/1101
Gambia	**1980/1963**		1979/302
Georgia	**2004/3325**	Malaysia	**1997/2987**

Country	SI/SR & O	Country	SI/SR & O
	2010/2971	Sierra Leone	**1947/2873**
Malta	**1995/763**		1968/1104
Mauritius	**1981/1121**	Singapore	**1997/2988**
	1987/467		2010/2685
	2003/2620		2012/3078
	2011/2442	Slovak Republic[3]	**1991/2876**
	2018/840	Slovenia[2]	**2008/1796**
Mexico	**1994/3212**	Solomon Islands	**1950/748**
	2010/2686		1968/574
Moldova	**2008/1795**		1974/1270
Mongolia	**1996/2598**	South Africa	**2002/3138**
Montenegro[2]	**1981/1815**		2011/2441
Montserrat	**1947/2869**	Spain	**2013/3152**
	1968/576	Sri Lanka	**1980/713**
	2011/1083	Sudan	**1977/1719**
Morocco	**1991/2881**	Swaziland	**1969/380**
Myanmar	**1952/751**	Sweden	**2015/1891**
Namibia	**1962/2352**	Switzerland	**1978/1408**
	1962/2788		1982/714
	1967/1489		1994/3215
	1967/1490		2007/3465
Netherlands	**2009/227**		2010/2689
	2013/3143		2012/3079
New Zealand	**1984/365**	Taiwan	**2002/3137**
	2004/1274	Tajikistan	**2014/3275**
	2008/1793	Thailand	**1981/1546**
Nigeria	**1987/2057**	Trinidad and Tobago	**1983/1903**
Norway	**2013/3144**	Tunisia	**1984/133**
Oman	**1998/2568**	Turkey	**1988/932**
	2010/2687	Turkmenistan	**2016/1217**
Pakistan	**1987/2058**	Tuvalu (and Kiribati)	**1950/750**
Panama	**2013/3149**		1968/309
Papua New Guinea	**1991/2882**		1974/1271
Philippines	**1978/184**	Uganda	**1993/1802**
Poland	**2006/3323**	Ukraine	**1993/1803**
Portugal	**1969/599**	United Arab Emirates	**2016/754**
Qatar	**2010/241**	Uruguay	**2016/753**
	2011/1684	USA	**2002/2848**
Romania	**1977/57**	Uzbekistan	**1994/770**
Russian Federation	**1994/3213**		2018/628
St Kitts and Nevis	**1947/2872**	Venezuela	**1996/2599**
Saudi Arabia	**2008/1770**	Vietnam	**1994/3216**
Senegal	**2015/1892**	Zambia	**2014/1876**
Serbia[2]	**1981/1815**	Zimbabwe	**1982/1842**

[1]   Treaty replaces 1967/25 with effect from 1 January 2011 or 6 April 2011 depending on type of income. However, where a resident of Germany was, before 30 December 2010, in receipt of a UK pension (including State Pension) or annuity relievable under Article X of prior treaty 1967/25, the individual may elect for the terms of the prior treaty to continue to apply to the pension or annuity.

[2]   *SI 1981/1815* (former Yugoslavia agreement) treated as remaining in force between the UK and, respectively, Bosnia-Herzegovina, Croatia and Serbia and Montenegro until superseded by new agreements. (SP 3/04.) The agreement was also treated as applying to Kosovo. New Croatia agreement came into force on 19 November 2015. New Kosovo agreement came into force on 16 December 2015.

[3]   *SI 1991/2876* (former Czechoslovakia agreement) treated as remaining in force between the UK and, respectively, Czech Republic and Slovak Republic. (SP 5/93.)

[4]   Hong Kong Special Administrative Region has its own agreement.

[5]   The 2018 treaty replaces SI 1997/2986 but where, immediately before the entry into force on 18 September 2018, an individual is entitled to the benefits of the 1997 agreement and was in receipt of pensions or other similar remuneration, or pensions paid and other payments made under a public scheme which is part of the social security system of a Contracting State, a political subdivision or a local authority thereof, the provisions of the 1997 agreement will continue to apply to such pensions and payments.

Tax information exchange agreements in force

Country	SI	Country	SI
Anguilla	2010/2677	Isle of Man	2009/228
Antigua and Barbuda	2011/1075	Jersey	2009/3012
Aruba	2011/2435	Liberia	2011/2434
Bahamas	2010/2684	Liechtenstein	2010/2678
Belize	2011/1685	Macao	2015/801
Bermuda	2018/518	Monaco	2015/804
British Virgin Islands	2009/3013	San Marino	2011/1688
Curaçao, Sint Maarten and BES Islands (formerly the Netherlands Antilles)	2011/2433	St Christopher and Nevis	2011/1077
Dominica	2011/1686	St Lucia	2011/1076
Gibraltar	2010/2680	St Vincent and Grenadines	2011/1078
Grenada	2011/1687	Turks and Caicos Islands	2010/2679
Guernsey	2009/3011	Uruguay	2014/1358

Tax information exchange agreements signed but not in force

Marshall Islands	Jersey Exchange of Letters[1]	British Virgin Islands Exchange of Letters[1]
Brazil	Guernsey Exchange of Letters[1]	Turks and Caicos Islands Exchange of Letters[1]
	Gibraltar Exchange of Letters[1]	Anguilla Exchange of Letters[1]

[1]   These will amend the existing tax information exchange agreements.

Tax information exchange agreements in force — EU savings directives

Country	SI	Country	SI
Aruba	2005/1458	Isle of Man	2005/1263
British Virgin Islands	2005/1457	Jersey	2005/1261
Gibraltar	2006/1453	Montserrat	2005/1459
Guernsey	2005/1262	former Netherlands Antilles (now known as Curaçao, Sint Maarten and BES Islands)	2005/1460

International agreements in force to improve tax compliance

Isle of Man, Guernsey, Jersey, Gibraltar	2014/520
USA	2015/878

Agreements in force covering shipping and air transport profits

Country	SI/SR & O	Country	SI/SR & O
Brazil	1968/572	Iran (air)	1960/2419
Cameroon (air)	1982/1841	Lebanon	1964/278
China (air)	1981/1119	Saudi Arabia (air)	1994/767
Congo Democratic Republic	1977/1298		

Agreements in force covering estates, inheritances and gifts

France*	1963/1319	Pakistan*	1957/1522
India*	1956/998	South Africa	1979/576
Ireland	1978/1107	Sweden	1981/840
Italy*	1968/304		1989/986
Netherlands	1980/706	Switzerland	1994/3214
	1996/730	USA	1979/1454

*   Agreements pre-date UK inheritance tax/capital transfer tax.

Overseas income – basis of assessment

SEE TOLLEY'S TAX COMPUTATIONS 23.1.
(ITTOIA 2005 Pt 8; ITEPA 2003 ss 573–576A, 642, 642A; ITA 2007 ss 809A–809Z10)

	Professions, trades, etc	Pensions	Other income
Non-residents	Exempt	Exempt	Exempt
Residents			
(1) **Foreign domicile**[2]	Remittance	Remittance	Remittance
(2) **UK domicile**	Arising	100%[1]	Arising

[1] 90% arising basis before 6 April 2017. Pensions paid by the governments of the Federal Republic of Germany, Austria, and from 6 April 2016 the Netherlands, to certain victims of WW2 persecution are exempt.

[2] Where an individual not domiciled in the UK who has overseas income (or, for non-domiciles only, gains) in excess of £2,000 claims the remittance basis, he will not qualify for personal allowances or the capital gains tax annual exemption. The claim for remittance basis must be made annually. If the individual is not UK domiciled in a year and has been resident in the UK for at least seven out of the last nine tax years and has overseas income or gains in excess of £2,000, there is an additional charge of £30,000. From 6 April 2015 this charge is £60,000 for non-domiciles who have been UK resident for at least twelve tax years in the previous fourteen (£50,000 from 6 April 2012 to 5 April 2015), and, before 6 April 2017, £90,000 for non-domiciles who have been UK resident for at least seventeen tax years in the previous twenty. From April 2017 an individual who has been resident in the UK for more than 15 of the last 20 tax years is deemed UK-domiciled for tax purposes and hence the £90,000 charge no longer applies. It is also no longer possible for an individual born in the UK to parents who are UK-domiciled to claim non-domicile status if they leave but then return and take up residency in the UK.

Employment income liability of non-resident employees see p 96.

Tax-free (FOTRA) securities

(FA 1996 s 154; FA 1998 s 161; ITTOIA 2005 ss 713, 714; CTA 2009 s 1279)

Interest on all government stock is exempt from tax where the beneficial owner is not resident in the UK. Except in the case of 3^1/$_2$% War Loan 1952 or after, the exemption does not apply where the securities are held for the purposes of a trade or business carried on in the UK.

Social security benefits

Taxable state benefits

	Weekly 6.4.20	Total 2020–21 (52 weeks)	Weekly 8.4.19	Total 2019–20 (52 weeks)
	£	£	£	£
Bereavement benefits — deaths before 6 April 2017[1]				
Bereavement allowance: standard rate	121.95	6,341	119.90	6,234
Widowed parent's allowance	121.95	6,341	119.90	6,234
Carer's allowance	66.95	3,481	66.15	3,439
– Adult dependency increase[7]	–	–	38.90	2,022
Employment and support allowance[6]				
–under 25	58.90	–	57.90	–
–25 or over	74.35	–	73.10	–
Incapacity benefit[6]				
Long-term (after 52 weeks)	114.15	5,935	112.25	5,837
– Adult dependency increase	66.30	3,447	65.20	3,390
– Age increase: higher rate	12.10	629	11.90	618
lower rate	6.70	348	6.60	343
Short term				
– Under pension age: higher rate	101.90	–	100.20	–
– Adult dependency increase	51.65	–	50.80	–
– Over pension age: higher rate	114.15	–	112.25	–
– Adult dependency increase	63.80	–	62.75	–
Industrial death benefit[2]				
Widow's pension: higher rate	134.25	6,981	129.20	6,718
lower rate	40.28	2,094	38.76	2,015
Widower's pension	134.25	6,981	129.20	6,718
Invalidity allowance[3]				
Higher rate	23.30	1,211	22.90	1,190
Middle rate	14.90	774	14.70	764
Lower rate	7.45	387	7.35	382
Jobseeker's allowance[4]				
Single: under 25	58.90	–	57.90	–
25 or over	74.35	–	73.10	–
Couple: both under 18	58.90	–	57.90	–
both under 18 higher rate	89.00	–	87.50	–
one under 18, one under 25	58.90	–	57.90	–
one under 18, one 25 or over	74.35	–	73.10	–
both 18 or over	116.80	–	114.85	–
State pension — retired before 6 April 2016				
Single person (Category A or B)	134.25	6,981	129.20	6,718
Single person (Category B lower) based on spouse's or civil partner's insurance	80.45	4,183	77.45	4,027
Adult dependency increase[7]	–	–	70.00	3,640
Non-contributory pension				
– single (Category C (higher) or Category D)	80.45	4,183	77.45	4,027
– single (Category C (lower))	–	–	–	–
Age addition (over 80) (each)	0.25	13	0.25	13
State pension — retired after 5 April 2016				
Rate	175.20	9,110	168.60	8,767
Statutory adoption pay				
Rate[5]	151.20	–	148.68	–
Earnings threshold	120.00	–	118.00	–
Statutory maternity pay				
Rate[5]	151.20	–	148.68	–
Earnings threshold	120.00	–	118.00	–

	Weekly 6.4.20	Total 2020–21 (52 weeks)	Weekly 8.4.19	Total 2019–20 (52 weeks)
	£	£	£	£
Statutory parental bereavement pay				
Rate[5]	151.20	–	–	–
Earnings threshold	120.00	–	–	–
Statutory paternity pay				
Rate[5]	151.20	–	148.68	–
Earnings threshold	120.00	–	118.00	–
Statutory shared parental pay				
Rate[5,10]	151.20	–	148.68	–
Earnings threshold	120.00	–	118.00	–
Statutory sick pay				
Rate	95.85	–	94.25	–
Earnings threshold	120.00	–	118.00	–

[1] Paid to widows, widowers and the civil partner of the deceased for up to 52 weeks. For deaths on or after 6 April 2017 bereavement support payments replace bereavement benefits and are non-taxable (see p 137).

[2] For deaths before 11 April 1988 only.

[3] When paid with retirement pensions. See note below on non-taxable benefits on p 136.

[4] Where the allowance exceeds the amount shown above, the excess is not taxable.

[5] The allowance is 90% of average weekly earnings if less than the above amount. In the first six weeks the rate of SMP and SAP is 90% of average weekly earnings even if higher than the standard rate.

[6] Employment and support allowance replaces incapacity benefits for new claimants on or after 27 October 2008. Only contributory employment and support allowance is taxable. Income related allowance is not taxable.

[7] Not available to new retirees or new carer's allowance claimants from 6 April 2010 and withdrawn completely on 5 April 2020.

[8] **A cap is placed on the total amount of benefit** that most people aged 16 to 64 can receive. The cap applies to the total amount that the people in a household receive from certain benefits. From 7 November 2016, the cap is £384.62 a week or £442.31 in Greater London for couples (with or without children living with them), and for single parents whose children live with them, and £257.69 a week or £296.35 in Greater London for single adults who do not have children, or whose children do not live with them. See www.gov.uk/benefit-cap/benefit-cap-amounts.

[9] **Universal credit** is being phased in gradually from 29 April 2013. It replaces some of the benefits above. For current rates see table of non-taxable benefits on p 136. See www.gov.uk/universal-credit.

[10] Statutory shared parental pay (ShPP) is available for eligible parents (the mother and her partner) whose baby was due on or after 5 April 2015 or where a child is placed for adoption (the parental equivalents are the primary and secondary adopter) on or after the same date.

Non-taxable state benefits

Weekly rates from		6.4.20	8.4.19
		£	£
Attendance allowance			
Higher rate (day and night)		89.15	87.65
Lower rate (day or night)		59.70	58.70
Child benefit[3]			
Eldest child		21.05	20.70
Each subsequent child		13.95	13.70
Child dependency addition			
Paid with state pension; widowed mother's/parent's allowance; short-term incapacity benefit - higher rate or over state pension age; long-term incapacity benefit; carer's allowance; severe disablement unemployability supplement		11.35	11.35
Disability living allowance[2]			
Care component	higher rate	89.15	87.65
	middle rate	59.70	58.70
	lower rate	23.60	23.20
Mobility component	higher rate	62.25	61.20
	lower rate	23.60	23.20
Personal independence payment[2]			
Daily living component	enhanced rate	89.15	87.65
	standard rate	59.70	58.70
Mobility component	enhanced rate	62.25	61.20
	standard rate	23.60	23.20
Guardian's allowance		17.90	17.60
Incapacity benefit (short-term)[1]			
Under pension age – lower rate (first 28 weeks)		86.10	84.65
– Adult dependency increase		51.65	50.80
Over pension age – lower rate (first 28 weeks)		109.50	107.65
– Adult dependency increase		63.80	62.75
Maternity allowance (where SMP not available)			
Standard rate		151.20	148.68
MA threshold		30.00	30.00
Severe disablement allowance[7]			
Basic rate		80.85	79.50
Age-related addition	higher rate	12.10	11.90
	middle rate	6.70	6.60
	lower rate	6.70	6.60
– Adult dependency increase		39.75	39.10

See next page for universal credit amounts

Amount payable per assessment period[5] in:		2020–21	2019–20
		£	£
Universal credit[5]			
Universal credit amounts			
Standard allowance	single under 25	**342.72**	251.77
	single 25 or over	**409.89**	317.82
	joint claimants both under 25	**488.59**	395.20
	joint claimants either 25 or over	**594.04**	498.89
Child element[6]	first child	**281.25**	277.08
	second/ subsequent child	**235.83**	231.67
Disabled child additions	lower rate addition	**128.25**	126.11
	higher rate addition	**400.29**	392.08
Limited capability for work element		**128.25**	126.11
Limited capability for work and work-related activity element		**341.92**	336.20
Carer element		**162.92**	160.20
Childcare cost element	maximum for one child	**646.35**	646.35
	maximum for two or more children	**1,108.04**	1,108.04
Non-dependants' housing cost contributions		**75.15**	73.89
Work allowances			
Higher work allowance (no housing element)	single, no dependent children	**Nil**	Nil
	single, one or more children	**512.00**	503.00
	single, limited capability for work	**512.00**	503.00
	joint claimant, no dependent children	**Nil**	Nil
	joint claimant, one or more children	**512.00**	503.00
	joint claimant, limited capability for work	**512.00**	503.00
Lower work allowance	single, no dependent children	**Nil**	Nil
	single, one or more children	**292.00**	287.00
	single, limited capability for work	**292.00**	287.00
	joint claimant, no dependent children	**Nil**	Nil
	joint claimant, one or more children	**292.00**	287.00
	joint claimant, limited capability for work	**292.00**	287.00

1 Incapacity benefit replaced invalidity allowance from April 1995. The benefits are taxable except those paid in the first 28 weeks of incapacity and those paid to persons already receiving invalidity benefit on 13 April 1995 so long as they remain incapable of work.

2 Personal Independence Payment (PIP) started to replace Disability Living Allowance (DLA) for new claims by eligible people aged 16 to 64 from 8 April 2013. PIP will be introduced in stages over a number of years for existing DLA claimants.

3 See note on p 78 regarding the income tax charge arising to certain child benefit claimants from 7 January 2013.

4 **A cap is placed on the total amount of benefit** that most people aged 16 to 64 can receive. The cap applies to the total amount that the people in a household receive from certain benefits. From 7 November 2016, the cap is £384.62 a week or £442.31 in Greater London for couples (with or without children living with them), and for single parents whose children live with them, and £257.69 a week or £296.35 in Greater London for single adults who do not have children, or whose children do not live with them. See www.gov.uk/benefit-cap/benefit-cap-amounts.

5 **Universal credit** is being phased in gradually from 29 April 2013. It replaces some of the benefits listed in the above tables. An assessment period is a calendar month from effective date of claim. See www.gov.uk/universal-credit.

6 The child element of universal credit is no longer awarded for third and subsequent children born after 6 April 2017. This also applies to families claiming universal credit for the first time after April 2017. The restriction does not apply to disabled children and multiple births.

7 Severe disablement allowance has been replaced with employment and support allowance except for those who reached retirement age before 6 April 2014.

See next page for Other non-taxable benefits

	2020–21	2020–21	2019–20	2019–20
Bereavement support payments — deaths on or after 6 April 2017[1]	**First payment**	**Monthly**	First payment	Monthly
	£	**£**	£	£
With children under 20 in full-time education	**3,500**	**350**[1]	3,500	350[1]
Without children under 20 in full-time education	**2,500**	**100**[1]	2,500	100[1]

[1]　Paid to widows, widowers and the civil partner of the deceased. For deaths on or after 6 April 2017 bereavement support payments replace taxable bereavement benefits (see p 133). Monthly payments paid for up to 18 months.

Other non-taxable benefits include:

Bereavement payment (lump sum £2,000)
Back to Work bonus

Child tax credit (see Tax Credits, p 107)
Christmas bonus (with retirement pension)
Cold weather payments
Housing benefit (income related)
Income support (income related)
Industrial injuries disablement pension

Pension credit
Pneumoconiosis, byssinosis and miscellaneous disease benefits
Social fund payments
Vaccine damage (lump sum)
War pensions
Winter fuel payment
Working tax credit (see Tax Credits, p 107)

Stamp taxes

Stamp duty land tax

(FA 2003 Schs 2A–9; FA 2019 ss 42–46)

Stamp duty land tax does not apply in Scotland to transactions with an effective date on or after 1 April 2015, from which date land and buildings transaction tax applies (see table below), subject to transitional provisions in particular in relation to contracts entered into on or before 1 May 2012. Stamp duty land tax does not apply in Wales to transactions with an effective date on or after 1 April 2018, from which date land transaction tax applies (see table below), subject to transitional provisions in particular in relation to contracts entered into on or before 17 December 2014.

Land transactions					
	Residential property[5]	Rate[3]	Higher rate applying to certain purchases[7]	Non-residential or mixed property	Rate
Effective date	**From 1.4.16**			**From 17.3.16**	
	On band of consideration[2]			On band of consideration[2]	
	Up to £125,000[3]	**Nil**	**3%**	**Up to £150,000**	**Nil**
	£125,001–£250,000[3]	**2%**	**5%**	**£150,001–£250,000**	**2%**
	£250,001–£925,000[3]	**5%**	**8%**	**£250,001 or more**	**5%**
	£925,001–£1,500,000	**10%**	**13%**		
	£1,500,001 or more	**12%**	**15%**		
	On total consideration[1]				
Non-natural persons[1,6]	**£500,001 or more**	**15%**			
Effective date	4.12.14–31.3.16			4.12.14–16.3.16	
	On band of consideration[2]			On total consideration[1]	
	Up to £125,000	Nil		Up to £150,000	Nil
	£125,001–£250,000	2%		£150,001–£250,000	1%
	£250,001–£925,000	5%		£250,001–£500,000	3%
	£925,001–£1,500,000	10%		£500,001 or more	4%
	£1,500,001 or more	12%			
	On total consideration[1]				
Non-natural persons[1,6]	£500,001 or more	15%			
Effective date	20.3.14–3.12.14			20.3.14–3.12.14	
	On total consideration[1]			On total consideration[1]	
	Up to £125,000	Nil		Up to £150,000	Nil
	£125,001–£250,000	1%		£150,001–£250,000	1%
	£250,001–£500,000	3%		£250,001–£500,000	3%
	£500,001–£1,000,000	4%		£500,001 or more	4%
	£1,000,001–£2,000,000	5%			
	£2,000,001 or more	7%			
Non-natural persons[1,6]	£500,001 or more	15%			

Land transactions				
	Residential property[5]	**Rate**	**Non-residential or mixed property**	**Rate**
Lease rentals	*On net present value (NPV) of rent over term of lease (applying a discount rate of 3.5%)*[4]			
Effective date	**Residential property**	**Rate**	**Non-residential or mixed property**	**Rate**
From 17.3.16	**Up to £125,000**	**Nil**	**Up to £150,000**	**Nil**
	£125,001 or more	**1%**	**£150,001– £5,000,000**	**1%**
			£5,000,001 or more	**2%**
1.1.10–16.3.16	Up to £125,000	Nil	Up to £150,000	Nil
	£125,001 or more	1%	£150,001 or more	1%

Premiums
The same tax is payable for a premium granted as for a land transaction. Special rules applied before 17 March 2016 to a premium in respect of non-residential property where the rent exceeds £1,000 a year. For transactions before 12 March 2008, the rules applied to all property where the rent exceeded £600 a year.

1. Rates apply to the full consideration, not only to that in excess of the previous band.
2. Rates are charged on the portion of the consideration that falls within each rate band. Where the change from calculations based on total consideration to those based on band of consideration took place for residential property from 4 December 2014, and for non-residential property from 16 March 2016, in certain circumstances the taxpayer could elect for the new rules not to apply.
3. **With effect from 22 November 2017, residential property purchases by first-time buyers attract a nil rate of SDLT for purchase consideration up to £300,000. Purchase consideration over £300,000 up to and including £500,000 attracts 5% SDLT. Where the purchase consideration is in excess of £500,000, no relief is due and standard rates above apply.**
4. Rates apply to the amount of NPV in the slice, not the whole value.
5. With effect from 19 July 2011, where a purchaser (or a connected person) of residential property acquires more than one dwelling from the same vendor (or a connected person) and makes a claim, the rate of SDLT will be calculated based on the mean consideration for each property, subject to a minimum rate of 1%. For leases granted on or after 26 March 2015 relief may be claimed in respect of superior interests in dwellings subject to a long lease, where the transaction is the lease element of a "lease and leaseback" funding arrangement entered into by a housing association or other qualifying body.
6. From 21 March 2012 a 15% rate applies to certain non-natural persons (ie companies, partnerships with at least one company member, and collective investment schemes) acquiring a residential property where consideration exceeds a specified threshold, which is £500,000 from 20 March 2014. Relief is available for certain acquisitions so that the charge is at the lower percentage. See p 64 for the annual tax on enveloped dwellings and capital gains tax charge which also apply to such properties.
7. From 1 April 2016 (for contracts exchanged after 25 November 2015) a higher rate applies broadly to purchases of additional residential property by individuals, and to purchases of residential property by companies and trusts other than bare trusts and interest in possession trusts. It does not apply to purchases of property under £40,000 or to purchases of caravans, mobile homes and houseboats. If there is a period of overlap in ownership of a main residence, a refund of the higher rate can be obtained if the previous main residence is sold within 36 months following the purchase of the new. Relief is available in certain circumstances when someone gets divorced, exchanges a property with a spouse, adds to an existing interest in their main residence or is a child whose affairs are subject to the Court of Protection.

Exemptions and reliefs

No SDLT (or, where relevant, stamp duty) is chargeable on:
(1) transfers to charities for use for charitable purposes.
(2) transfers to bodies established for national purposes.
(3) gifts inter vivos.
(4) certain transfers on divorce or dissolution of a civil partnership.
(5) transfers of property to beneficiaries under a will or an intestacy.
(6) land transfers within groups of companies.
(7) land transferred in exchange for shares on company reconstruction and acquisitions.
(8) certain transfers to or leases granted by registered providers of social housing. (Although the relief is repealed for the old stamp duty rules for instruments executed on or after 6 April 2013, it still applies to stamp duty land tax).
(9) sale and leaseback and lease and leaseback arrangements involving commercial and residential property.
(10) certain acquisitions of residential property by house building companies or property traders from personal representatives, or when people move into a new dwelling or a chain of transactions break down, or by employers involving employee relocations.
(11) from 22 November 2017 purchases of residential property by first-time buyers for consideration of not more than £500,000 (see p 140).
(12) demutualisation of building societies and insurance companies.
(13) incorporation of limited liability partnerships.
(14) transfers of land between public bodies under a statutory reorganisation.
(15) compulsory purchase of land facilitating redevelopment.

(16) land transactions in compliance with planning obligations enforceable against the vendor and made within five years of the obligation where the purchaser is one of certain public authorities.

(17) transfers by a local constituency association in consequence of a reorganisation of parliamentary constituencies.

(18) purchases or leases of certain diplomatic or consular premises or headquarters premises of certain international organisations.

(19) from 15 September 2016, transfer of properties into an authorised PAIF or CoACS within an initial period if conditions are met.

(20) from 12 February 2019 certain transfers of securities, property and land from a failed institution to the appointed temporary holding entity under a Bank of England stabilisation power, and on transfers of securities to bondholders following exercise of the bail-in stabilisation power.

Relief from SDLT may also apply on:

(a) right to buy transactions, shared ownership leases and rent to loan transactions.

(b) alternative property finance schemes.

(c) exercise of collective rights by leaseholders.

(d) crofting community right to buy.

(e) certain arrangements relating to land transactions involving public or educational bodies.

(f) acquisitions of interests in land by certain National Health Service bodies.

Land and buildings transaction tax (Scotland)

(Land and Buildings Transaction Tax (Scotland) Act 2013; Land and Buildings Transaction Tax (Amendment) (Scotland) Act 2016; SSI 2015/126; SSI 2017/233; SSI 2018/372; SSI 2020/24)

Land and buildings transaction tax applies in Scotland instead of stamp duty land tax from 1 April 2015.

Land transactions					
Effective date	*Residential property*	Rate[2, 3]	**Effective date**	*Non-residential or mixed property*	Rate[2]
	On band of consideration[1]			On band of consideration[1]	
From 1.4.15	**Up to £145,000[3]**	**Nil**	**From 25.1.19[4]**	**Up to £150,000**	**Nil**
	£145,001–£250,000[3]	**2%**		**£150,001–£250,000**	**1%**
	£250,001–£325,000	**5%**		**£250,001 or more**	**5%**
	£325,001–£750,000	**10%**			
	£750,001 or more	**12%**			
From 1.4.15	Up to £145,000[3]	Nil	1.4.15–24.1.19	Up to £150,000	Nil
	£145,001–£250,000[3]	2%		£150,001–£350,000	3%
	£250,001–£325,000	5%		£350,001 or more	4.5%
	£325,001–£750,000	10%			
	£750,001 or more	12%			

Lease rentals

LBTT is applied to non-residential leases. Residential leases are generally exempt from LBTT with the exception of certain long leases which are qualifying leases. Before 7 February 2020, where a lease is chargeable the amount of tax payable is 1% of the amount of net present value (NPV) of the rent above £150,000. For transactions with an effective date on or after 7 February 2020, where contracts were entered into on or after that date and subject to some exceptions for further returns, the rate is 1% of the NPV between £150,000 and £2m, and 2% above £2m[5]. Licences to occupy property are exempt interests, except licences that are of a description prescribed under Land and Buildings Transaction Tax (Scotland) Act 2013 s 53(1).

Premiums

The same tax is payable for a premium granted as for a land transaction, subject to the exemption for residential leases other than qualifying leases (see above). Special rules apply to a premium in respect of non-residential property where the rent exceeds £1,000 a year.

[1] Rates are charged on the portion of the consideration that falls within each rate band.

[2] For land transactions with an effective date on or after 25 January 2019 (other than where contracts were entered into before 12 December 2018), an additional amount of LBTT of 4% (previously 3% for transactions with an effective date on or after 1 April 2016 where contracts were entered into after 27 January 2016) of the consideration applies to transactions which consist of or include the acquisition of an additional dwelling by individuals or which consist of or include the acquisition of a dwelling by certain businesses, companies and trusts. It does not apply to purchases of property under £40,000. If there is a period of overlap in ownership of a main residence, a refund of the higher rate can be obtained if the previous main residence is sold within 18 months following the purchase of the new. Relief is available in

certain circumstances when two buyers jointly buy a new dwelling and previously lived together as a married couple, civil partners or cohabitants in a dwelling owned by either one of them solely.

[3] **With effect for contracts entered into after 8 February 2018, where the effective date of the transaction is after 29 June 2018 relief for first-time buyers applies a nil rate to the first £175,000 of purchase consideration resulting in first-time buyers benefiting from the relief up to a maximum of £600.**

[4] Revised rates apply only to contracts entered into from 12 December 2018.

[5] Rates apply to the amount of NPV in the slice, not the whole value.

Exemptions and reliefs

There are various exemptions and reliefs from LBTT, see 'LBTT3010 - Tax Reliefs' and 'LBTT3002 - Exempt Transactions' at www.revenue.scot.

Land transaction tax (Wales)

(Land Transaction Tax and Anti-avoidance of Devolved Taxes (Wales) Act 2017; SI 2017/953; SI 2018/126)
Land transaction tax applies in Wales instead of stamp duty land tax from 1 April 2018.

Land transactions					
Effective date	*Residential property*	Rate	*Higher rate applying to certain purchases*[2]	*Non-residential or mixed property*	Rate
	On band of consideration[1]			On band of consideration[1]	
From 1.4.18	Up to £180,000	Nil	3%	Up to £150,000	Nil
	£180,001–£250,000	3.5%	6.5%	£150,001–£250,000	1%
	£250,001–£400,000	5%	8%	£250,001–£1,000,000	5%
	£400,001–£750,000	7.5%	10.5%	£1,000,001 or more	6%
	£750,001–£1,500,000	10%	13%		
	£1,500,001 or more	12%	15%		

Lease rentals
LTT is applied to non-residential leases and the amount of tax payable is 1% of the amount of net present value (NPV) of the rent between £150,000 and £2m, and 2% above £2m[3].

Premiums
The same tax is payable for a premium granted as for a land transaction. Special rules apply to a premium in respect of non-residential property where the rent exceeds £9,000 a year.

[1] Rates are charged on the portion of the consideration that falls within each rate band.

[2] A higher rate applies broadly to purchases of additional residential property by individuals, and to purchases of residential property by companies and trusts other than bare trusts and interest in possession trusts. It does not apply to purchases of property under £40,000. If there is a period of overlap in ownership of a main residence, a refund of the higher rate can be obtained if the previous main residence is sold within 36 months following the purchase of the new. Relief is also available where immediately before the purchase the buyer's spouse or civil partner owns a major interest in the same dwelling and that dwelling will be the buyer's only or main residence immediately before and after the purchase.

[3] Rates apply to the amount of NPV in the slice, not the whole value.

Exemptions and reliefs

There are various exemptions and reliefs from LTT, see Land Transaction Tax and Anti-avoidance of Devolved Taxes (Wales) Act 2017 Schs 3, 9–22.

Stamp duty

(FA 1986 Part III; FA 1999 Sch 13)

Shares, etc	
Shares put into depository receipts or put into duty free clearance systems[5]	1.5%
Purchase of own shares by company	0.5%
Transfers of stock or marketable securities	0.5%
Takeovers, mergers, demergers, schemes of reconstruction and amalgamation (except where no real change of ownership)	0.5%

[1] Stamp duty is rounded to the next multiple of £5.

2   For instruments executed after 11 March 2008 stamp duty is not chargeable where the amount or value of the consideration is less than £1,000.
3   From April 2014 transfers of interests in exchange traded funds will be exempt from stamp duty and stamp duty reserve tax.
4   From 28 April 2014 no stamp duty or stamp duty reserve tax is due on trades in 'recognised growth markets' such as the Alternative Investment Market and the ISDX Growth Market.
5   For options entered into on or after 25 November 2015 and exercised on or after 16 March 2016, where UK securities are deposited with a depositary receipt issuer or clearance service following the exercise of an option, the transfer will be chargeable to stamp duty or stamp duty reserve tax (SDRT) at 1.5% of the higher of the market value or the option strike price at the date the instrument is executed (for stamp duty) or the date of transfer (for SDRT).

Fixed duties

Instruments affecting land transactions	£5

From 13 March 2008 fixed duties are generally abolished other than as above. The £5 rate applies to instruments effected from 1 October 1999.

Stamp Duty Reserve Tax (SDRT)

(FA 1986 Part IV)

Agreements to transfer chargeable securities for money or money's worth (eg renounceable letters of allotment)[1]	0.5%
Chargeable securities put into a clearance service[2] or converted into depositary receipts where the transfer is not an integral part of an issue of share capital[4,7]	1.5%
Dealings of units in unit trusts and shares in open-ended investment companies before 30 March 2014[3]	0.5%
Transfers of foreign currency bearer shares and agreements to transfer sterling or foreign currency convertible or equity-related loan stock issued by UK companies	0.5%

1   If the transaction is completed by a duly stamped instrument within six years from the date on which the charge is imposed, the SDRT will be cancelled or repaid.
2   Where the operator of a clearance service elects to collect and account for SDRT on the normal rate of 0.5% on dealing within the system the higher SDRT charge of 1.5% does not apply.
3   From 6 April 2001 transfers of units in a unit trust and surrenders of shares in open-ended investment companies are exempt when held within individual pension accounts. From 30 March 2014 the exemption applies to all transfers of units in a unit trust and all surrenders of shares in open-ended investment companies, although the charge will remain on non pro-rata in specie redemptions.
4   Following the cases of HSBC Holdings plc and the Bank of New York Mellon Corporation v HMRC and HSBC Holdings plc and Vidacos Nominees Limited v Commissioners for HMRC, SDRT of 1.5% is no longer applicable on issues of UK shares to depositary receipt issuers and clearance services. Claims for repayment of SDRT may be made.
5   From April 2014 transfers of interests in exchange traded funds will be exempt from stamp duty and stamp duty reserve tax.
6   From 28 April 2014 no stamp duty or stamp duty reserve tax is due on trades in 'recognised growth markets' such as the Alternative Investment Market and the ISDX Growth Market.
7   For options entered into on or after 25 November 2015 and exercised on or after 16 March 2016, where UK securities are deposited with a depositary receipt issuer or clearance service following the exercise of an option, the transfer will be chargeable to stamp duty or stamp duty reserve tax (SDRT) at 1.5% of the higher of the market value or the option strike price at the date the instrument is executed (for stamp duty) or the date of transfer (for SDRT).

Interest on unpaid tax

Stamp duty land tax. *From 1 March 2019*: Interest runs from the end of 14 days (previously 30 days) after the effective date of transaction (normally completion), or the date of a disqualifying event, until the tax is paid. In the case of a deferred payment, interest runs from the date the payment is due until the tax is paid. A penalty carries interest from the date determined until the date of payment.

Stamp duty. *For instruments executed from 1 October 1999*: Interest runs from the end of 30 days after the date the instrument is executed until the tax is paid. Amounts less than £25 are not charged.

Stamp duty reserve tax. *From 1 January 2015*: The harmonised interest regime applies, see p 4.

Rates: see pp 4, 5.

Land and buildings transaction tax (Scotland). *From 1 April 2015*: Interest runs broadly from the filing date of the return and is charged at the same rate as under the harmonised interest regime but paid to Revenue Scotland — see p 4.

Land transaction tax (Wales). *From 1 April 2018*: Interest runs broadly from the filing date of the return and is charged at the same rate as under the harmonised interest regime but paid to the Welsh Revenue Authority — see p 4.

Repayment supplement / Interest on overpaid tax

Stamp duty land tax. *From 26 September 2005*: Interest is added to repayments of overpaid stamp duty land tax and runs from the date tax was paid or an amount was lodged with HMRC, or the date a penalty was made, to the date the order for repayment is issued.

Stamp duty. *For instruments executed from 1 October 1999*: Interest is added to repayments of overpaid stamp duty and runs from 30 days after the date the instrument is executed or the date of payment if later. Amounts less than £25 are not paid.

Stamp duty reserve tax. *From 1 January 2015*: The harmonised interest regime applies, see p 4.

Rates: see pp 4, 5.

Land and buildings transaction tax (Scotland). *From 1 April 2015*: Interest runs from the date the tax, penalty or interest was paid or an amount was lodged with Revenue Scotland, to the date repayment is made. It is paid by Revenue Scotland and up to 1 August 2018 it was paid at the same rate as under the harmonised interest regime — see p 4. From 2 August 2018 it is paid at 0.75%.

Land transaction tax (Wales). *From 1 April 2018*: Interest runs from the date the tax, penalty or interest was paid, to the date repayment is made. It is paid by the Welsh Revenue Authority and up to 1 August 2018 it was paid at the same rate as under the harmonised interest regime — see p 4. From 2 August 2018 it is paid at 0.75%.

Stamp tax penalties

Offence	Penalty
Stamp duty land tax and stamp duty reserve tax	
Inaccuracy in return or other document (FA 2007 Sch 24).	See **Penalties — modernised penalty regime** on p 10
Inaccuracy in return or other document as a result of third party providing incorrect (or withholding) information (FA 2007 Sch 24).	See **Penalties — modernised penalty regime** on p 10
Failure to notify HMRC of an error in an assessment (within 30 days) (FA 2007 Sch 24).	See **Penalties — modernised penalty regime** on p 11
Failure to comply with HMRC investigatory powers with effect from 1 April 2010 (FA 2008 Sch 36).	(a) Initial penalty of £300; (b) if failure/obstruction continues, a further penalty of up to £60 per day; (c) if failure/obstruction continues after penalty under (a) imposed, a tax-related amount determined by the Upper Tribunal.
Provision of inaccurate information or document when complying with an information notice with effect from 1 April 2010 (FA 2008 Sch 36).	Up to £3,000 per inaccuracy.
Stamp duty reserve tax – for charges due and payable from 1 January 2015	
Failure to make returns on time (FA 2009 Sch 55)	See **Penalties — modernised penalty regime** on p 12
Failure to make payments on time (FA 2009 Sch 56)	See **Penalties — modernised penalty regime** on p 12
Stamp duty – for instruments executed from 1 October 1999	
Failure to present instrument for stamping within 30 days after execution (or the day in which it is first received in the UK if executed outside the UK) (Stamp Act 1891 s 15B; SI 1999/2537). (Extended to instruments executed from 24 July 2002 for transfers of UK land and buildings, wherever executed (FA 2002 s 114)). From 1 October 2014 HMRC guidance to penalty amounts applies.	Documents submitted late for stamping **on or after 1 October 2014**: If presented within one year after the end of the 30-day period: 10% of the unpaid duty capped at £300. If presented more than one year after the end of the 30-day period but not more than two years after: 20% of the amount of unpaid duty. If presented more than two years after the end of the 30-day period: 30% of the unpaid duty. For delays of one year or more, penalty rate may be higher if there is evidence that the failure to submit documents was deliberate. Before 1 October 2014: If presented within one year after the end of the 30-day period: the lower of £300 or the amount of the unpaid duty. If presented more than one year after the end of the 30-day period: the greater of £300 or the amount of unpaid duty.
Stamp duty land tax – contracts completed after 30 November 2003	
Failure to deliver a land transaction return by the filing date (FA 2003 Sch 10 paras 3, 4).	£100 if return delivered within three months of filing date, otherwise £200. If not delivered within 12 months, penalty up to amount of tax chargeable.
Failure to comply with notice to deliver return within specified period (FA 2003 Sch 10 para 5).	Up to £60 for each day on which the failure continues after notification.
Failure to keep and preserve records under FA 2003 Sch 10 para 9 or Sch 11 para 4 (FA 2003 Sch 10 para 11, Sch 11 para 6).	Up to £3,000 unless the information is provided by other documentary evidence.
Failure (From 1 August 2005) to disclose certain SDLT proposals or arrangements (TMA 1970 s 98C; SI 2005/1868; SI 2005/1869; SI 2010/2743).	(a) Up to £600 per day during 'initial period' (but tribunal can determine a higher penalty up to £1 million); (b) further penalty up to £600 per day while failure continues. Both the initial penalty in (a) above and the secondary penalty in (b) above can be increased up to £5,000 per day that failure continues from 10 days after the order is made.
Failure (From 1 August 2005) to provide prescribed information relating to disclosure certain SDLT proposals or arrangements (TMA 1970 s 98C; SI 2005/1868; SI 2005/1869; SI 2010/2743).	(a) Initial penalty up to £5,000; (b) further penalty up to £600 per day while failure continues. This can be increased up to £5,000 per day after a tribunal has issued a disclosure order.

Offence	Penalty
Failure (From 1 August 2005) to provide scheme reference number relating to certain SDLT proposals or arrangements (TMA 1970 s 98C; SI 2005/1868; SI 2005/1869; SI 2010/2743);	(a) Penalty of £100 in respect of each scheme to which the failure relates;
for second failure, occurring within three years from the date on which the first failure began;	(b) penalty of £500 in respect of each scheme to which the failure relates;
for subsequent failures, occurring within three years from the date on which the previous failure began.	(c) penalty of £1,000 in respect of each scheme to which the failure relates.
Land and buildings transaction tax (Scotland) from 1 April 2015	
Inaccuracy in return or document (RSTPA 2014 ss 182, 183)	Careless inaccuracy — maximum 30% of tax lost Deliberate inaccuracy — maximum 100% of tax lost
Failure to make returns on time (RSTPA 2014 ss 160–163)	The penalty rates applying are as for stamp duty reserve tax **Penalties — modernised penalty regime** on p 12, though reductions for disclosure differ. Penalties are payable to Revenue Scotland.
Failure to make payments on time (RSTPA 2014 s 169)	The penalty rates applying are as for stamp duty reserve tax **Penalties — modernised penalty regime** on p 13, though for some types of payment penalty is due as soon as tax is late. Penalties are payable to Revenue Scotland.
Land transaction tax (Wales) from 1 April 2018	
Inaccuracy in return or document (TCMWA 2016 s 130)	Careless inaccuracy — 30% of tax lost Deliberate inaccuracy — 100% of tax lost
Failure to make returns on time (TCMWA 2016 ss 118–121)	Initial penalty £100 Failure continues for more than 6 months — greater of 5% of the tax due and £300 12 months late and return deliberately withheld — greater of £300 or up to 95% of tax due 12 months late and return not deliberately withheld — greater of 5% of the tax due and £300 Reductions for disclosure Penalties are payable to the Welsh Revenue Authority.
Failure to make payments on time (TCMWA 2016 s 122)	5% of unpaid tax Further 5% of any outstanding amount 6 months after return filing date Further 5% of any outstanding amount 12 months after return filing date Reductions for disclosure Penalties are payable to the Welsh Revenue Authority.

Value added tax

Value added tax rates

(VATA 1994 s 2)

	From 4.1.11	
	Rate	VAT fraction
Standard rate	**20%**	**1/6**
Reduced rate (see p 152)	**5.0%**	**1/21**
Flat-rate scheme for farmers	**4.0%**[1]	

[1]   Flat rate addition to sale price. It is proposed from 1 January 2021 to have entry and exit thresholds for the scheme of £150,000 and £230,000 respectively. These thresholds are the same as those applying to the flat-rate scheme for small businesses on p 150.

[2]   The first 10p of the standard VAT rate and the first 2.5p of the reduced VAT rate raised in Scotland will be assigned to the Scottish Parliament from a date to be determined. A methodology for calculating Scottish VAT receipts has been developed and is in a transitional phase during which Scottish VAT is forecast and calculated, but with no impact on the Scottish budget.

Registration limits

UK taxable supplies

(VATA 1994 Sch 1 para 1, Sch 1A para 1)

A person who is UK-established[3] and makes taxable supplies is liable to be registered:
  (a)   at the end of any month, or
  (b)   at any time, if:

	(a) turnover in the past year[1] (b) turnover in the next 30 days[2] exceeds:	Unless, in the case of (a), turnover for next year not expected to exceed:
1.4.17 onwards[4]	**£85,000**	**£83,000**
1.4.16–31.3.17	£83,000	£81,000
1.4.15–31.3.16	£82,000	£80,000

[1]   The value of taxable supplies in the year then ending.
[2]   If there are reasonable grounds for believing the value of taxable supplies will exceed limit.
[3]   Non-UK established businesses are required to register for VAT regardless of the value of taxable supplies made in the UK.
[4]   The VAT limit is proposed to be unchanged before 1 April 2022.

Supplies from other EC countries ('distance selling')

(VATA 1994 Sch 2)

A business person in another EC country not registered or liable to be registered in the UK is liable to be registered on any day if, in the period beginning with 1 January in that year, the value of supplies by that person to non-taxable persons in the UK exceeds:

1.1.93 onwards	£70,000

[1]   The distance selling rules may be repealed after the end of the Brexit implementation period (subject to the terms of the future relationship). EU-wide changes are also expected to apply from 1 January 2021.

Acquisitions from other EC countries

(VATA 1994 Sch 3)

A person not registered or liable to be registered under the above rules is liable to be registered:

    (a)   at the end of any month if, in the period beginning with 1 January in that year, the value of taxable goods acquired by that person for business purposes (or for non-business purposes if a public body, charity, club, etc) from suppliers in other EC countries exceeds the following limits; or

    (b)   at any time, if there are reasonable grounds for believing the value of such acquisitions in the next 30 days will exceed the following limits:

1.4.17 onwards[1]	**£85,000**
1.4.16–31.3.17	£83,000
1.4.15–31.3.16	£82,000

[1]   The VAT limit is proposed to be unchanged before 1 April 2022. It is anticipated that 'acquisitions' may be broadly abolished at the end of the Brexit implementation period (subject to the terms of the future relationship).

Deregistration limits

UK taxable supplies

(VATA 1994 Sch 1 para 4)

A registered taxable person who is UK-established[1] ceases to be liable to be registered if, at any time, HMRC are satisfied that the value of taxable supplies in the year then beginning will not exceed the limit below, unless the reason for not exceeding the limit during that year is that the person will cease making taxable supplies or suspend making taxable supplies for 30 days or more:

1.4.17 onwards[2]	£83,000
1.4.16–31.3.17	£81,000
1.4.15–31.3.16	£80,000

[1]   Non-UK established businesses are required to register for VAT regardless of the value of taxable supplies made in the UK.
[2]   The VAT limit is proposed to be unchanged before 1 April 2022.

Supplies from other EC countries ('distance selling')

(VATA 1994 Sch 2)

A person registered under these provisions ceases to be liable to be registered if, at any time:
    (a)   relevant supplies in year ended 31 December last before that time did not exceed following limit; and
    (b)   HMRC are satisfied that value of relevant supplies in year immediately following that year will not exceed following limit:

1.1.93 onwards	£70,000

[1]   The distance selling rules may be repealed after the end of the Brexit implementation period (subject to the terms of the future relationship). EU-wide changes are also expected to apply from 1 January 2021.

Acquisitions from other EC countries

(VATA 1994 Sch 3)

A person registered under these provisions ceases to be liable to be registered if, at any time:
    (a)   relevant acquisitions in year ended 31 December last before that time did not exceed the following limits; and
    (b)   HMRC are satisfied that value of relevant acquisitions in year immediately following that year will not exceed the following limits:

1.4.17 onwards[1]	£85,000
1.4.16–31.3.17	£83,000
1.4.15–31.3.16	£82,000

[1]   The VAT limit is proposed to be unchanged before 1 April 2022. It is anticipated that 'acquisitions' may be broadly abolished at the end of the Brexit implementation period (subject to the terms of the future relationship).

Annual accounting scheme

(SI 1995/2518 regs 49–55)

A business may, subject to conditions, complete one VAT return a year. Quarterly or monthly interim payments to be made.

	Can join if taxable supplies in next year not expected to exceed:	Must leave at end of accounting year if taxable supplies exceeded:
1.4.06 onwards	£1,350,000	£1,600,000

Cash accounting scheme

(SI 1995/2518 regs 56–65)

A business may, subject to conditions, account for and pay VAT on the basis of cash paid and received. It can join the scheme at any time as follows.

	Can join if taxable supplies in next year not expected to exceed:	Must leave at end of VAT period if taxable supplies in previous year exceed:	Unless turnover for next year not expected to exceed:
1.4.07 onwards	£1,350,000	£1,600,000	£1,350,000

Flat-rate scheme for small businesses

(SI 1995/2518 regs 55A–55V)

A business which expects its taxable supplies in the next year to be no more than £150,000 can opt to join a flat-rate scheme. The appropriate percentage below is applied to total turnover generated, including exempt income, to calculate net VAT due. Once in the scheme a business may continue to use it until its total business income exceeds £230,000, and if income does exceed this limit, the business can still remain in the scheme if the income in the following year is estimated not to exceed £191,500.

From 1 April 2017 a 16.5% rate applies to a 'limited cost trader', that is a trader whose VAT-inclusive expenditure on goods used for business purposes (excluding capital expenditure, food and drink for consumption by the business or its employees, and certain vehicles, vehicle parts and fuel) is less than 2% of turnover, or greater than 2% of turnover but less than £1,000 per year. Any trader which is not a limited cost trader continues to use the flat rate based on the categories of business detailed below.

Category of business	Appropriate %
	From 4.1.11
Accountancy or book-keeping	14.5
Advertising	11
Agricultural services	11
Any other activity not listed elsewhere	12
Architect, civil and structural engineer or surveyor	14.5
Boarding or care of animals	12
Business services that are not listed elsewhere	12
Catering services, including restaurants and takeaways	12.5
Computer and IT consultancy or data processing	14.5
Computer repair services	10.5
Entertainment or journalism	12.5
Estate agency and property management services	12
Farming or agriculture that is not listed elsewhere	6.5
Film, radio, television or video production	13
Financial services	13.5
Forestry or fishing	10.5
General building or construction services[1]	9.5
Hairdressing or other beauty treatment services	13
Hiring or renting goods	9.5
Hotel or accommodation	10.5
Investigation or security	12
Labour-only building or construction services[1]	14.5
Laundry or dry-cleaning services	12
Lawyer or legal services	14.5
Library, archive, museum or other cultural activity	9.5
Management consultancy	14
Manufacturing fabricated metal products	10.5
Manufacturing food	9
Manufacturing that is not listed elsewhere	9.5
Manufacturing yarn, textiles or clothing	9

Category of business	Appropriate %
	From 4.1.11
Membership organisation	8
Mining or quarrying	10
Packaging	9
Photography	11
Post Offices	5
Printing	8.5
Publishing	11
Pubs	6.5
Real estate activity not listed elsewhere	14
Repairing personal or household goods	10
Repairing vehicles	8.5
Retailing food, confectionery, tobacco, newspapers or children's clothing	4
Retailing pharmaceuticals, medical goods, cosmetics or toiletries	8
Retailing that is not listed elsewhere	7.5
Retailing vehicles or fuel	6.5
Secretarial services	13
Social work	11
Sport or recreation	8.5
Transport or storage, couriers, freight, removals and taxis	10
Travel agency	10.5
Veterinary medicine	11
Wholesaling agricultural products	8
Wholesaling food	7.5
Wholesaling that is not listed elsewhere	8.5

[1] That is, services where value of materials supplied is less than 10% of turnover of such services; any other services are 'general building or construction services'.

Partial exemption

SEE TOLLEY'S TAX COMPUTATIONS **408.1, 408.2**.

(SI 1995/2518 regs 106–107)

A registered person who makes taxable and exempt supplies is partly exempt and may not be able to deduct (or reclaim) all his input tax. Where, however, input tax attributable to exempt supplies in a prescribed accounting period or tax year is within the de minimis limits below, all such input tax is attributable to taxable supplies and recoverable (subject to the normal rules).

De minimis limits	£625 per month on average and 50% of all input tax for the period concerned

Capital goods scheme

See Tolley's Tax Computations 402.1.
(SI 1995/2518 regs 112–116)

Input tax adjustment following change in taxable use of capital goods

Item	Value	Adjustment period
Computer equipment	£50,000 or more	Five years
Ships, boats or other vessels[1]	£50,000 or more	Five years
Aircraft[1]	£50,000 or more	Five years
Land and buildings	£250,000 or more[2]	Ten years (for adjustment periods commenced before 1 January 2011, five years where interest had less than ten years to run on acquisition)

[1] Applies for goods acquired on or after 1 January 2011.
[2] Figure reduced to £1 where owner ('O') of item or a person to whom O has granted an interest in that item:
   (a) uses that item to make a grant falling within VATA 1994 Sch 9 Group 1 Item 1(ka) (self-storage facilities excluded from exemption);
   (b) decides, no later than 31 March 2013, to treat the item as a capital item; and
   (c) makes a written record to that effect, specifying the date of the decision.

Adjustment formula where adjustment period begins on or after 1 January 2011

$$\frac{\text{Total VAT on item}}{\text{Length of adjustment period}} \times \text{adjustment percentage}$$

The adjustment percentage is the percentage change in the extent to which the item is used (or treated as used) in making taxable supplies between the first interval in the adjustment period and a subsequent interval. (The first interval generally ends on the last day of the tax year in which the input tax was incurred.) For goods acquired on or after 1.1.11 total VAT includes any non-business VAT and the extent to which a capital item is used for business purposes must be determined when ascertaining taxable use for each subsequent interval.

Zero-rated supplies

A zero-rated supply is a taxable supply, but the rate of tax is nil (VATA 1994 Sch 8).

Group 1 – Food
Group 2 – Sewerage services and water
Group 3 – Books etc including e-publications from 1 May 2020
Group 4 – Talking books for the blind and disabled and wireless sets for the blind
Group 5 – Construction of buildings etc
Group 6 – Protected buildings
Group 7 – International services
Group 8 – Transport
Group 9 – Caravans and houseboats
Group 10 – Gold
Group 11 – Bank notes
Group 12 – Drugs, medicines, aids for the disabled etc
Group 13 – Imports, exports etc
Group 15 – Charities etc
Group 16 – Clothing and footwear
Group 18 – European Research Infrastructure Consortia
Group 19 – Women's sanitary products (from 1 January 2021)

Reduced rate supplies

(VATA 1994 Sch 7A)

Group 1 – Domestic fuel and power
Group 2 – Installation of energy-saving materials
Group 3 – Grant-funded installation of heating equipment or security goods or connection of a gas supply
Group 4 – Women's sanitary products (to be reduced to zero-rated from 1 January 2021)
Group 5 – Children's car seats and bases
Group 6 – Residential conversions
Group 7 – Residential renovations and alterations
Group 8 – Contraceptive products
Group 9 – Welfare advice or information
Group 10 – Installation of mobility aids for the elderly
Group 11 – Smoking cessation products
Group 12 – Caravans
Group 13 – Cable-suspended transport systems

Exempt supplies

(VATA 1994 Sch 9)

Group 1 – Land

Group 2 – Insurance

Group 3 – Postal services

Group 4 – Betting, gaming, dutiable machine games and lotteries

Group 5 – Finance

Group 6 – Education

Group 7 – Health and welfare

Group 8 – Burial and cremation

Group 9 – Subscriptions to trade unions, professional and other public interest bodies

Group 10 – Sport, sports competitions and physical education

Group 11 – Works of art etc

Group 12 – Fund-raising events by charities and other qualifying bodies

Group 13 – Cultural services etc

Group 14 – Supplies of goods where input tax cannot be recovered

Group 15 – Investment gold

Group 16 – Supplies of services by groups involving cost sharing

EC Sales Lists

(SI 1995/2518 regs 2, 21–23)

All VAT-registered businesses in the UK must provide HMRC with details of goods and services supplied to a VAT-registered customer in another EU country. The requirement for returns is as follows:

Supplies of		Frequency
Goods	Supplies of goods are in excess of £35,000 in any of the current or last four quarters	Monthly
Goods	Supplies of goods are below £35,000 per quarter in the current and previous four quarters	Quarterly on 31 March, 30 June, 30 September and 31 December
Services supplied to a business where the place of supply is where the customer belongs		Quarterly as above
Goods and services where a business is required to submit monthly lists for goods		Monthly for all supplies, or monthly for goods and quarterly for services
Goods or services supplied by a business completing annual VAT returns	Total annual taxable turnover does not exceed £145,000; annual value of supplies to other EU countries not more than £11,000 (and do not include *New Means of Transport*)	On application — annual on agreed due date
Goods only supplied	Total annual taxable turnover does not exceed the VAT registration threshold plus £25,500; annual value of supplies to other EU countries not more than £11,000 (and do not include *New Means of Transport*)	On application — annual in simple format on agreed due date

The due date for returns is 21 days after the end of the period if submitted online and 14 days after the end of the period if submitted on paper.

Country	Code
Austria[10]	AT
Belgium	BE
Bulgaria	BG
Croatia	HR
Cyprus[9]	CY
Czech Republic	CZ
Denmark[2]	DK
Estonia	EE
Finland[3]	FI
France[4]	FR
Germany[5]	DE
Greece[11]	EL
Hungary	HU
Ireland	IE
Italy[6]	IT
Latvia	LV
Lithuania	LT
Luxembourg	LU
Malta	MT
Netherlands[12]	NL
Poland	PL
Portugal[7]	PT
Romania	RO
Slovak Republic	SK
Slovenia	SI
Spain[8]	ES
Sweden	SE

[1] Countries not listed in the table above are not part of the EU VAT area and so sales to those countries should not be included on the EC sales list. The following are not part of the EU VAT area; Andorra, The Channel Islands, Gibraltar, Mount Athos, San Marino, and Vatican City. The UK and the Isle of Man are part of the EU VAT area, but sales to these should not be included on the list.

[2] Does not include the Faroe Islands and Greenland.

[3] Does not include Aland Islands.

[4] Includes Monaco; excludes Martinique, Guadeloupe, Reunion, St Pierre & Miquelon, and French Guiana.

[5] Does not include Busingen and Isle of Heligoland.

[6] Does not include communes of Livigno and Campione d'Italia and the Italian waters of Lake Lugano.

7   Includes the Azores and Madeira.
8   Includes the Balearic Islands but excludes Ceuta, Melilla, and the Canary Islands.
9   Includes British sovereign base areas of Akrotiri and Dhekelia, but excludes those areas in United Nations buffer zone and to the north of that where the Republic of Cyprus does not have effective control.
10   Includes Jungholz and Mittelberg.
11   Excludes Mount Athos.
12   Excludes Antilles (now Curaçao, Sint Maarten and BES Islands).
13   After the end of the Brexit implementation period it is expected that there will no longer be a requirement to submit EC Sales Lists in the UK (subject to the terms of the future relationship).

Intrastat

(SI 1992/2790)

All VAT-registered businesses in the UK must complete boxes 8 and 9 on the VAT return showing the total value of goods supplied to and acquired from EU member states respectively. Businesses with a total value of such supplies (dispatches) or acquisitions (arrivals) exceeding a threshold must make supplementary declarations containing further information each month. Thresholds are set for each calendar year and recent thresholds are shown below. If a person's dispatches or arrivals in the previous calendar year exceeded the current year's threshold, supplementary declarations must be made for the full current year. If the cumulative total of dispatches or arrivals in a year exceeds that calendar year's threshold, supplementary declarations must be made for the rest of the year, starting in the month in which the threshold is exceeded. Additional delivery terms information must be provided on the supplementary declaration only if the annual value of arrivals or dispatches exceeds the delivery terms threshold, and the information must be submitted from the start of the next calendar year. If the delivery terms threshold for arrivals is exceeded, but not that for dispatches, delivery terms must be provided for arrivals only, and vice versa. Declarations must be submitted electronically and will be due 21 days after the end of the month in which there is EU trade to declare. Businesses unable to submit the declaration on 21 April 2020 as a result of the COVID–19 (coronavirus) pandemic could email intrastatenquiries@hmrc.gov.uk.

Year	Supplies (dispatches) threshold per calendar year	Acquisitions (arrivals) threshold per calendar year	Delivery terms threshold per calendar year
From 1.1.15	£250,000	£1,500,000	£24,000,000

Some of the EU country codes and the areas included for intrastat purposes differ from those used for EC sales list purposes. The intrastat codes are as follows.

Country	Code
Austria	AT
Belgium	BE
Bulgaria	BG
Croatia	HR
Cyprus[9]	CY
Czech Republic	CZ
Denmark[2]	DK
Estonia	EE
Finland[3]	FI
France[4]	FR
Germany[5]	DE
Greece[10]	GR
Hungary	HU
Ireland	IE
Italy[6]	IT
Latvia	LV
Lithuania	LT
Luxembourg	LU
Malta	MT
Netherlands	NL
Poland	PL
Portugal[7]	PT
Romania	RO
Slovak Republic	SK
Slovenia	SI
Spain[8]	ES
Sweden	SE
United Kingdom[11]	GB

1   Andorra and Liechtenstein are both outside the customs territory (and therefore the statistical territory) of the EU.
2   Does not include the Faroe Islands.
3   Includes Aland Islands.
4   Includes Monaco, but excludes all French Overseas departments and territories. Martinique, Guadeloupe,

Reunion, Mayotte, and French Guiana are part of the statistical territory of France but because customs documentation is still required for exports to, or imports from, these territories HMRC continue to collect trade statistics from that documentation and it must not be declared on the intrastat.

[5] Includes Isle of Heligoland but excludes Busingen.

[6] Does not include communes of Livigno and Campione d'Italia, the Italian waters of Lake Lugano and the Vatican. Livigno is part of the statistical territory of Italy but because customs documentation is still required for exports to, or imports from, this territory HMRC continue to collect trade statistics from that documentation and it must not be declared on the intrastat.

[7] Includes the Azores and Madeira.

[8] Includes the Balearic Islands but excludes Ceuta, Melilla, and the Canary Islands. The Canary Islands are part of the statistical territory of Spain but because customs documentation is still required for exports to, or imports from, these territories HMRC continue to collect trade statistics from that documentation and it must not be declared on the intrastat.

[9] Includes UK sovereign base areas but excludes Northern Cyprus.

[10] Includes Mount Athos.

[11] Includes the Isle of Man and the Channel Islands but excludes Gibraltar.

[12] After the end of the Brexit implementation period obligations to submit Intrastat returns may be impacted (subject to the terms of the future relationship).

VAT Mini One Stop Shop (VAT MOSS)

(VATA 1994 Sch 4A paras 15, 16; SI 2018/1194; HMRC Brief 46/2014)

From 1 January 2015 the place of supply for business-to-consumer (B2C) supplies of broadcasting, telecommunications and e-services (digital services) is determined by the location of the consumer unless, from 1 January 2019, such annual supplies across the EU are less than €10,000. This applies to all businesses that supply digital services above that threshold to consumers (ie private individuals), whether or not they are registered for UK VAT. Any business supplying digital services above the €10,000 limit to a consumer in another member state therefore has to charge VAT on the supply in that member state and register for VAT in that member state. Supplies of digital services to businesses only (including the self-employed) are not affected by these rules.

To avoid having to register for VAT in every EU member state where digital services are supplied, a business may opt to use the VAT Mini One Stop Shop online service (VAT MOSS). Using the VAT MOSS online service means a business can submit a single calendar quarterly VAT MOSS return and payment covering all its EU digital service supplies. If the business registers for the VAT MOSS online service in the UK, HMRC will send an electronic copy of the appropriate part of the VAT MOSS return, and the related VAT payment, to each relevant member state's tax authority.

After the end of the Brexit implementation period it is unlikely that VAT MOSS (or the digital services threshold) will be available in the UK (subject to the terms of the future relationship).

Car fuel

SEE TOLLEY'S TAX COMPUTATIONS 406.1.

(VATA 1994 ss 56, 57, Schs 4, 6; FA 2013 Sch 38)

Where an employer pays mileage allowances, he may use the advisory fuel rates on p 88 to calculate the input VAT to reclaim on the fuel element. Receipts must still be retained.

VAT-inclusive scale figures can be used to assess VAT due on fuel provided at no cost for private journeys by registered traders or their employees, where the fuel has been provided from business resources. The figures represent the tax-inclusive value of the fuel supplied to each individual and relate to return periods beginning on the dates shown. If the trader or employer opts to use the scale figures he must use them for all supplies of fuel for private use made for no consideration in the prescribed accounting period. The scale charge may also be used as an alternative to accounting for VAT on the required open market value where the fuel is supplied for a consideration below that value.

	12 months £	3 months £	1 month £
From 1 May 2020: CO_2 band			
120 or below	581	144	48
125	870	218	72
130	930	231	76
135	986	246	81
140	1,047	261	87
145	1,103	275	91
150	1,163	290	96
155	1,219	305	101
160	1,279	319	106
165	1,335	334	111
170	1,396	348	115
175	1,452	362	120
180	1,512	377	125
185	1,568	392	130
190	1,628	406	135
195	1,684	421	140
200	1,745	436	144
205	1,801	450	149
210	1,861	464	154
215	1,917	479	159
220	1,977	493	164
225 or above	2,033	508	168

	12 months £	3 months £	1 month £
1 May 2019–30 April 2020: CO_2 band			
120 or below	592	147	49
125	886	222	73
130	947	236	78
135	1,004	250	83
140	1,066	265	87
145	1,123	280	93
150	1,184	296	98
155	1,241	310	103
160	1,303	325	107
165	1,360	340	113
170	1,421	354	117
175	1,478	369	122
180	1,540	384	128
185	1,597	399	132
190	1,658	414	137
195	1,715	429	143
200	1,777	444	147
205	1,834	458	152
210	1,895	473	157
215	1,952	487	162
220	2,014	502	167
225 or above	2,071	517	172

	12 months £	3 months £	1 month £
1 May 2018–30 April 2019: CO_2 band			
120 or below	562	140	46
125	842	210	70
130	900	224	74
135	954	238	79
140	1,013	252	84
145	1,067	266	88
150	1,125	280	93
155	1,179	295	98
160	1,238	309	102
165	1,292	323	107
170	1,350	336	111
175	1,404	351	116
180	1,463	365	121
185	1,517	379	125
190	1,575	393	130
195	1,630	407	135
200	1,688	421	140
205	1,742	436	145
210	1,801	449	149
215	1,855	463	154
220	1,913	477	159
225 or above	1,967	491	163

	12 months £	3 months £	1 month £
1 May 2017–30 April 2018: CO_2 band			
120 or below	563	140	46
125	842	211	70
130	901	224	74
135	955	238	79
140	1,013	252	84
145	1,068	267	88
150	1,126	281	93
155	1,180	295	98
160	1,239	309	102
165	1,293	323	107
170	1,351	337	111
175	1,405	351	116
180	1,464	365	121
185	1,518	379	125
190	1,577	393	131
195	1,631	408	136
200	1,689	422	140
205	1,743	436	145
210	1,802	449	149
215	1,856	463	154
220	1,914	478	159
225 or above	1,969	492	163

	12 months £	3 months £	1 month £
1 May 2016–30 April 2017: CO_2 band			
120 or below	467	116	38
125	699	175	58
130	747	186	61
135	792	197	65
140	841	209	69
145	886	221	73
150	934	233	77
155	979	245	81
160	1,028	256	85
165	1,073	268	89
170	1,121	279	92
175	1,166	291	96
180	1,214	303	101
185	1,259	314	104
190	1,308	326	108
195	1,353	338	112
200	1,401	350	116
205	1,446	362	120
210	1,495	373	123
215	1,540	384	128
220	1,588	396	132
225 or above	1,633	408	135

	12 months £	3 months £	1 month £
1 May 2015–30 April 2016: CO_2 band			
120 or below	536	133	44
125	802	200	66
130	857	213	70
135	909	227	75
140	965	240	80
145	1,016	254	84
150	1,072	267	88
155	1,123	281	93
160	1,179	294	97
165	1,231	308	102
170	1,286	320	106
175	1,338	334	111
180	1,393	347	115
185	1,445	361	119
190	1,501	374	124
195	1,552	388	129
200	1,608	401	133
205	1,660	415	138
210	1,715	428	142
215	1,767	441	146
220	1,822	455	151
225 or above	1,874	468	155

Value added tax interest and penalties

Default interest

(VATA 1994 s 74)

Interest runs on the amount of any VAT assessed (or paid late by voluntary disclosure):
- from the reckonable date (normally the latest date on which a return is required for the period in question);
- until the date of payment (although in practice it runs to the date shown on the notice of assessment or notice of voluntary disclosure if paid within 30 days of that date).

The period of interest cannot commence more than three years before the date of assessment or payment.

The rates of interest are as follows:

Period	Rate
from 7 April 2020	2.60%
30 March 2020–6 April 2020	2.75%
21 August 2018–29 March 2020	3.25%
21 November 2017–20 August 2018	3.00%
23 August 2016–20 November 2017	2.75%
29 September 2009–22 August 2016	3.00%

Note: As a result of the COVID–19 (coronavirus) pandemic businesses are not required to make a VAT payment during the period from 20 March 2020 until 30 June 2020 and will be given until 31 March 2021 to pay any liabilities which have accumulated during the deferral period. Interest and penalties will not be charged on any amounts that have been deferred.

Interest on VAT overpaid in cases of official error

(VATA 1994 s 78)

Where VAT has been overpaid or underclaimed due to an error by HMRC, then on a claim HMRC must pay interest:
- from the date they receive payment (or authorise a repayment) for the return period in question;
- until the date on which they authorise payment of the amount on which interest is due.

This provision does not require HMRC to pay interest on an amount on which repayment supplement is due.

The rates of interest are as follows:

Period	Rate
from 29 September 2009	0.50%

Repayment supplement – VAT

(VATA 1994 s 79)

Where a person is entitled to a repayment the payment due is increased by a supplement of the greater of:
- (i) 5% of that amount; or
- (ii) £50.

The supplement will only be paid if:
- (a) the return or claim is received by HMRC not later than the last day on which it is required to be made;
- (b) HMRC do not issue a written instruction making the refund within the relevant period; and
- (c) the amount shown on the return or claim does not exceed the amount due by more than 5% of that amount or £250, whichever is the greater.

The 'relevant period' is 30 days beginning with the receipt of the return or claim or, if later, the day after the last day of the VAT period to which the return or claim relates.

Penalties and surcharges

Offence	Penalty
Inaccuracy in return or other document (FA 2007 Sch 24)[1].	See **Penalties — modernised penalty regime** on p 10.
Failure to notify obligation to register for VAT, change in supplies made by person exempted from registration, acquisition affecting exemption, acquisition of goods from another member state and unauthorised issue of an invoice (FA 2008 Sch 41).	See **Penalties — modernised penalty regime** on p 10.
Inaccuracy in return or other document as a result of third party providing incorrect (or withholding) information (FA 2007 Sch 24).	See **Penalties — modernised penalty regime** on p 10.
Failure to inform HMRC of an error in an assessment within 30 days of the date of the assessment (FA 2007 Sch 24).	See **Penalties — modernised penalty regime** on p 11.
Failure to comply with HMRC investigatory powers with effect from 1 April 2009 (FA 2008 Sch 36).	(*a*) Initial penalty of £300; (*b*) if failure/obstruction continues, a further penalty of up to £60 per day; (*c*) if failure/obstruction continues after penalty under (*a*) imposed, a tax-related amount determined by the Upper Tribunal.
Provision of inaccurate information or document when complying with an information notice (FA 2008 Sch 36).	Up to £3,000 per inaccuracy.
Failure to submit a return electronically if required to do so by SI 1995/2518 reg 25 for prescribed accounting periods starting on or after 1 April 2012. Before 1 April 2012, failure of a *specified person* to make a *specified return* using an electronic return system for prescribed accounting periods ending on or after 31 March 2011 (SI 1995/2518 reg 25A). 'Specified person' was broadly a person registered for VAT on or after 1 April 2010, or one registered before that date who at 31 December 2009 or any later date has an annual VAT exclusive turnover of £100,000 or more. Penalty will only apply to prescribed accounting periods ending on or after 31 March 2013 where the person is required to make an electronic return only as a result of the removal of the turnover test from 1 April 2012.	Annual VAT exclusive turnover of: £22,800,001 or more — £400 £5,600,001 to £22,800,000 — £300 £100,001 to £5,600,000 — £200 £100,000 or under — £100
Failure to submit return or pay VAT due within time limit (where a return is late but the VAT is paid on time or no VAT is due, a default is recorded but no surcharge arises) (VATA 1994 s 59)[2]. Failure to pay tax due under the payment on account scheme on time (VATA 1994 s 59A).	The greater of £30 and a specified percentage of outstanding VAT for period, depending on number of defaults in surcharge period: first default in period 2%, second default 5%, third default 10%, fourth and further defaults 15%. (Surcharge assessments are not issued for sums of less than £400 unless the rate of the surcharge is 10% or more.) *Proposals to replace with a penalty regime for late submission and late payment have been postponed.*
Issuing incorrect certificate stating that certain supplies fall to be zero-rated or taxed at the reduced rate (VATA 1994 s 62).	Difference between tax actually charged and tax which should have been charged.
Material inaccuracy in EC sales statement (VATA 1994 s 65).	£100 for each material inaccuracy in two-year penalty period (which commences following notice of second material inaccuracy).
Failure to submit an EC sales statement (VATA 1994 s 66).	Greater of £50 or a daily penalty (maximum 100 days) £5 for the first, £10 for the second, £15 for the third or subsequent failure in the default period.
Breach of walking possession agreement (VATA 1994 s 68).	50% of VAT due or amount recoverable.
Failure to preserve records, including digital records, for prescribed period (VATA 1994 ss 69, 69B).	£500.
Failure to preserve records specified in HMRC direction (VATA 1994 ss 69, 69B).	£200 for each day of failure (maximum 30 days).
Breaches of regulatory provisions, including failure to notify cessation of liability or entitlement to be registered, failure to keep records and non-compliance with any regulations made under VATA 1994 (VATA 1994 s 69).	Greater of £50 and a daily penalty (maximum 100 days) of a specified amount depending on number of failures in preceding two years: £5* per day if no previous failures; £10* per day if one previous failure; £15* per day if two or more previous failures.
Where failure consists of not paying VAT or not making a return in the required time.	*1/6, 1/3 and 1/2 of 1% of the VAT due respectively, if greater.

Offence	Penalty
Breaches of regulatory provisions involving failure to pay VAT or submit return by due date (VATA 1994 s 69).	Greater of £50 and a daily penalty (for no more than 100 days) of a specified amount depending on number of failures in preceding two years: greater of £5 and 1/6 % of VAT due if no previous failures; greater of £10 and 1/3% of VAT due if one previous failure; greater of £15 and 1/2% of VAT due if two or more previous failures.
Failure to comply with the requirements of the investment gold scheme (VATA 1994 s 69A).	17.5% of the value of transactions concerned.
Import VAT (FA 2003 ss 24–41):	
– failures relating to non-compliance	maximum penalty of £2,500
– evasion.	maximum penalty equal to VAT sought to be evaded.
Evasion of VAT: conduct involving dishonesty (VATA 1994 ss 60, 61). Does not apply to acts or omissions relating to an inaccuracy in a document or failure to notify HMRC of an under-assessment (to which penalties under FA 2007 Sch 24 apply).	Amount of tax evaded or sought to be evaded (subject to mitigation).
Transactions connected with fraudulent evasion of VAT (VATA 1994 ss 69C–69E).	30% of potential lost VAT.
Failure to notify the use of a designated avoidance scheme (VATA 1994 Sch 11A paras 10, 11).	*15% of the tax avoided (applies to businesses with supplies of £600,000 or more).* **Replaced from 1 January 2018, see below**.
Failure to disclose certain schemes within 30 days of the due date or the first return affected (VATA 1994 Sch 11A paras 10, 11).	*£5,000 (applies to businesses with supplies exceeding £10 million).* **Replaced from 1 January 2018, see below**.
Failure from 1 January 2018 to notify details of, or notify use of, a notifiable proposal which enables a person to obtain a tax advantage within 31 days of the making of the proposal (F(No 2)A 2017 Sch 17).	Penalty up to £600 per day in 'initial period' A continuing penalty not exceeding £600 for each day on which the failure continues after imposition of initial penalty (but a tribunal can determine a higher penalty up to £1 million).
Failure from 1 January 2018 to provide HMRC with the reference number and related information in relation to notifiable arrangements above (F(No 2)A 2017 Sch 17).	Penalty not exceeding £5,000 in respect of each scheme to which the failure relates For second failure within three years of first, penalty not exceeding £7,500 in respect of each scheme For subsequent failures within three years of previous, penalty not exceeding £10,000 in respect of each scheme.

[1] In relation to VAT MOSS returns, a penalty under FA 2007 Sch 24 only applies when the recipient of the supply is in the UK. If an inaccuracy on a UK return relates to a supply to a recipient in another member state, there is no penalty under UK legislation, but a penalty may apply in that other member state in which the recipient is located. If an inaccuracy on (say) a French VAT return relates to a supply to a recipient in the UK, there could be a penalty under UK legislation.

[2] In relation to VAT MOSS returns, a penalty for a late return or late payment could be charged by each member state in which the supplies are deemed to be made.

Index

A

Accounts, inheritance tax
  due dates 110
  excepted estates 110
Advisory fuel rates 88
Advisory electricity rate 90
Age allowance 80
Aggregates levy 67
Agricultural property relief 112
Air passenger duty 67
Alternative finance investment bonds 26
Annual accounting scheme, VAT 150
Annual exempt amount, capital gains tax 35
Annual exemption, inheritance tax 112
Annual tax on enveloped dwellings 64
Apprenticeship levy 100
Approval applications 27
Authorised mileage rates 90
Average exchange rates 125

B

Bank base rates 1
Bank levy 65
Bank corporation tax surcharge 65
Basic rate of income tax 75
Basis of assessment
  employment income 96
  overseas income 132
Benefits, employee 91–94
Benefits, social security 133–137
Blind person's allowance 80
Bus services 85, 91
Business asset disposal relief 37
Business property relief 112

C

Capital allowances
  cars 29
  claims, time limits 23
  dredging 29
  elections, time limits 23
  enterprise zones 32
  know-how 29
  mineral extraction 29
  patent rights 29
  plant and machinery 30–33
  rates 29–32
  renovation of business premises 32

Capital allowances – *cont.*
  research and development 32
  structures and buildings 32
Capital gains tax
  annual exempt amount 35
  ATED properties 64
  business asset disposal relief 37
  chattel exemption 35
  claims, time limits 22
  due date 2
  elections, time limits 22
  employee-ownership trusts 38
  employee shareholder shares 38
  enterprise investment scheme (EIS) 39
  entrepreneurs' relief 37
  exemptions 35
  high value UK residential property 36
  hold-over relief for gifts 39
  incorporation relief 40
  indexation allowance 42–59
  investors' relief 38
  late payment interest 4
  leases 62
  non-resident CGT 1, 9, 36
  payment of tax 1
  penalties 10–20
  personal representatives 35, 36, 40
  rates 36
  reliefs 38
  retail prices index 60–61
  returns, penalties 10–14
  roll-over relief 40
  seed enterprise investment scheme (SEIS) 40
  share identification rules 37
  social investment tax relief 40
  trustees 35, 36, 41
  venture capital schemes 40
Capital goods scheme, VAT 152
Capped income tax reliefs 104
Cars
  advisory fuel rates 88
  advisory electricity rates 90
  authorised mileage rates 90
  benefit 82
  capital allowances 29
  capital gains exemption 39
  fuel for private use
    taxable benefit 85
    VAT 157
  hired: restricted allowances 85
  mileage allowances 88
  private use 82
Carbon price floor 69

Cash accounting scheme, VAT 150
Certificates of tax deposit 7
Charities and CASCs
    capital gains exemption 38
    gift aid 79
    gift aid small donations 79
    gifts in kind 79
    gifts to, inheritance tax relief 112
    payroll giving scheme 79
Chattels, capital gains exemption 35
Cheap loans to employees 91
Child benefit income tax charge 78
Child tax credit 107
Claims, time limits
    capital allowances 23
    capital gains tax 22
    corporation tax 23
    income tax 22
Clearance applications 27
Clearing houses 26
Climate change levy 69
Community investment tax relief 100
Company share option plans 107
Compensation, capital gains exemption 38
Computer equipment 94
Construction industry scheme
    deduction of tax 78
    security, failure to provide 21
Corporation tax
    annual tax on enveloped dwellings 64
    bank corporation tax surcharge 65
    claims, time limits 23
    disincorporation relief 63
    diverted profits tax 65
    digital servivces tax 63
    due date 2
    elections, time limits 23
    gifts of pre-eminent objects 64
    instalments of tax 1
    interest on overdue tax 5
    interest on overpaid tax 6
    marginal relief 63
    patent box 64
    payment of tax 1
    penalties 10–20
    rates 63
    real estate investments trusts 64
    reliefs 63
    research and development expenditure 64
    restitution interest 66
    returns, penalties 10–13
    security, failure to provide 21
Cycles and cycle safety equipment 85

D

Default interest, VAT 161
Default surcharge, VAT 162
Deregistration limits, VAT 149
Direct recovery of debt 6
Disabled employees, equipment 92

Disincorporation relief 63
Diverted profits tax 65
Digital services tax 65
Dividends 77
Dividend allowance 77
Double taxation agreements
    air transport profits 131
    capital taxes 131
    income and capital gains 129
    shipping profits 131
    tax compliance agreements 131
    tax information exchange agreements 131
Dredging allowances 29
Due dates of tax 2–3

E

Elections, time limits
    capital allowances 23
    capital gains tax 21
    corporation tax 23
    income tax 21
Employees
    accommodation, supplies etc used in employment duties 91
    amounts which would be otherwise deductible 91
    assets given to employees 91, 122
    bus services for 85, 91
    car benefits 82
    cheap loans 91
    childcare 92
    Christmas parties, annual functions 92, 122
    clothing and uniforms 122
    computers provided for private use 94
    credit cards and tokens 92, 122
    cycles and cycle safety equipment 85
    disabled, equipment etc 92
    electricity for an electric car 85
    emergency vehicles 85
    employees' liability insurance 92
    entertaining 122
    eye tests 92
    fixed-rate expenses 98
    flat rate expenses 98
    fuel benefits 82, 123
    holidays 122
    homeworkers 92
    incidental overnight expenses 92
    living accommodation 92
    living expenses 93
    loan benefits 91, 123
    long service awards 93
    meals 93, 123
    medical check-ups 93
    medical insurance, etc. 93, 123
    medical treatment 93
    mileage rates 88, 90
    mobile phones 94, 123
    national living wage 96
    national minimum wage 96
    notional payments 123

Employees – *cont.*
parking facilities for 85, 123
payments in kind 123
pensions advice 93
personal expenses 93, 123
relocation benefits 94, 123
round sum allowances 123
scholarships and school fees 94, 123
share schemes 106
shareholder status 38, 102
subscriptions 94
tax paid for 123
telephone costs 123
third party gifts 94
trivial benefits 94
use of employer's assets 94
van benefits 85
vouchers 94, 123
Employee shareholder status 38, 102
Employment benefits and expenses
  payments 91–94
Employment exemption 95
Employment income 95
basis of assesment 96
due dates of tax 2
fixed rate expenses 98
termination payments 97
Employee-ownership trusts 38, 95
Enterprise investment scheme (EIS)
capital gains exemption 39
income tax relief 100
Enterprise management incentives (EMIs) 106
Enterprise zones 32
Entrepreneurs' relief 37, 38
Environmental taxes and other levies 67–73
Excepted estates, inheritance tax 110, 111
Excepted transfers 110
Exchange rates
average 125
year end 128
Exchanges
alternative finance investment bonds 26
recognised foreign exchanges 26
recognised futures exchanges 25
recognised investment exchanges 26
recognised stock exchanges 24
Exempt supplies, VAT 153

F

Filing dates 8
Fixed rate expenses 98
Flat rate scheme for small businesses,
  VAT 150
Flat rate scheme for farmers, VAT 147
Flexible benefit arrangements 94
Foreign exchange rates
average 125
year end 128
Foreign income
basis of assessment 132
employment income 96

Foster carers 102
FOTRA securities 132
Fuel duty 70
Fuel for private use
income tax 85
VAT 157
Futures exchanges 25

G

Gift aid 79
Gift aid small donations 79
Gifts in kind 79
Gifts of land, shares etc 79
Gifts of pre-eminent objects 39, 64, 103

H

Harmonised interest regime 4
Help to buy: ISAs 102
High value UK residential property 36, 64, 139
Hired cars and motorcycles 85
Hold-over relief for gifts 39

I

Income tax
capped reliefs 104
claims, time limits 22
due dates 2
elections, time limits 22
late payment interest 4
lease premiums 62
payment of tax 2
penalties 10–20
personal allowances 80
rates 75
reliefs 80, 102
repayment interest 4
returns, penalties 10–20
Incorporation relief 40
Indexation allowance 42–59
Individual savings accounts (ISAs) 101
Inheritance tax
agricultural property relief 112
annual exemption 112
business property relief 112
charitable gifts, exemption 112
due dates for accounts 110
due dates for tax 3
excepted transfers estates and
  settlements 110
gifts, reliefs 112
interest on overdue tax 5
marriage/civil partnership gifts, exemption 112
national purposes, gifts exemption 112
nil rate bands 109
non-domiciled spouse/civil partner 113

Inheritance tax – *cont.*
payment of tax 2
penalties 10–20
political parties, gifts exemption 112
potentially exempt transfers 112
quick succession relief 113
rates 109
reliefs 112
small gifts exemption 113
tapering relief 113
Insurance premium tax 70
Insurance premiums, life 103
Interest rates
bank base rates 1
capital gains 4
certificates of tax deposit 8
corporation tax 4–6
default, VAT 161
income tax 4
income tax on company payments 5
inheritance tax 5, 6
land and buildings transaction tax
(Scotland) 141
land transaction tax (Wales) 142
late payment interest 4
national insurance contributions 4–6
official, cheap loans 91
overpaid tax 6
repayment interest 4
stamp duties 4, 5
unpaid tax 4, 5
VAT 161
Investment exchanges 26
Investment reliefs
community investment tax relief 100
enterprise investment scheme (EIS) 100
help to buy: ISAs 102
individual savings accounts (ISAs) 101
junior ISAs 102
lifetime ISAs 102
seed enterprise investment scheme
(SEIS) 100
social investment tax relief 101
urban regeneration companies 101
venture capital trusts (VCTs) 101
Investors' relief 38

J

Junior ISAs 102

K

Know-how, capital allowances 29

L

**Land and buildings transaction tax
(Scotland)** 141
Land transaction tax (Wales) 142
Landfill disposals tax (Wales) 71
Landfill tax 71
Landfill tax, Scottish 71
Late payment interest 4
Leases
depreciation table 62
premiums 62
stamp duties 139–142
Life assurance premium relief 103
Lifetime ISAs 102
Local authority members, travel expenses 90
Loans to employees 91
Loans to participators
payment of tax 1
tax charge 66

M

Machinery and plant allowances 30–33
cars 29
rates 30
Maintenance payments 103
Managed services companies 95
Marginal relief, corporation tax 63
**Marriage/civil partnership gifts, inheritance
tax relief** 112
Married couple's allowance 80
Mileage allowances 88
Minimum wage, national 96
Misdeclarations, VAT 162
Mobile phones 94
Motorcycles 85

N

National insurance contributions
apprentices under age 25 115
Class 1 115, 123
Class 1A, 1B 115, 123
Class 3 121
Classes 2 and 4 3, 80, 121
employees under age 21 115
employers' contributions on benefits 123
employment allowance 115
interest on overdue contributions 4
interest on overpaid contributions 6
payment of 3
rates 115
weekly and monthly thresholds 95
National living wage 96

National minimum wage 96
Nazi persecution, pensions to victims 132
Non-domiciled individuals
employment income 96
overseas income 132
spouses/civil partners, inheritance tax 113
Non-residents
employment income 96
overseas income 132
Non-resident CGT
filing date 9
payment of tax 1
rate of tax 36

O

Official rate of interest, employee loans 91
Offshore matters, penalties, territory
categories, transfers 10, 11, 13–16
Optional remuneration arrangements 94
Overseas income, basis of assessment
employment income 95
overseas income 132

P

Parking facilities 85
Partial exemption, VAT 151
Participators, loans and benefits to
payment of tax 1
tax charge 66
Patent rights, capital allowances 29
Patent box 64
Payment dates of tax 1–3
PAYE
payment of 3
penalties 10–20
security, failure to provide 21
settlement agreements 95
weekly and monthly thresholds 95
Payroll giving scheme 79
Penalties
asset-based for offshore inaccuracies etc 16
deliberate enablers of offshore evasion etc 16
generally 10–20
interest on 4, 20
mitigation of 20
offshore matter asset moves 15
offshore matter, territory categories 14, 15
special information returns 17
stamp taxes 145
VAT 162
Pension provision 104
Personal allowances 80
Personal pension schemes 104
Personal representatives 35, 36, 40
Personal savings allowance 75
Personal service companies 95
Plant and machinery allowances
rates 30–33

Potentially exempt transfers 112
Premiums on leases
capital gains tax 62
income tax 62
stamp taxes 140, 142
Property allowance 102
Publishing details of
deliberate tax defaulters 21
enablers of offshore evasion 21
persistently uncooperative large
businesses 21
serial tax avoiders 21

Q

Qualifying corporate bonds 39
Qualifying care relief 102
Quick succession relief 113

R

Rates of tax
annual tax on enveloped dwellings 64
capital gains tax 35
corporation tax 63
diverted profits tax 65
digital services tax 65
environmental taxes and other levies 67–73
income tax 75
inheritance tax 109
non-resident CGT 36
stamp taxes 139–143
VAT 147
Real Estate Investment Trusts 64
Recognised clearing houses 26
Recognised futures exchanges 25
Recognised investment exchanges 26
Recognised stock exchanges 24
Reduced rate supplies, VAT 152
Registration limits, VAT 147
Reliefs
capped income tax reliefs 104
capital gains 37, 38
corporation tax 63
income tax 80, 100, 102
inheritance tax 112
Remission of tax 6
Renovation of business premises 32
Rent, stamp duties 139, 140, 142
Rent-a-room relief 103
Repayment interest 4
Repayment supplement, general 5
Repayment supplement, stamp duty 144
Repayment supplement, VAT 161
Research and development 32, 64
Restitution interest 66
Retail prices index 60–61
Retirement pensions 104
Return filing dates 8–9

Roll-over relief 40

S

Salary sacrifice arrangements 94
Save as you earn (SAYE) share option schemes 106
Scottish income tax 75
Scottish landfill tax 71
Scottish VAT 147
Seafarers' deduction 96
Securities, tax-free for non-residents 132
Security, failure to provide 21
Seed enterprise investment scheme (SEIS) 40, 100
Share identification rules 37
Share incentive plans 106
Share schemes 106
Shared lives carers 102
Small gifts relief 113
Simple assessment 9
Simplified fixed rate deductions 104
Social investment tax relief 40, 101
Social security benefits
  cap on benefits 134, 136
  non-taxable 135
  taxable 133
Special relief 6
Stamp taxes
  exemptions 140
  fixed 143
  interest 4, 5, 143, 144
  land and buildings transaction tax (Scotland) 141
  land transactions 139, 142
  land transaction tax (Wales) 142
  leases 140, 141
  penalties 145
  premiums 140, 141, 142
  rates 139–143
  reliefs 140–141
  rent 139–142
  repayment supplement 5, 144
  stamp duty 142
  stamp duty land tax 139
  stamp duty reserve tax 143
  stock transfers 142–143
State benefits
  cap on benefits 134, 136
  non-taxable 135
  taxable 133
Stock exchanges 24
Structures and buildings 32
Student loans 7–8
Subscriptions 27, 94
Supplement VAT 161

T

Tapering relief, inheritance tax 113

Tax credits 107
Tax information exchange agreements 131
Termination payments 97
Time limits, claims and elections 21
Trading allowance 102
Travel expenses, local authority members 90
Trustees
  capital gains annual exempt amount 35
  expenses allowable for CGT 41
Trusts
  capital gains tax rates 36
  income tax rates 75

U

Universal credit 136
Urban regeneration companies 101

V

Van, employee benefit 85
VAT
  annual accounting scheme 150
  capital goods scheme 152
  car fuel advisory rates 157
  car fuel for private use 157–160
  cash accounting scheme 150
  default interest 161
  default surcharge 162
  deregistration limits 149
  EC sales lists 154
  EU country codes 154, 155
  evasion 162
  exempt supplies 153
  failure to notify liability 162
  flat-rate scheme for farmers 147
  flat-rate scheme for small businesses 150
  interest on overpaid tax 161
  intrastat 155
  Mini One Stop Shop (MOSS) 156
  partial exemption 151
  penalties 162
  rates 147
  reduced rate supplies 152
  registration limits 147
  repayment supplement 161
  Scottish VAT 147
  zero-rated supplies 152
Vehicle excise duty 72
Venture capital trusts (VCTs)
  capital gains exemptions 40
  income tax reliefs 101

W

Welsh income tax 76
Withdrawal of self assessment 9

Working tax credit 107

Z

Zero-rated supplies, VAT 152